THE HUMAN WHISPERER

THE HUMAN WHISPERER

mastering the art of understanding, connecting with, and influencing others

Steven Keyl

Whispering Press

ISBN: 0999515209
ISBN 13: 9780999515204

To my beloved full-volume Whisperers,
Margaret and Nicole

Table of Contents

Acknowledgements

During a Midwest winter of the 1970's, a father convinced his kids to buy for their mother a half-inch thick paddle with which to spank them when they misbehaved. (This was in the days when corporal punishment was not only tolerated, but in most quarters expected.) Better yet, it was to be a Christmas gift! The kids had a few misgivings about this plan... OK, more than a few. But they did it anyway. Christmas came and their mother received this lovely stenciled paddle. The boy and girl had plenty of toys to keep themselves occupied so everything was right with the world.

The first time "the board of education met the seat of understanding" (December 26, 1976) the boy had two thoughts: this gift was a bad idea...a very bad idea. His primary thought, however, was how in the world did their father ever talk them into such a poorly thought out plan?

This sparked his first curiosity about the concepts of influence and persuasion, although he didn't yet know their names. After all, he was only seven. It was just a nagging question of how a person could get someone to do something that ran so counter to their own self-interest. That question has followed the boy into adulthood.

It was a painful beginning that marked my entry into the fascinating world of Human Whispering. An eye-opening journey that, through my professional career, has led me full-circle.

Did that boy ever find out how his father convinced him to purchase such an ill-advised present? He sure did. And he hasn't forgotten those lessons since. Thanks, Mom and Dad.

Thanks also to my friends and family in whose support has bestowed the strength to persevere. Thanks to Margaret, Nicole, Barb, Rhonda, Dan, Rob, Ryan, Michael, Sara, Ken, Bea, Heidi, Allen, Emily and Chris.

Fellow Intelligence Community members Jennifer Elkhouri, Bob Kelly, and Drew Thompson have been true resources that I've called upon time and again. Not just in writing the book, but in every avenue of endeavor they have been endlessly encouraging, willing sounding boards, and although undeserving, they have never wavered in their belief in me.

Throughout my time in the Intelligence Community, it's been my great privilege to work alongside countless men and women whose dedication to our country and mission are a never-ending source of pride. Many of these people in whom I've placed my faith have expanded my understanding of thoughts and behaviors, not only through example, but in a few cases, trial-and-error! So, to my fellow compatriots Joel Ashman, Dominic Carhart, Bob Coleman, Jon Eskenazi, Joe Fox, Nekia Freeman, David Grondzki, Craig Hassan, John T. Smith, Jim Thompson, Darryl Trent, and Bobby Welsh, I offer my sincerest thanks.

During the research phase, while collecting and culling the material, it was always clear that I stood on the shoulders of giants. Of course, people like Edward de Bono, Robert Cialdini, Paul Ekman, and Joe Navarro created works that have left a profound impression on me. This led to further reading from myriad authors and researchers, whose pages each filled in another missing piece of the puzzle.

In terms of the writing itself, my primary support system rested on Linda Boyd and Jeff Quintilian.

Linda came on board about half-way through the project. After seeing her initial redlines, almost no hint of the original writing was left! It became my secret hope that she would abandon this project due to either her perception of my incompetence or just a lack of interest—either would have sufficed. But no, she stayed true to the task, and after more than a few tense conversations, we eventually found our rhythm. Her red pen has made more than a few passes over this manuscript and as a result, has a readability and flow that would not have otherwise been present.

Jeff, as it happens, is one of the most intelligent people I've ever met. He's done it all throughout this process: sounding board, editor, proofreader, willing participant in traveling down whatever rabbit hole I had fallen into, such as spending hours talking about creative options for the cover, and being a constant source of help and encouragement. Each time I asked him to re-read a chapter for the umpteenth time, he never complained, he never said "not again!" He just rolled up his sleeves and got to work. Of far greater value than his significant contribution to the book, is our 30+ year friendship, which, if memory serves, started over a discussion of a Jethro Tull album.

Teller, from famed magic duo "Penn and Teller" once remarked (and yes, he does actually speak) that, "neuroscientists are novices at deception." Magicians plumb the depths of misdirection, deception and how are senses can be used to fool us in subtle, unconscious ways. For those who work in the magical arts, whose writings and conversations have filled in more than a few missing gaps, I'm grateful to Banachek, Scott Barden, Lew Brooks, Bob Cassidy, Mark Elsdon, Marc Paul, Barrie Richardson, Peter Turner, and Greg Wilson.

For the muggles who offered blind faith in me when none was warranted, I'd like to thank Kathleen Bassett, Dan Behrns, Kari King, Rhonda Mansfield, Kimberly A. Robinson, Dawn Rockwell, April Thompson, and J. Scott Vangor.

The most astute observer of the human condition that I've ever met was Salvatore Victor Emmanuel. I was his janitorial assistant for three short months back in the summer of 1989. He knew more about people than anyone I've ever known. Few were aware that a veritable genius was at work underneath those rumpled clothes and tousled hair. Though we hadn't spoken in nearly 30 years, the lessons he taught me are indelibly etched into my mind. I've only recently learned that he passed away earlier this year. Farewell, Sal, and thank you.

How to read this book

While most of the chapters *may* stand alone, this book is meant to be read sequentially. The concepts build on one another, so if you jump headlong into persuasion and bypass earlier sections, you lose foundational principles designed to make step-by-step implementation as easy as possible.

Additionally, you will find some chapters contain a heavier dose of complex information. To help you get the most from the material, timeouts are placed strategically so you can visualize implementation into your own life in smaller incremental steps.

TIMEOUT: This indicates a stopping point to put down the book and ponder the questions posed. Relate the material to your life and how you might make use of the information.

You will also see Whisper Alerts throughout the book. These highlight principles which must be remembered to be the most effective Whisperer possible. The alerts are succinct and easy to remember.

WHISPER ALERT: Interactive reading is more than clicking a mouse!

Dog-ear pages. Highlight and underline text. Make marginal notes on principles you want to implement. Note areas where deeper research would be beneficial. Keep pad and pen handy to fully write out answers to the Timeout questions.

* * *

FORGET-ME-NOTS

- These are bulleted summaries at the end of each chapter
- High-level recaps are what you'll find here; not every topic is mentioned again
- Where applicable, this also points to the relevant appendix to find more information

*   *   *

Introduction

What is a *Whisperer?*

There are lion, tiger and bear whisperers ("OH MY"), and even a skunk whisperer! *The Horse Whisperer* was made famous through the novel and subsequent movie starring Robert Redford and the *Dog Whisperer* through the television series with Cesar Millan.

Cesar hosted a show where he worked to overcome dogs' troublesome behavior and temperament. The show was popular not only because we love dogs, but as Mr. Millan plied his craft we were fascinated watching the profound effect he had over a problem pet. People contending with unruly animals for years sought out Cesar. He would show up at their doorstep and in a matter of hours (OK, with video editing, just a few minutes), their dogs were loving and obedient in a way their owners had never seen before.

His <u>understanding</u> of dogs allowed him to create a <u>bond</u> with which he <u>influenced</u> their behaviors. For all Whisperers, the methods are necessarily different, but the sequence and goals are the same:

- Develop a deep understanding of the psychology of the animal
- Forge an emotional bond drawing them to the Whisperer
- Influence thoughts and behaviors

For most of us, the animals we spend the most time with are other people. To become a "Human Whisperer" we must *<u>understand</u>* people, *<u>connect</u>* with them, and use that connection to *<u>influence</u>* their actions and even their thoughts.

If you can improve your ability in even one of these areas, you *will* find greater success in your personal and professional relationships. This holds true with strangers, acquaintances, work colleagues and even your closest friends and family.

THE VALUE GUARANTEE

If you find just one concept that resonates and you *apply it*, then your time will have been well spent. All too often, we read a "self-improvement" book and enjoy it, but as soon the last page is turned we say, "Done." It gets put on a shelf to collect dust until we can exclaim to a houseguest, "I read that!" The goal here is more than bragging rights. Whether you make a concerted effort to apply the principles outlined or you discover information that interprets a previous mystery, this book has proven its worth.

Becoming an effective "Human Whisperer" is a lifetime pursuit. We can always improve our effectiveness in dealing with people, no matter our starting point. Some may have already developed processes (even subconsciously) that accomplish these goals while others may realize their virtual toolbox is empty and would like to fill it with effective techniques. In either case, you're in the right place.

* * *

Successful Whispering requires a diverse set of skills. Reading (understanding) people, connecting with them, and wielding influence all work together to create a stable footing to get the most out of your relationships–both professional and personal.

SO WHAT'S NEW?

The Human Whisperer is different from similar books on the basis of both *scope* and *context*.

Some sources limit the focus to one topic like either body language or how to influence people. Many of these books are great reads but the limited *scope* carries two drawbacks. First, it doesn't provide a full toolbox in how to understand, connect with, and influence; it only reveals part of the picture. Second, the massive length and depth devoted to a single topic creates an overload in the reader, who at the end of the journey, is hard-pressed to remember much of what was read, let alone how to apply it.

Some books are written within a specific *context*. The authors relate the material to a narrow sphere of influence, such as sales or law enforcement. They are so concentrated in a specific area that the general reader cannot apply the principles and ideas to the everyday world around them.

For example, books that deal with <u>reading</u> others, particularly body language, are geared toward conversations in controlled environments like interrogation rooms. Much of the information is not as practical in the more typical environments most of us experience. "The Human Whisperer" covers nonverbal communication in a non-criminal context and uncovers deeper truths by adapting investigative techniques to casual conversations.

*   *   *

Before this book was published, people would find out I was writing a book and would ask what it was about. My "elevator pitch" was that it helps you become more effective in dealing with people. The reply to this would often be, "Oh, like the Dale Carnegie book *How to Win Friends and Influence People!*"

This is a great book on creating a <u>connection</u> with people and the principles are as valuable now as when they were written. Some of the advice, however, is dated and doesn't translate as well to the 21st century. The section on flattery, for example, would be seen as insincere today. So while its popularity is testament to its greatness, much of it would be considered "common sense" now. "The Human Whisperer" details the latest science and psychology of persuasive techniques, giving the practitioner principles to better read thoughts and motivations of others. These topics were left uncovered in the Carnegie book, as it doesn't take into account all of the psychological principles we've learned since 1936.

*   *   *

There are likewise no shortage of books discussing <u>influence</u>. Most are focused exclusively on the effect of sales and marketing through mass media. Moreover, these books are not attempting to create more persuasive individuals; rather, they seek to educate readers on how to avoid persuasive traps set by others seeking to part you from your money.

Without the proper context of how these techniques can work in one-on-one situations, they are of limited value. This results in frustration because these ideas don't seem to "work in the real world." These books also lump all influence together without articulating that *different types of requests* require different persuasive tools. Once we know when and how to use the right tool for the job we come to realize these techniques <u>*can*</u> and <u>*do*</u> work in the real world. In fact, they have been working for hundreds of years for those with the ability to tap into the most basic elements of human nature.

Persuasion in "The Human Whisperer" is tackled from a goal-oriented approach. First, decide what you're trying to accomplish, then figure out the best tools for the job. Whether you're trying to get someone to do you a favor or change an opinion or even a more deeply held belief, you need to use the right technique for the task.

Not written by or for the academic community, *The Human Whisperer* borrows ideas from far-flung disciplines and adapts them for everyday use. Interrogation techniques of law enforcement are used to separate truth from lies. The "cold reading" techniques of psychics are used to facilitate genuine connections. The techniques of social engineers and con men are used, not to steal from people, but to better understand them. Sales techniques are used to modify the decision making process. The one thing they all have in common is that they further our objectives–reading, connecting, influencing.

WHISPERS NOT SHOUTS

The "*Whisper*" in *The Human Whisperer* means speaking softly, not shouting. The softness of the voice is a metaphor for the gentle nature in which the Whisperer operates. This is not about coercion, manipulation, or behaving unethically. It is about subtlety, tact, and sincerity.

If you are unable to operate within a Whisper, your efforts will not bear fruit. We will revisit this topic, but put your mind at ease that you're not being asked to act immorally or unethically.

Whispering is neither solely about influence nor "tricking people into doing stuff." It's about being more effective with people–to conduct ourselves with more skill, grace, and finesse. Knowing what to say and how to act in the moment, and not 20 minutes after the conversation has ended.

"Honestly, I find the writing trite and pedantic."

Nor does Whispering mean cloak-and-dagger level secrecy. Contrary to how it sounds, a Human Whisperer is not someone that hides in the shadows or acts behind the scenes pulling people's strings like a crazed puppeteer. They are affable people to whom others gravitate because they are charismatic. Generating charisma is a fundamental skill that transcends Whispering and is therefore valuable in every aspect of your life, so that's where our journey begins.

Before *you* say a word

"Signs don't shout, they whisper."

– A.D. POSEY

Before every conversation, you're assessing someone, and they're assessing you. The outset of every in-person interaction is visual. Consciously or not, you either bolster or harm that image by how you carry yourself.

Bringing our nonverbal behaviors under conscious control is the first stop in our quest to become Human Whisperers because our nonverbal behaviors generate one of the most misunderstood yet most desired interpersonal traits...*Charisma*.

Before learning how to boost your charisma, however, we must take a broader look at the principles of nonverbal behaviors, or *body language*, because this is the foundation on which to build a more charismatic you. There are a few misperceptions and counterintuitive ideas about body language that should first be explored.

BODY LANGUAGE

How big a role do nonverbals really play?

In the 1950's, Albert Mehrabian famously declared that communication is 7% the words we use, 38% the tone of our voice, and 55% nonverbal. Though an oft-cited statistic, the study was flawed because it:

- Combined data inappropriately from multiple studies
- Analyzed only *positive* emotions
- Contained only women
- Excluded nonverbal communication such as body language and posture

Since that time others have studied communication to provide more clarity on the proportional impact of both verbal and nonverbal channels. The one thing these studies have in common is that none draw the same conclusions. One comprehensive study found nonverbals had over four times the impact of the verbal channel. A different study found that words alone had over four times the impact of the nonverbals (Argyle, Hsee).

Variability is high because these studies suffer from the faulty premise–that it is possible to discern exactly how much of a message comes from the nonverbal channel. In any given interaction, the answer depends on how well the participants can transmit and receive the nonverbal signals. When we say a person is *perceptive*, we are referring to their ability to receive and decode nonverbal signals. If a person isn't perceptive, the message they receive comes primarily from spoken words alone.

Another variable is the context in which the communication takes place. Listening to a tour guide drone on while visiting the "Pencil Museum" (yes, this is a real place) won't engage as many nonverbal behaviors as two drivers yelling at each other over a premium parking space.

Even if absolutes are scarce, general trends can still be observed. Analysis of thousands of sales interviews shows that body language has significant impact around a negotiating table. This is why the stronger argument wins when negotiating over the phone–because our decisions rest solely on what we hear; whereas in person, it is more likely the visuals that determine the outcome.

The classic example of this phenomenon goes back to the first televised Presidential debate between John F. Kennedy and Richard Nixon in 1960. Kennedy understood the new medium and made sure he looked his best and appeared calm and in command. Nixon didn't see the need for a televised debate and his refusal to let anyone apply makeup to his face resulted in him looking pale and washed out when under the lights. A majority of those watching the debate on *television* scored it as a victory for Kennedy, but a majority of those listening on the *radio* scored it as a victory for Nixon. The power of nonverbal communication cannot be overestimated.

Most studies conclude that 60-80% of our opinion of someone is cemented within the first 4 minutes of our initial meeting. Certain traits like trustworthiness and attractiveness are determined almost immediately with other traits added over the next few minutes until a fixed first impression is formed (Willis, Todorov). Thereafter everything we see and hear is interpreted through that lens, so a great first impression reaps rewards throughout the life of the relationship. Conversely, a poor first impression can be nearly impossible to overcome.

Even if specifics are impossible to quantify, every Whisperer knows the *ability to influence others begins long before the conversation starts*. How you dress, how you enter a room, how you conduct yourself, and the myriad of nonverbal signals before, during, and after the conversation affects your potential to connect with and influence others. These nonverbals can signal joy, insecurity, nervousness, boldness, confidence, sadness, deception, and flirtation, to name a few. By consciously controlling these signals you can create a positive first impression *before you say a word*.

Nature vs. Nurture

Many basic communication signals are the same across all cultures because they are inborn and not subject to cultural modification, such as head nodding to signify agreement[1], which is also done by people born blind. Shaking the head "no" may not be inborn, strictly speaking, but when a baby has had enough to eat they will shake their head from side to side to stop the feeding process. This head shaking is then extended to other situations. The "shoulder shrug" is universal and displays: exposed palms to show nothing is hidden, hunched shoulders, and raised eyebrows to show submission.

Other gestures such as greetings are highly cultural, the most common being the handshake. In places other than the US, one or two kisses is the norm. Even the number of "handshake pumps" can vary by country. In the US, five to seven pumps is common, in the UK it is three to five pumps, and in Germany it's "one and done!"

How much touching is acceptable varies highly between cultures and even regionally here in the US.

In the US, holding the tips of index finger and thumb together while allowing the other three fingers to point up loosely signifies "OK", in Japan it means money, in France it means zero, and in Turkey and Brazil it signifies...let's just say... a part of the anatomy. The "thumbs-up" sign can mean anything from "good" to "up yours" depending on the country in which you see it.

Our focus is on *universal body language* and not behaviors specific to a single region. Not only does this make our discussion more globally applicable, but these innate

---

1 With a couple notable exceptions, like in Greece and Albania, where nodding the head actually means "no."

behaviors tell us so much because they normally operate outside of our conscious control.

Your unconscious emotional state controls your body language

When performed <u>unconsciously</u>, *body language is an outward reflection of a person's emotional state*. Feeling defensive, elated, unhappy, or wishing to escape is conveyed through body movements and recognized by the astute observer.

The brain's *necessity* to align thought with behavior is known as <u>cognitive dissonance</u>. How and why this works, and the specific behaviors involved, is the focus of chapter 3.

Your conscious body language controls your emotional state

Here we will focus on bringing *our* body language under <u>conscious</u> control to convey the desired message.

Nonverbal behaviors normally show a person's emotional state, such as fingers drumming on a table to indicate boredom. What is less intuitive is the reverse. *Your emotional state changes to align with your existing body language!* If you consciously exhibit positive, happy, upbeat body language, these behaviors will have a substantive impact on your mental state.

A genuine smile has been shown to create positive feelings not only in the people that observe the smiler, but in the smiler as well. This is supported by findings that women injected with botox, and *therefore unable to frown*, reported feeling happier and less anxious. More importantly, they did not report feeling any more attractive, suggesting the emotional effects were not driven by the end result of the treatment (Wenner). *Because* they did not frown, their attitude was more positive and happy. The nonverbal behavior created the corresponding emotional state in the smiler.

Conversely, negative body language can engender negative feelings. Folding one's arms is often a sign of defensiveness, disengagement, apathy, and/or nervousness. By folding one's arms in the absence of these emotions, the mind assumes a mental state that aligns with this negative body language. In other words, folding your arms *produces* the defensiveness and detachment that normally causes arms to become folded in the first place! For example: researchers found in a lecture series that a group instructed to keep their arms crossed over their chest retained 38% less information than the control group. Further, these listeners had a more negative view of the speaker and found the lecture less valuable than those instructed to keep their arms uncrossed (Pease).

This illustrates a person's need for mind and body to be in sync. Body language not only *reflects* the mind but may *change* it as well. This is all a part of your brain's way of maintaining congruence between thoughts and actions in order to maintain cognitive harmony. We can change how we *feel* by changing our body language? Yes! If you are feeling defensive and notice your arms crossing… STOP! Force yourself to uncross and maintain an open posture. If your conscious mind is forcing an open posture, to prevent cognitive dissonance, your defensiveness will diminish.

A common reaction is, "yes, but I'm just more comfortable when I cross my arms!" Sure, but any position is comfortable when it aligns with your attitude. If you're relaxing with your friends or are having a fun night out, folding your arms won't seem nearly as natural or comfortable because it creates a cognitive dissonance with your present emotional state. If you find you routinely cross your arms in most settings "because it is more comfortable", then perhaps this is because defensiveness (or perhaps detachment) has become your default setting.

TIMEOUT: What are my default gestures? Do I need to consider alternatives?

Aside from our emotional state, eliminating cognitive dissonance works on our *preferences* as well. Test subjects listened to a recording of what they believed to be their own heartbeat, then they were instructed to look at Playboy centerfolds. When "their heartbeats" sped up, even though the heartbeat sound was artificial, their judgment of the centerfolds' attractiveness increased along with the rate of the heartbeat. Even 2 months later, their opinions persisted on which centerfolds were most attractive (Valins). This is further evidence of the strong need for congruence between mind and body.

Even neutral body language is forced to harmonize with our thoughts. When test subjects were asked to furrow their brows while viewing photographs of celebrities, the celebrities were perceived as less famous because the brow-furrowing action itself *inferred mental exertion* to think of who the celebrity was, even if they were already known to the subject (Strack, Neumann).

As we look at *charismatic* nonverbal behaviors, it is important to remember that it isn't enough to *know* what they are, you need to *use* them to the point they become natural. As you incorporate this body language, your thoughts and feelings will follow.

WHAT'S THIS GOT TO DO WITH CHARISMA?

Charisma is generated by specific *nonverbal behaviors*, and not some intangible or magical quality (Erez). This means, in practical terms, that **charisma is a skill you can learn!**

Knowing how to generate charisma is better than any persuasive technique. When using tools of persuasion, you are trying to get someone to *do* something or *think* a certain way. When you have charisma, *people want to do what you want them to do.*

Charismatic people draw others to them. You feel good when you are around them and even better when they pay attention to you. Charisma is not only important to world leaders and captains of industry but to anyone wanting to be more effective with people.

But it is a skill unlike other learned proficiencies. Through *The Human Whisperer* you will select elements to develop based on your strengths and weaknesses as related to principles of nonverbal behavior.

*   *   *

The three traits all charismatic people nonverbally project are *power*, *warmth* and *presence* (Cabane, p.13). The more balanced power and warmth are, the more pronounced the effect. If you are strong in one, but weak in the other, your full potential will never be realized. Presence underscores both of the other traits and needs to be maximized in all situations.

It is a myth that you must be effervescent or extroverted to be charismatic. Society places so much emphasis on being outgoing that introverts can feel they never quite "measure up." In fact, introverts can have a strong charismatic advantage in dealing with certain types of people where extroverts come off too strong. None of the three charismatic traits depend on how outgoing you are. So for all of you introverts out there, know that you too can exude charisma in a natural way that doesn't require you to change the fundamental way you behave or interact with others.

Power isn't limited to projecting authority. It means affecting the world through *prestige*. One can be seen as powerful if they have more money, knowledge, intelligence or social status than those around them. Even if you are not traditionally seen as powerful, you can be empowered by your expertise on topics or through another avenue.

If you can't find that power within you it's not a problem, because you don't need power to have charisma, you only need to *appear* powerful. People accept whatever we project, both positively and negatively. Sharp clothing and a confident posture leads us to *assume* a powerful person just as friendly body language and warm smiles lead us to *assume* good intentions.

Warmth is easiest to define–having a friendly and charitable disposition. Warmth lets others know that our power will be used benevolently. Warmth entails more than just being nice; nice people complain they are taken advantage of because they are too nice. Most often, this is an incorrect self-assessment; they *allow* themselves to be taken advantage of. Being a warm person does not equate to being treated badly by others. You can be warm and still stand up for yourself.

Power and warmth need to be present in roughly equal measure. Warmth without power is likeable but comes across as over eager, subservient, and desperate to please. Power without warmth is impressive but isn't charismatic as it appears arrogant, cold and detached. As with power, you don't need to *be* warm to be charismatic, you only need to *appear* warm. A room-lighting smile and welcoming eyes create the appearance of warmth even when true intentions are anything but warm and friendly.

Presence is the most difficult to accomplish because, unlike power and warmth, it is not enough to *appear* to have presence–it must be genuine. Presence means staying connected to a person instead of getting caught up in our own thoughts. When we aren't fully present in a conversation, people see it. We've all spent time talking to someone who wasn't listening. It is perceived as inauthentic and dismissive, making it impossible to generate trust and rapport.

Staying present in a conversation is not an easy thing to do because our brains are conditioned to focus on novel stimuli. When engaging someone in a long conversation it is natural for our minds to wander. In our modern society, the problem is even more pronounced and is getting worse. Technology distracts us through a constant influx of stimulation, leading to a state of *continuous partial attention*, where we become incapable of devoting all our attention to any one thing. With our phones, tablets, computers, wearable tech, etc., it's a wonder we ever speak to one another at all. Even a tiny boost in your presence can have a dramatic impact on others, which makes you memorable.

WHISPER ALERT: Exuding charisma is demonstrating power and warmth in equal measure, permeated with presence.

PROJECT CHARISMA TO BECOME CHARISMATIC

Unfortunately, micromanaging charismatic body language (no matter how skilled you think you are or how well you try to remember all the signals) is impossible because you send out dozens, and even hundreds, of signals beyond your conscious control. Rather, you must *focus on a small subset* of behaviors proven to achieve two effects simultaneously.

First, these behaviors must *externally* project the attributes of power, warmth and presence. By demonstrating these traits with your body language you will be seen by others as a charismatic person.

Second, these behaviors will create the corresponding mental states so you not only appear charismatic, but *internally* adopt the feelings of power, warmth and presence. Remember our minds are controlled by our body language as much as our body language is controlled by our minds. By consciously engaging in body language that defines these charismatic traits, our minds follow suit. Once you are in the right frame of mind, your body's many nonverbal behaviors will manifest naturally so mind and body create cognitive harmony. This is a natural way to project how you wish to be seen–by seeing yourself the same way. *Once you are seen as naturally charismatic you have taken a big step in becoming a Human Whisperer.*

Following are strategies to boost these attributes in the general order they will be noticed in conversation. As easy as they sound, some may find them difficult to do without concerted effort. My advice is to put in the effort, as the benefit far outweighs the cost. So how do we demonstrate POWER, WARMTH and PRESENCE?

Smile!

> *"Most of the time... when you're crying, nobody notices your tears. Most of the time... when you're worried, nobody feels your pain. Most of the time... when you're happy, nobody sees your smile. But when you fart just one time..."*

-ANONYMOUS

You're smiling right now! The first thing people notice is your smile, which is the easiest way to boost your warmth, both inside and out. Before you say "yeah, yeah, I've heard this all before", please stay tuned and read on. You will find out a few things about the simple smile that you never knew, and with luck, it may just keep that smile on your face!

Smiling comes more easily for some than others. If you don't smile often, this behavior will be among the most difficult to habituate, but if you can do it, you will reap *substantial* interpersonal rewards by brightening others' lives and your own. Smiling needs to become routine, even if it feels foreign or unnatural. If you can work toward making smiling your default state, you can boost your charisma and likeability in all situations.

There are two types of smiles: the "real" one and the "fake" one. Think about it for a moment. The smile you use when re-connecting with a loved one differs greatly from the smile you use when saying "thank you" for a present you *know* you will return. *(Note: sweater vests are NEVER good gift ideas.)*

A real smile is called a "zygomatic" smile - the entire face is involved, and it shows. This smile pulls the mouth back while the muscles around the eyes cause them to narrow and create "crow's feet". It is a genuine smile and is interpreted warmly by anyone seeing it. When you smile genuinely, there is no effort involved, and it feels natural.

Smiling is so important that we have come up with a fake smile to help smooth over what might otherwise be socially unpleasant situations. Politicians and snake oil salesmen (sometimes they're not the same thing) are known for their fake smiles. These fake smiles use different muscles to push the edges of the mouth horizontally. *We* know the smiles are fake, *they know we know* the smiles are fake and yet we all do it anyway.

Why? Because it still creates the impression of warmth, even if we know the smiles aren't genuine.

A real smile is easy to spot by wrinkle lines around the eyes. If you don't see those lines, and if the eyes and the rest of the face are not involved in the smile, it is not a genuine smile. It doesn't mean the person isn't feeling emotions consistent with a smile, but rather they most likely don't feel it to the same degree as shown by a real smile. Hillary Clinton offers an excellent contrast between these smiles. Note in the first image how the entire face is involved in the smile: the muscles all around the face and eyes are engaged and you can easily tell this is a genuine smile. The second image shows a smiling politician ("a smile for the camera"). Look at how uninvolved the rest of the face is. The eyes appear as if she weren't smiling at all.

* * *

Although it is intuitive, smiling affects those around you in a positive way. Smiling is contagious and will influence people to smile back (Hatfield). For the non-smilers out there, how many times have you met a person's gaze who was smiling right at you and without thinking you returned the smile? Even if it only lasted a second, it is proof we are positively impacted by such a gesture.

When you are happy, or you see someone else smile, a part of your brain (the cingulate cortex) automatically and unconsciously triggers a smile (O'Doherty). This part of your brain contains "mirror neurons" that recognize faces and cause an instant "mirroring" reaction. What is even more impressive is that this mirroring response works *even when you are both using fake smiles*! <u>Remember, nobody smiles, but almost everybody smiles back</u>. When you smile at someone and they *don't* smile back, it is because they are making a *conscious* effort not to do so.

Smiling makes you more attractive to people and you will be treated better as a result. You're also viewed as more relaxed, reliable and sincere. Another study reports that "seeing an attractive smiling face activates the region in your brain that processes sensory rewards" (O'Doherty). This means when you smile at someone, it elevates their emotional state in a positive direction and creates the impression of warmth.

* * *

Smiling and attraction

While you appear more attractive when smiling, there are exceptions in courtship rituals. Early studies show that women find men less sexually attractive when smiling when compared to non-smilers who looked proud and arrogant. Men rated women more sexually attractive when they smiled a lot. Why the disconnect? Because smiling in certain contexts is a submission signal. Women prefer men of higher power and status, which is conveyed in part by smiling less. Men often prefer mates that show submissive traits. This does not mean that women do not value a sense of humor. Quite the opposite. The best results come when a man can show a sense of humor while showing the correct level of pride and status.

More recent studies, however, run counter to these classical notions and find that women find men more attractive who smile more. This is likely due to cultural and generational shifts in mate selection. So, if you're trying to maintain an air of status and mystery for someone you find particularly fetching, it would still behoove you to smile more than your natural instincts indicate.

So the best advice in all contexts, not just romantic ones, is "when in doubt, smile!"

* * *

Smiling affects not only others' perceptions of you, it also affects your health and happiness. The physical act of smiling activates neuropeptides that help fight off disease and ease stress (Seaward). Dopamine, endorphin, and serotonin (the brain's "feel-good" chemicals) are all released when you smile. The dopamine relaxes your body, lowering your heart rate and blood pressure (Lane, p.345–370). The endorphin acts as a natural pain reliever while the serotonin acts as a natural antidepressant. Antidepressant pharmaceuticals work primarily by artificially raising the level of serotonin in your brain. By smiling you can achieve this effect naturally. Happy people that smile a lot also get sick less often than people that are chronic complainers. This makes perfect sense, as the endorphins released by smiling have a tranquilizing effect on the nervous system and help to build up the immune system. All of this leads to the conclusion that by smiling you will actually live longer! (Abel)

* * *

Degree. A smile can be bigger or smaller depending on what we're smiling about. Smiling "too big for the moment" is seen as fake at best, and at worst, psychotic. Thanking a cashier for ringing up a pack of gum doesn't require a smile turned up to "10" (or for you fans of the movie *Spinal Tap*, "11"). Smiling is not an on/off condition; rather, it is a continuum where successful smilers have learned the appropriate level to apply for a given situation. Practice smiling so it comes across naturally and doesn't look forced. If you find that your smile feels forced or artificial, don't abruptly stop smiling. Just try smiling a little less and see if that makes you feel more at ease.

"Eyebrow flash". It is a quick staccato brow raise associated with *positive emotions* or surprise. The eyebrow flash is a universal social greeting signal (except in Japan where it is improper because of sexual connotations). Using an eyebrow flash increases the potency of a smile and can achieve likeability faster and more effectively than a smile alone. For friends and acquaintances, you can hold the eyebrows up for slightly longer than just an instant as it signals how much you like the person's company. Holding your eyebrows up for too long may make you look more than a little unbalanced! So be judicious.

In professional contexts: People smile more around authority figures in general but those in authority only smile in friendly situations. When things get tense, the dominant person in the room will be the last to smile. If you're in a tense business situation where you wish to be seen as *less* submissive, an easy way to achieve this is to smile less. If you are in the dominant role in a meeting, however, try smiling more to achieve specific benefits. First, it helps put others at ease even when the situation is charged. Second, the strongest psychological impact can be felt when a friendly smile disappears behind a disapproving question or comment. It allows more leeway to create a greater "command of the room."

WHISPER ALERT: To warm and soften your persona, smile more. To increase projection of power, smile strategically.

Caution, ladies! Women need to be particularly aware of smiling as a submission signal. Research indicates women smile more than men. Some claim it is because they have been traditionally placed in subordinate roles. Studies show baby girls smile more than baby boys by eight weeks of age, so it is probably instinctual, but is further reinforced through cultural conditioning. If women smile more, it projects a submissive, less authoritative demeanor. For women in business contexts, smile less to be taken more seriously. When you do smile, make sure not to smile more often than your male counterparts. For men to be more persuasive, they should generally smile more.

TIMEOUT: Do I smile too rarely or excessively? Should I modify my smiling behavior?

The habit of smiling is important because it not only makes you *appear* warmer, it influences your emotional state so you actually *become* warmer. If you appear warmer, others will respond favorably. If you become warmer, you will be in the right frame of mind to become charismatic, which is one of the most powerful tools in your quest to become a Human Whisperer. Work on making a smile your default state–it will change your life and the lives of those around you. Enormous impact for minimal effort!

The handshake

The most primitive greeting was to hold arms out with palms exposed to show no hidden weapon. In more recent Roman times, to prevent the possibility of a concealed dagger, the forearm grasp became a common greeting. The modern handshake started in the 19th century to conclude business deals between men. It has only become a widespread greeting over the last 100 years. Now it is used universally across all business and personal contexts. In order to make the most of this first impression opportunity, consider both the position of the hands and the strength of grip.

Position of the hands: To create rapport with others make sure your hands are vertical so no one has the "upper hand." Apply the same pressure you receive so you can avoid the impression you're either giving them a "wet fish" or a vice-grip like handshake, both of which are to be avoided.

The "double hander" is a favorite of politicians and used car salesmen and is *supposed* to instill confidence but has the opposite effect. There are several varieties of this handshake. The left hand might come to rest on the back of the other person's hand, wrist, forearm, elbow or upper arm. The farther the reach, the more personal and intimate a greeting it becomes. Only use a double-handed handshake if you already have a personal relationship with the person. In the wrong context, it generates immediate mistrust and negative feelings. In the right context, and when performed gently, this can generate warmth and positive feelings, particularly in situations when a hug would be too intimate but a handshake too formal.

It is not uncommon to encounter the "fingertip grab" where either you or the other party grab too soon and end up gripping only fingers. In either case, you want to correct the situation by saying in a light, almost comical, yet sincere way, "let's try that again." If you are on the receiving end of such a handshake, you might need to use your other hand to grip their wrist so you can readjust the handshake-in-progress. Failing to fix this situation can signal the beginning of an awkward conversation, especially if this is a person you do not know well.

Pressure and Strength: The handshake is particularly well suited to displaying power and confidence at the outset of a conversation. People that use a firm handshake are seen as more outgoing and emotionally expressive and make better first impressions. Soft handshakers are seen as shy and neurotic.

Women with a strong handshake are considered more open-minded. This contradicts the commonly held belief that assertive women are more negatively regarded than their male counterparts (Chaplin). Gender aside, working on developing a solid, firm handshake is an easy way to exude power and confidence, even in situations where you feel less than powerful.

To be seen as more powerful, even dominant, turn your hand palm down in the handshake. The hand will not be parallel to the floor but at about a 45-degree angle. In one business study, only 31% of superior women used the "palm down thrust" as opposed to 88% of the men. Women aren't generally looking to establish their dominance, which accounts for most of that disparity. Using the palm down thrust isn't advisable unless you don't exude power through other nonverbal means; otherwise, it is easy to appear aggressive and cocky.

Whether or not you decide to use it, it is still a good idea to know how to counter the palm down thrust when someone offers it to you. The easiest option is a double handed shake where your right hand enters from a palm up position to take his hand. Place your left hand on the back of his right hand to achieve the "double hander." In this position you can move all hands firmly to a vertical position while you start the handshake motion. This silently, but forcefully, shows strength and confidence while maintaining social equality.

Another counter to the palm down thrust is the "power handshake". This one gets your whole body involved. First, though it will feel unnatural, step forward slightly with your *left* foot. Then step forward with your right leg moving across the person's body and into their personal space. Finish by moving your left foot next to your right foot to complete the action. This automatically moves you into a vertical, and dominant, position. As a position check, your body should be inside their personal space at about a 45-degree angle. Another helpful note here is that you want to maintain slightly *more* pressure than they exert (Pease p. 47-9). (If you can't visualize this maneuver, go to http://www.stevenkeyl.com for a demonstration.)

Two clarifications about the power handshake. First, the movements should be small and subtle. Large movements come across as aggressive instead of confident. Second, execute the movements with a big smile and positive body movements. This reinforces your good intentions and gets the meeting off on the right foot (pun intended).

Fun but not normally appropriate: Besides the traditional handshake, there are many types of informal greetings that serve the same purpose, many of which started in professional sports in the 1950's like the high (and low) five, the palm clasp, and the fist bump (which was allegedly started by germophobe Stan Musial). These greetings were used because athletes felt that after a major victory, a handshake was just too muted of a congratulatory response (Stephey). By the 1970's the fist bump achieved common use in urban, predominantly black neighborhoods, but by the 80's and 90's these greetings were common throughout the United States. One of the latest evolutions of these greetings is the "pound hug", also known as the "bro hug" or the "man hug", where during a handshake or palm clasp, two men give each other an off-center one arm hug. Unlike the traditional hug which symbolically and physically removes barriers and unites two people, the pound hug maintains the obstacle of the two right arms.

Though some disagreement remains on the origins of these greetings, all of them are informal and used only by people that know each other well. It is a common mistake to greet strangers, or potential customers, in one of these familiar ways. It is quite a presumptuous breach of social etiquette to meet someone for the first time and provide anything other than a traditional handshake. If they feel comfortable enough with you to offer a palm clasp or fist bump or even a bro hug, then you should warmly reciprocate. Let them make their level of comfort known and then follow suit. Mirroring their greeting will put them at ease which is vital if you want to create true rapport.

Listening

"Many a man would rather you heard his story than granted his request."

-Philip Stanhope

We all have a powerful need to be heard and understood. <u>Mastering listening skills is a requirement</u> in becoming a Human Whisperer. If you can show others you are listening *and* understand what is being said, you illustrate your "presence"–your ability to be (and stay) in the moment.

It is a misconception that great persuaders are smooth talkers. Some are, but *all* people of influence are great listeners. *You communicate more through nonverbals when listening*, because the speaker is highly sensitive to the nonverbal behavior of the listener. People feel good when your body language says, "tell me more." They feel heard, and it's a great way to find out what's important to them.

"Presence" means being fully engaged with another person, and so, for the duration of the conversation, they should feel important to you. Checking your messages, texting, taking a phone call, looking around the room, or engaging in any activity that pulls you away from the conversation undermines your presence and destroys your chance to build rapport and generate charisma.

Listening starts with the willingness to stay present, pay attention, and focus on what is being said. If you let your mind wander, the lack of presence will show on your face and damage your chances of creating rapport. To help prevent your mind from wandering, focus on your breathing, blinking rate, the temperature in the room, or some other physical sensation that will, or at least *appear* to, keep you in the moment.

*   *   *

Good listeners know the golden rule of listening–"Never interrupt." For some, this is a near impossible goal, but to excel as a listener you must suppress the urge to cut someone off while they are speaking. Even if that urge stems from the positive excitement from what is being said, interrupting leaves the speaker feeling incomplete because they could not express their thoughts fully.

This doesn't mean that there is no place for dynamic, free-flowing conversation. In larger families, for instance, when sitting around the dinner table, if you don't interrupt you may never get a word in. The goal here isn't "communication" per se, but rather reinforcing social bonds. Any informal dynamic like this one, with friends or family, discussing nothing in particular and having a great time doing it, is not about charismatic listening. The "golden rule of listening" applies to situations where the listener must actively demonstrate charismatic principles.

Great listeners not only don't interrupt, they let the other person interrupt them! Of course, no one should interrupt, but one shouldn't draw attention to another's faux pas because it impedes the flow of conversation. So let it pass, because the thought they want to vocalize is preventing them from listening to what you're saying anyway. Set aside your need to be heard, and nurture someone else's.

Supreme listeners pause before answering. This is such an important and often overlooked point, I will say it again. *The greatest listeners pause before answering.* This allows you to absorb fully what you've heard and shows the speaker you've heard them.

After two seconds nod slowly to show you've not only heard the information, but you've understood it. These actions flow together... pause and nod. Too many people look like bobble heads when trying to show they're listening to someone. If you nod too quickly or too often, it comes across as an artificial affectation designed to trick people into thinking you're paying attention to them. When nodding, do it slowly and deliberately. Pause and nod. These actions together demonstrate you've heard them, assimilated the information and understand what they are saying.

There is a world of difference between "hearing" and "listening." Most conversations are exercises in "hearing"– two people politely waiting for the other to stop talking so they can continue with their own important point. Neither is listening to the other, and neither seems to care. True listening does not mean simply waiting for the other person to stop speaking so you can talk again. "Hearers" are easily identified when the response ignores or talks over the other's point. Failure to listen flatlines your presence and kills any hope of generating charisma.

You need to **listen**. Stop thinking about what you will say next. Focus your effort and energy into understanding what is being said.

Concentrating on their message and not on what to say next creates a natural pause. Not only does the pause show you've heard their thought, but you respond to what they've said rather than continuing your independent train of thought. You have really heard and understood them. You will *become* a better listener through this process, instead of just *appearing* to be a better listener.

TIMEOUT: Do I "hear" or "listen"? Do I control my inclination to interrupt? Does my reply demonstrate that I have truly listened?

As a test, engage a friend or family member in a topic you know will create a nice back-and-forth conversation. During this time, stay present and focused on what the other person is saying. Note how different the structure and flow of the discussion is from your normal conversational rhythms. The person you're speaking with will probably report this conversation as more satisfying and fulfilling than your "run-of-the-mill talks."

Before trying out the experiment, remember:

- Don't interrupt them, but let them interrupt you
- Pause and nod for a full 2 seconds before you speak, and do so slowly and deliberately
- Don't think about what to say until the other person is done speaking. Process what you've heard and only then think about responding.

With these simple tips it is possible to exude charisma in any conversation. Many people report they already unconsciously use one or more of these techniques but until now may not have understood why they work.

Speaking

What to say and *how* to say things to enhance your ability to connect with and persuade others is covered in later chapters. But word choice and delivery, discussed here, can also boost your charisma.

Increase your vocabulary: Linguistic studies show a relationship between *apparent* intelligence, status, prestige and one's vocabulary; therefore, one way to amplify your power is to improve your vocabulary. The "word-a-day" calendars are popular because they are a simple way of strengthening your linguistic toolbox.

An important part of learning $3.00 words is knowing when, *and when not,* to use them. If someone uses big words to convey ideas and the listener can keep pace, then the word choices are appropriate. For maximum impact, tailor your word choice to be at, or slightly above, the level of your audience.

It's fine to use an occasional word that someone may not know *as long as its meaning can be easily inferred by context.*

Using too many big words comes across as arrogant. If your word choice would be indecipherable to your listener, or if a simple word would work equally well, then drop the big word. This not only boosts message clarity but facilitates rapport and liking through mirrored speech.

Allow me to pellucidly articulate this (recondite) conceptualization: Your puissance is not made manifest through sesquipedalian pursuits because your gasconading circumlocution makes you look pusillanimous instead of perspicacious.

"Forbidden" words: On the other end of the linguistic spectrum are curse words. A judicious amount of bad language can be good, while too much makes you look unintelligent and inarticulate. Note I didn't suggest that you *eliminate* cursing, because it does have a role in language. Sometimes a curse word used at the right place and time can drive home your point in a way not achievable through other means. The keys are that cursing must:

- Not be overused
- Be a conscious choice
- Be used in an appropriate setting

We all know someone who can't form a sentence without adding three expletives. If you find it difficult to relate a story or concept without swearing, work on eliminating it entirely. Once you can speak curse-free without effort, then begin adding it back as appropriate.

Those that don't swear at all shouldn't start now. Adding curse words into speech must sound and feel natural. People that don't swear suddenly dropping a curse word into conversation can sound stilted and unnatural. The rule of thumb is that if you do swear, try to do it less, and if you don't swear at all, keep it that way.

* * *

My mother taught English at the university level. Whereas many of my friends' families disallowed any cursing at all, that wasn't the case in our house. As youngsters, my sister I weren't allowed to swear. As we got older, though, my mother didn't mind "proper cursing." She taught us that swearing is a part of language and it's important to know how to use it effectively. Since it wasn't taboo, we learned how to swear, around whom we could (and could not) swear, and in what situations.

She said, "You must be able to express every thought in your head without swearing. Swearing is a spice, not the main course. By very occasionally peppering it into your speech you can emphasize points and grab the listener's attention. The less you use it, the stronger it is."

Knowing how to swear naturally is an acquired skill. I had a parent willing to let us learn early on how to do it right. Thanks, Mom.

* * *

Beyond word choice, the voice itself can project power and warmth. When delivering a message people are proven to be more influenced by *how* things are said rather than *what* is said (Perry). Learn to control your voice to improve the chances your message is favorably received.

Pitch. The lower the pitch of your voice, the more resonant and powerful it sounds. Don't artificially lower the tone, but work to keep your voice on the lower end of your normal speech register. Lowering the intonation at the end of sentences also projects power in both the speaker and in the message being delivered. (Raising your intonation at the end of sentences makes every statement sound like a question creating the impression you are unsure of yourself, and it tends to irritate the listener.)

Volume. Power can also be projected through greater volume. Being too loud comes across as obnoxious, so learn to fill the space you're in with an appropriate intensity. Warmth can be added by reducing volume slightly below your typical level.

Tempo. Confidence is transmitted when using slow and measured speech. Speaking too quickly undermines perceived confidence and makes it harder to understand the overall message. Frequent use of pauses is another way to transmit that confidence. Pauses generate anticipation and subtly communicate that your message is important enough to continue uninterrupted, because only someone confident enough in the substance of their message would risk being interrupted by pausing.

Smile. The best way to project vocal warmth is to smile. We've already looked at the importance of the smile in face-to-face interactions but it's just as important to smile when you can only be heard. When you're on the phone, for example, people can "hear your smile." One study even found that listeners could detect 16 kinds of smiles from the voice alone! (Drahota)

* * *

When speaking, "it's not all about you." A command of language is important for creating an impression of intelligence and standing, but *appropriate* word choice is a key element in demonstrating presence. By expressing thoughts slightly above the listener, you exhibit respect without condescension. Sensitivity to objectionable language is always a must so "when in doubt, throw it out." Finally, vocal elements of speech can be used to increase listenability, warmth and confidence. It's not just the message, it's also delivery.

Eye contact

When speaking to someone, it is important to maintain an appropriate level of eye contact. This does not mean *never* breaking eye contact. Anyone that stares at someone 100% of the time is considered confrontational and their behavior inappropriate.

When looking at someone in conversation, various gazes can be used. With the *social gaze*, you meet someone's eyes ⅔ of the time and the rest of that time is spent scanning their face in the triangle formed between their eyes and their mouth. This is how we normally speak to others in a non-threatening environment. Most people only look each other in the eyes 30-60% of the time, so if you can follow the ⅔ rule, you will boost your presence. Depending on how welcoming and sincerely you form that eye contact, a social gaze can also project warmth.

Eye contact is not just for boosting presence and warmth, you can boost power as well.

The *power gaze* runs betweens the eyes and extends in a triangle upward to the center of the forehead. The same ⅔ rule applies, so don't make too much or too little eye contact. The impact this gaze can have on a discussion is striking. It projects strength and changes any conversation into a no-nonsense exchange. If you aren't being treated seriously at work, try this out when presenting your ideas and you will surprise yourself with how well it can work. (Power is also elevated because your head will rise slightly above its normal conversational angle, which *projects* confidence and authority and also enhances your *internal* feeling of power.)

A first cousin of the power gaze is the *power stare*. This is when your eyes move from person to person without blinking. When your gaze moves to the next person you stare them directly in the eye until you shift your gaze to the next person. This projects immediate authority and has an unnerving effect on anyone watching you. This is best used selectively when speaking to a group of people. If in a one-on-one situation, use a "blinkless power gaze" as an alternative and it will serve the same purpose. A softer approach that still shows strength is to make a conscious effort to blink less often.

When someone else is using a power gaze, or just making too much eye contact, it may be a sign they are trying to assert their dominance and authority. If you want to equalize this nonverbal attempt at gaining the upper hand, meet their gaze as consistently as they meet yours and use a power gaze of your own. In most cases, they will capitulate and move into a more normal social gazing behavior at which point you should follow suit.

*   *   *

Inappropriate in any business context (but in the interest of completeness) the *intimate gaze* is the triangle which runs between the eyes and down the body. Both sexes engage in this gaze but women have a wider peripheral vision and are more subtle, which allows them to avoid being noticed. Men have tunnel vision which is why his up and down gaze is obvious. Research shows that women use the intimate gaze more, but men are accused of this more often because they keep getting caught (Pease, p. 183). If someone is looking at you with an intimate gaze...well, that's outside the scope of this modest book, so you'll have to handle that one yourself, but good luck!

Movements and gestures

More educated people rely on words over gestures to communicate ideas. The greater socioeconomic status one has, the fewer body movements one tends to make.

An overabundance of gestures detracts from the overall message. Reducing gestures such as hair grooming, drumming fingers and/or tapping toes will increase your status (and power) in the eyes of others. By consciously eliminating fidgeting and restless movements, your mind will instead focus on gestures that project confidence and power.

Taking up Space: Using your body to occupy space projects confidence and authority. Sitting slightly askew on chairs or putting your arm on the back of an adjacent chair are simple ways to claim that space.

"Arms akimbo," also known as "The Wonder Woman pose", asserts dominance and projects authority. This is when your elbows are bent and your hands are resting on your hips. For women particularly, this is a powerful display to use in a board room, professional workplace, or any setting to show she is standing her ground, confident, and unwilling to be bullied.

"Hand steepling" is when the fingertips of one hand all lightly touch the fingertips of the other hand. Sometimes the palms will also come together to form a praying-type gesture to appear less smug and more pious. This shows a confident and self-assured attitude, most often seen while seated at a table. Another variation is "the church steeple," which is formed by starting with the regular hand steeple but then interlocking all the fingers of each hand except for the thumbs and index fingers.

Clasping your hands behind your back is another behavior that shows superiority, confidence and power. Doing this when stressed, like before a public speech or legal proceeding, will make you feel powerful and self-assured.

"Hooding" is another territorial display of high confidence. This is when your hands are clasped together and place behind your head. It is most often accompanied by leaning back in one's chair. It shouts to all observers "I'm in charge here" and it may be what you want to convey, but be judicious when using this gesture.

Displaying confident body language makes you look and *feel* more powerful. People assuming strong, confident postures and strong speaking voices produce a biochemical reaction that make them feel more confident and powerful (Carney). Evidence again that *conscious* control over body language can affect our mental state just like our mental state can *unconsciously* affect our body language.

(Caution: Learn how to look comfortable taking more space. All of these power gestures can be interpreted, in some cases, as anti-social and arrogant. To avoid this, only use these techniques if you need to boost your power to align with your warmth and presence; otherwise, you risk alienating the people you're trying to win over. If you normally come across as overbearing, then consider adding more gestures when you speak to *reduce* the amount of power you project.)

Mirroring

Mirroring is the act of mimicking the body language of others, boosting presence and warmth. It generates trust and rapport as it makes others feel at ease. Mirroring takes place unconsciously and is rarely noticed by either the person engaging in mirroring or the one who is being mirrored. (No, the photo of first lady Michelle Obama and a university president has not been photo shopped! Dog-ear this page because later you will be asked to look at the picture again.)

Simultaneous blinking and pupil dilation are unconsciously mirrored, which is surprising given that these behaviors cannot be consciously mimicked. When done consciously, however, mirroring can activate deep instincts of trust and liking. Mirroring can get people to buy your products, give you a better deal, or just make you more physically attractive to others (Gueguen).

Though mirroring is a topic often discussed in books, magazines and by motivational speakers, one element often missed is that the mirroring needs to be done subtly and naturally. There is nothing more counterproductive than an attempt at mirroring which comes across as patronizing, self-serving, or worse, mocking. Mirroring behaviors must remain subliminal to be effective. Here are a few simple ways to make mirroring more subtle:

- *Be selective.* Only do what's comfortable for you. Some gestures are more gender-specific (hair grooming, throat touching), for example. Don't feel the need to mirror every movement.
- *Vary the magnitude.* If their gesture is too big, make a smaller one. You need not mimic the size of the gesture for the mirroring to be subconsciously perceived.
- *Wait.* Avoid immediate mirroring. Let a little time pass before mirroring their movements. It is still effective even if it takes to 20-30 seconds to move into a similar posture or pose.

Following these rules allow you to engage in mirroring behavior that will be consciously invisible but have a profound impact.

*   *   *

Mirroring isn't a recent invention, but part of our earliest experiences

When a parent imitates an infant's expressions while making sounds consistent with that emotion, the infant associates that emotion with a corresponding expression. This fosters self-awareness as they see their emotions reflected in the faces of their parents. Conversely, infants learn new emotions, expressions, and gestures by mirroring their parents' expressions. This may help promote social communication later in life (Kohut).

*   *   *

Mirroring is not restricted to our nonverbal behaviors but is employed in many social situations. When dining out, for example, each person may ask the other, "what are you going to order?" Even when not ordering identical meals, people choose complementary items. For example, if everyone else is ordering salad, and you wanted the 22 oz. Porterhouse steak and baked potato, you might not make it all the way back to a salad but end up ordering a soup and sandwich instead. If you have your heart set on dessert but everyone else passed, you will likely mirror the behavior of the others and skip dessert too.

Email greetings and closings are other "mirror-able" social behaviors. Emails might begin Mr. Keyl, Steven, Dear Sir, etc.. Closing an email contains just as much variety with Sincerely, Yours truly, etc. or just their name. Sometimes no greeting and/or closing is used. By mirroring, we match a common level of decorum for the exchange, neither too formal nor too relaxed.

Speech rate is another overlooked mirror behavior. *Don't speak faster than others as it makes them feel pressured and anxious.* If they speak more slowly, then you need to force yourself to slow down to more closely match their rate of speech. This is particularly important in sales. When providing too much information, salesmen speak so much faster than their customer that it hurts their chances of closing the deal. Mirroring applies to all of the speech variables like volume and pitch.

Caution: Be aware of gender specific differences in how we mirror. Women mirror each other four times as much as men mirror one another. Women routinely mirror men but men mirror women only when in "courtship mode." If you can get into the habit of mirroring people more often, you'll see a dramatic shift in how people treat you and how they think about you. One reason women can look across a crowded room and perceive disagreement, anger, or hurt feelings is because they are used to reading body language that men don't tend to notice.

Although women are better at mirroring they need to realize that men rarely use their face to signal their attitudes. So women, particularly very expressive women, are well-advised to reduce their facial expressions so as not to come across too strong. And don't mirror what you *assume* he is feeling; if you're wrong, it can come across as flighty, sarcastic, or belligerent, depending on context. In business contexts, women who listen with a more serious and less expressive face come across as more intelligent, astute and sensible.

Interpreting mirroring observed in others: A long-standing trick in the sales trade when presenting products or ideas to a couple is to notice who mirrors whom to determine who is the final decision maker. This concept can be extended to any situation where you are looking to find out "who wears the pants in the family" or who holds more power along the table in the boardroom. Once you know who is in charge or who is more influential, you can tailor your message accordingly.

Generally, avoid mirroring negative body language. But for people who are anxious, drawn into themselves and having difficulty finding the right words, <u>loosely</u> mirror their behaviors, i.e. how they're holding their head, tapping fingers, fidgeting with a button or cuff link, etc. and maintain this mirror for as long as they're speaking. When it's your turn to speak, add warmth through your eyes, voice and face. Slowly move into a more relaxed and open position *and they likely will mirror your more positive body language.* This "mirror-then-lead" strategy can calm people in a variety of settings and situations. However, if they are openly angry, defensive or defiant then any mirroring would only escalate tensions and is not advisable.

WHISPER ALERT: Look for the mirror. Mirroring is woefully underestimated as a charismatic tool.

Mirroring aids in establishing rapport which is essential in becoming a Human Whisperer. Remember subtlety is key. Mirroring actions, attitudes, and speech patterns shows you are more likely to be a friend and also more likely to hold similar beliefs and attitudes. It is not uncommon to begin by mirroring someone only to have the other person mirror you! Their mirroring behavior is a clear signal they agree with you and/ or like you. It shows they are comfortable and rapport is achieved.

Spacing

"Personal Space" is the area around a person perceived as "theirs." When this area is encroached upon, most people feel discomfort or anxiety. There are four levels of personal space with differing diameters, depending on the particular zone and individual comfort level:

- The "intimate zone" runs outward from 0-18 inches and is reserved for our closest friends and family.

- The "personal zone" is from 18 inches to 4 feet and is used for friends and close associates.
- The "social zone" is from 4-12 feet and is reserved for strangers, the cable guy, and the new guy at work.
- The "public zone" extends outward from 12 feet and is used for public speaking in larger groups.

In the personal zone, some are happy in the 18 inch range, while others aren't comfortable unless you have a larger buffer of 3 to 4 feet. These differences often depend on where we grew up. The farther a person reaches to shake your hand, the more space he wants maintained between the two of you. People brought up in urban environments don't reach as far as rural dwellers as they are more accustomed to being in close proximity with others. Interestingly, these distances increase between two men and shorten between two women.

Spacing rituals are learned behaviors *that some people can't seem to learn*! Most of these rituals follow a similar pattern. Look for the widest space available and choose a spot mid-way between them.

At a movie theater, you choose a seat mid-way between the nearest person and the end of the row. Failure to comply with these unwritten rules can be jarring. In a near-empty theater, if a stranger were to take the seat next to you, it would be unsettling because it is unexpected and violates the social norms for preserving our personal space.

In public restrooms, there is an entire world of etiquette that we never think about. Behavioral scientists, however, can predict with startling accuracy which bathroom urinals and stalls people will choose, based almost entirely on personal space rules.

These spacing rules are so ingrained that they persist in virtual reality as well. In online video games where players become characters in a connected world with other players, they respect spacing rules just as they would in real life! (Cabane p.150)

Crowding violates people's intimate zones, causing stress and anxiety. Behaviors are largely consistent across all crowding situations. In a crowded elevator, there is no talking, even with people you know. Violators of this rule are seen as breaking a social norm. Other typical behaviors are avoiding eye contact, maintaining a "poker face", pretending to be deeply engrossed in a newspaper or device, minimal or no body movement, and keeping your eyes on those floor numbers!

These same "elevator" behaviors can be seen by commuters and passengers on public transport causing them to be described as "miserable" and "unhappy." The blank, expressionless look on people's faces are misjudgments. They are people shielding the intrusion of their intimate zones in cramped quarters.

To keep people comfortable, relaxed and in a position to build rapport, make sure they are comfortable with your distance from them. When you meet someone, give them a confident and natural handshake, step back and see what happens next. If they step back, they are not comfortable being any closer so do not encroach on the space between the two of you. Let *them* decide the appropriate distance. This has an added benefit of allowing you to more naturally notice when they reduce the distance between you, meaning they are increasingly comfortable.

Another way to maintain comfort is to avoid a seating arrangement where people will be seated with their back to the door or other open space. Men, in particular, are less comfortable than they would be otherwise.

When making the choice of a chair for yourself, sitting in "someone else's seat" is a big mistake. Just the simple act of saying, "Which chair is yours?" is a great way to keep others feeling comfortable and engenders good will.

The amygdala (discussed in Chapter 3) is the part of the brain where we feel stress in response to violations of our personal space. These feelings are absent in people whose amygdala is damaged. Though not everyone disregarding spacing rules has a damaged amygdala, "space invaders" are often unaware that they are generating undesired anxiety and stress in others. Criminal interrogators occasionally use this technique to *cause* intentional stress and/or agitation from a potential suspect. For our purposes, however, it is beneficial to respect these boundaries to increase the level of rapport.

NONVERBAL BEHAVIOR TO AVOID

Engaging in *negative* nonverbal behavior will impact your ability to generate rapport, trust and influence. Your negative body language unconsciously registers with others to form a negative impression. Also, by holding these negative body postures you will feel the emotions connected to them.

Defensive behaviors are the easiest to recognize and consciously avoid. The most obvious is crossing the arms. Others' reaction to this is immediate and it not only outwardly signals defensiveness, detachment and disengagement but will *cause* those feelings to become your mindset.

As mentioned earlier, people who routinely cross their arms or legs say they are comfortable this way. They are comfortable *because it matches their emotional state.* One of the most difficult things to do is maintain relaxed body language when you are nervous, insecure or defensive. To be most effective, however, it is an essential skill to practice. You need to convey relaxed, confident, and open body language *regardless of how you feel.* You will be *perceived* as confident and *become* more confident in the process.

Avoid clenching of the hands, or rubbing the hands together even in tense situations as it will negatively impact any interaction. This extends to both versions of clenched hands where the fingers are interlocked and where each hand grasps the other with fingers held together. If this is something you do unconsciously, when you notice it, try relaxing all the pressure from the hands and fingers, so that your grip is loose. Continue loosening the tension until the hands come apart on their own. Do this each time you find yourself in this position and you will notice a decrease in its frequency.

Eliminate excessive or rapid nodding of the head. It makes you look subservient and eager to please. Concentrate on the slow and deliberate nodding described in the "Listening" section, and this should be easy to accomplish.

A first cousin to excessive nodding is excessive verbal affirmation. Saying, "uh-huh", "yeah", "OK", "Oh, I agree", "I see what you mean" after each thing someone says undercuts your power by making you look deferential and eager-to-please.

*   *   *

It is upon the pillars of power, warmth, and presence that charisma is built, and this charisma is a cornerstone of the Human Whisperer model.

Your goal is to ensure that <u>power</u> and <u>warmth</u> are proportionately represented through your body language. Overemphasizing a trait is just as bad as having a deficit. If you already project warmth, smiling more will not boost your charisma score. If you already project power, adding powerful body language will only make you *less* likeable as you appear more arrogant.

Presence needs to be as strong as possible.

The average man doesn't display enough warmth while the average woman doesn't display enough power. Presence is something that both men and women tend to lack. In my life, I fall into traditional gender roles and need to work on both my presence and warmth. Smiling more, using warm eye contact instead of a power gaze, and using the listening and mirroring skills allow me to boost my warmth and presence to not only *appear* more charismatic, but to *feel* that way, too.

These situations are fluid and may vary by situation and circumstance. If you are speaking to a group as a subject matter expert, for example, you may project more or less power (depending on your comfort with public speaking and your confidence in the subject), so be mindful of which behaviors to emphasize or minimize. Conversely, if you find you lack warmth or presence, focus on smiling, mirroring and listening skills, respectively. For quick reference, Appendix A summarizes the behaviors discussed in terms of the three attributes.

*   *   *

FORGET-ME-NOTS

- Our <u>unconscious</u> body language is a *reflection* of our mental state, whereas our <u>conscious</u> body language *determines* our mental state.
- Charisma is not an elusive quality. It is the positive balance of nonverbal behaviors that demonstrate power, warmth and presence. (A summary of these behaviors can found in Appendix A).
- By bringing our body language under proper conscious control, we will *project* charisma to others, and simultaneously, our minds will adopt the corresponding attitudes.

*   *   *

Now we know how, and in which ways, to *consciously* control <u>our</u> body language. The next step is to look at the *unconscious* body language of <u>others</u>, which cues us as to their emotional state.

3

Before *they* say a word

"When the eyes say one thing, and the tongue another, a practiced man relies on the language of the first."

- RALPH WALDO EMERSON

While our conscious body language *affects* our emotional state, our unconscious body language *reflects* our emotional state. People we call "intuitive" have learned to compare the verbal and nonverbal messages to more fully understand the communication–to know if something more is being said.

Interrogations aren't done over the phone. Couples still date. Even with emojis, text based conversations are still limited by too much inference. People still fly to business meetings in lieu of a conference call. The need to observe and express nonverbals is an integral part of communication. To forgo that component unduly impairs one's ability to understand and be understood. Both words and nonverbal behavior must be experienced together to correctly interpret a message.

The ability to ascribe specific nonverbal behaviors to emotions and thoughts allows you to see when others are unsure of your message, uncomfortable with you personally, nervous, anxious, defensive, not interested in what you're saying or just downright deceptive. Invaluable! This skill transcends your abilities as a Whisperer and is globally applicable to every conversation you will ever have. Working on *your* nonverbal behaviors is only the *first step* on the journey. So stamp your passport and travel on!

* * *

Many people (and studies) reduce the study of nonverbal behavior to a means of knowing when someone is lying. While this is important (so much so that chapter 6 is dedicated to detecting deception), understanding body language is much more than just knowing when someone is telling the truth. Gaining insight into a target's mental and emotional state can be of greater importance in the course of a typical interaction.

Gaining this insight requires that you have some understanding of the normal behavior of people with whom you are dealing; their "baseline". You informally absorb information about your friends, co-workers, peers, family and even competitors. They may be high energy, quiet, anxious, shy, gregarious, serious...the list goes on. You've observed their natural demeanor and seen them respond in a variety of situations. This knowledge is the baseline against which to determine alternate competing nonverbal interpretations.

HOW DOES IT WORK? (SPOILER ALERT: IT'S THE LIMBIC SYSTEM)

In simplest terms, think of the brain as a three story structure. The lowest level is referred to as the "reptilian brain". It houses the brain stem and deals with low-level functions like blood pressure, respiration and motor control. At the top lives the "human brain" housing the prefrontal cortex which is the cognitive part of our brain capable of complex problem solving and decision-making. These cognitive processes are also called *executive functions*. *Because* it is part of the brain capable of complex thought, it can and will be used to deceive others. Between these two, in that big beautiful middle, lies the limbic system or the "mammalian brain". Immune from the higher level influence of executive function, the limbic system responds reflexively to its surroundings. These reflex actions are "truthful" signals of a person's state of mind.

The limbic brain comprises many components, the most notable for our purposes is the amygdala, which controls our emotional response to stimuli. The limbic brain reacts instinctively before higher brain functions can analyze and short-circuit a reflexive action, so the initial limbic response to stimuli is genuine (Myers). These reactions are hardwired into our nervous system, making them difficult to disguise or eliminate (Goleman, 13-29).

The amygdala processes our response to stress and danger, both physical and emotional. It accounts for the "freeze, flight or fight" response, the life-saving reactions inherited from our primitive ancestors. Most people incorrectly call this "fight or flight". This is incorrect on two counts. First, the fight response is the brain's *last* option, not its first. Second, both options are preceded by the freeze response. So the correct term should really be "freeze, flight or fight." The brain doesn't care whether the cause is physical danger or anxiety-producing stress. The amygdala is instinctively wired to invoke the freeze, flight or fight response, and it is in these moments we can get a true reading of nonverbal signals. Let's look at this process in action.

Freezing is the first thing the body will do in moments of fear and panic. Even if this only lasts for a fraction of a second, it is a primitive instinct hardwired to ensure our survival. Accounts of the mass shootings at Columbine, Virginia Tech and Sandy Hook relate that many students survived by holding still and playing dead even though they were only a few feet away from a killer. Instinctively, the students adopted primal behaviors that saved their lives.

In Las Vegas when a tiger or lion walks on stage the people in the first row will reflexively become still because the limbic brain knows that movement attracts attention. People in row 20 are elbowing their neighbors to comment on the size of the great cat without a care in the world, confident that the beast's belly will be full by row 7 at the latest.

This freeze reflex occurs not only in the presence of killers and lions but also in less immediately life-threatening situations. When someone is being questioned about something that could get them into trouble, they will freeze in their chair. Shoplifters often hide by hunching over and restricting their movements which only makes them stand out. Psychologists and social workers recognize freezing behaviors of abused children. When in proximity to an abuser, a child's arms will go limp at their sides and they avoid eye contact, as if the lack of movement and submissive behavior will keep them safe by going unnoticed (Navarro, p. 112).

Flight response kicks in if freezing is not adequate to eliminate the danger. When experiencing board room meeting stress, however, one doesn't leap out of their chair and bound down the hallway like a panicked gazelle. "Blocking behaviors" are the successor to the traditional flight response, and while not as obvious, serve the same purpose. *Closing the eyes, rubbing the eyes, and placing the hands in front of the face* are all examples of a modern flight responses that seek to put distance between the stressed and the stressor. Even turning away from someone is a flight response. In business and social situations, blocking behaviors are the counterpart to fleeing behaviors in physically dangerous situations.

Fight is the final tactic of the limbic brain if you're not able to flee danger. This can manifest itself as aggression even if there is no physical contact. Posture, gaze, puffing out your chest, contemptuous sneer, verbal attacks and violating another's personal space are all examples of the fight response.

* * *

Beyond the freeze/flight/fight response of self-preservation, when perceiving *negative* stimuli, the limbic brain causes body language that shows signs of *stress* or "low confidence." Look for the limbic response clues! A limbic response to a negative experience will often be followed by a "pacifying behavior." Pacifying behaviors identify specific issues or subjects which trouble a person, so learning to recognize them is key.

Touching parts of the body, like the head, neck, arm, or leg in response to stress (like a tough question) are pacifying behaviors. None of these behaviors help us resolve the stress; they keep us calm so we can decide on our next move. Men have a tendency to touch their faces and/or stroke their beards. Women opt to touch their clothing and accessories, hair, and neck.

Other frequent pacifying responses to stress include touching or stroking the face, "leg cleansing" where the hands are placed on the thighs and then slid down toward the knee, whistling or talking to oneself, drumming the fingers on a tabletop or one's own leg, removing invisible lint, or tapping a pen or pencil against a hard surface like a table or desk. These behaviors occur quickly in response to a negative event and are all done to rid the body of tension and stress.

*   *   *

Learn to distinguish between defensive behaviors and pacifying ones. Defensive behaviors serve as the brain's way to deal with a *threat in progress*, such as a child's proximity to an abuser resulting in a behavioral change from animated to lifeless. Pacifying behaviors are the brain's way of reducing the *stress and anxiety* that is felt in the moment, through hand rubbing, neck and leg stroking, face touching, etc.

None of this information is useful unless you can follow the golden rule of deciphering nonverbal signals: *you must learn to link a pacifying behavior with the specific stressor that caused it.* Timely detection is crucial.

WHISPER ALERT: Pacifying behaviors are <u>immediate</u> responses to stressors.

We will return to this idea later.

We spent a great deal of time analyzing *our* smile, handshake, arm position and eye contact, among other things, and seen how and why nonverbals work. This is only part of what we need to know when observing *others*. Let's look at some specific behaviors in more detail. The best place to begin is at the bottom, and we will work our way up.

There is a lot of ground to cover here. Don't feel the need to memorize all of the signals. Look for "behavior clusters" from the feet to shoulders for a better overall picture of the target's emotional state. The more experience you get, the more signals you will incorporate into the assessment of your subjects.

LOWER BODY

When trying to read people, the feet and legs are the most overlooked and under-appreciated source of information. When entering a room or engaging in a conversation, watching the feet provides more information than any other part of the body. Why? As we move from the head to the feet, conscious control decreases, so we are *least* aware of what the feet are doing. Therefore, our lower limbs provide the most honest information.

Feet: When viewing the feet, look first at where they are pointed. *They will point away from an undesired object.* If we are not interested in a conversation, our feet will shift away from the person as a sign of disengagement. Our feet may also point toward other people in the room whose conversation we would prefer. In studying courtroom behavior, jurors turn their feet toward the exit when they don't like a particular witness. When seeing this nonverbal behavior, you must figure out *why* this person is eager to leave or quit the conversation.

The feet will also point *toward* positive objects of desire. If you observe a group of people in a loose circle, their feet will tell you who each person thinks is most interesting and/or attractive. By looking at additional body language you can determine if the feet are pointing *toward* something or pointing to get *away* from something.

When a third person attempts to access two people talking, watch the feet of those already in conversation. If their feet *and body* "open up" to create a triangle, the person has been welcomed into the group. If only their torsos open to admit the person while the feet stay locked in position, then they're being polite but consider this person an interloper.

Legs: When the legs splay outward, this is a territorial display meant to show dominance and confidence. In the photo above, President Putin of Russia provides a typical example of leg splaying behavior. President Obama's feet are not only pointing away from Putin, showing he has emotionally withdrawn from this exchange, but he is also mirroring the leg splaying behavior initiated by President Putin. This signals he will not be intimidated or cowed. (No chest puffing or contemptuous sneers were noticed. Dog-ear this page, too, because later you will be asked to analyze this picture with new information and guidelines.) These territorial displays are fairly easy to spot. If the legs start together and then gradually move apart, the person is feeling defensive or threatened by someone or some*thing*, which may just be the current topic of conversation. Understanding these behaviors *and the context in which they occur* will tell us a great deal about the emotional state of the observed.

Crossed legs can be a confusing signal. Some authorities say it's a high comfort display, others say it's a blocking signal that shows the person is defensive and/or closed off. It depends largely on context and positioning.

When standing, leg crossing means we feel comfortable and confident *if the weight is shifted onto one leg* and may also be accompanied by the person leaning against a wall or other stable surface. When crossing one leg in front of the other we dramatically reduce our ability to balance. The limbic brain only allows us to do this when we are comfortable. To illustrate the point, if a man is standing in this position alone in an elevator, the first thing he will do when a stranger enters is uncross his legs and plant both feet firmly on the ground. His limbic brain is telling him to be prepared for anything.

Legs crossed with *weight shifted more evenly on both feet* is a sign of a closed and defensive attitude. The photo examples at right show the difference between the two. Even though both people have their arms crossed, it is clear which one is more relaxed and which one is less open. Even if the man were not smiling in this photo, the relaxed nature of the rest of his body is a telling indicator he is comfortable.

When seated, crossed legs again is open to different interpretations. The American "Figure 4", where a seated man's leg rests on his other leg above the knee are perceived as not only more dominant, but more relaxed and youthful. However, studies show that people most often commit to a decision when both feet are on the floor, so the "figure 4" is *not* the right time to ask for a commitment. If this is accompanied by a "leg clamp", meaning that both hands are holding the upper leg in place, it often means that the person is completely dug into their position.

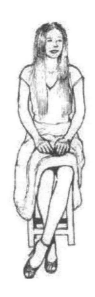

The "ankle lock" where the legs are crossed near the ankle is commonly associated with holding back a negative emotion and shows a withdrawn attitude (as the feet are hidden). Men combine this gesture with clenched fists or hands tightly gripping the armrests and take up *more* space. Women will have their feet to one side with hands resting in their lap and take up *less* space. As many women are taught to sit this way, they may do so out of habit which can be incorrectly read as a negative signal.

Asking non-threatening questions is a good way to get them to relax, unlock and engage in the conversation. Sometimes people claim they are just comfortable in this position, but they fail to realize it may be comfortable *because* they hold a negative or defensive mindset reflected in their posture.

The "leg twine", when one leg is wrapped almost completely around the other leg and the feet are hooked together, is exhibited almost exclusively by shy or timid women. A welcoming, easy-going style is needed when engaging with people in such a frame of mind.

If you're trying to persuade someone who is sitting in any crossed position, break that position before continuing. Have them lean forward to hold a piece of paper or brochure. Offering tea or coffee is another way to get them to uncross and become more receptive to your message.

High Confidence behaviors: Not all foot and leg displays indicate a negative attitude. Our lower limbs react to threats and emotions–both positive and negative. "Happy feet" are legs that wiggle and bounce with joy–this is a high-confidence tell. However, naturally jittery legs can be hard to differentiate from happy feet. In these cases the baseline will let you know if it is the former or the latter. If this person commonly exhibits nervous behaviors, it is not a link to negative emotions. Conversely, it may mean that the person is growing impatient with whatever is happening around them.

"Gravity defying" behaviors like a foot in the air with the heel on the ground is also a positive sign that the person is elated. The reverse of this, where the foot is on the ground and the heel is in the air, is known as "starter's position" and means the person is getting ready to *do* something. This will require further confirmation. They may want to leave or be interested and want to engage you further. Again, you need to rely on the context of the conversation to determine what action they are interested in taking.

If a woman dangles her shoes from the tips of her toes, she is very comfortable with her companion but will immediately stop when she is uncomfortable. Her feet will show how invested she is in the conversation, one way or the other.

The "knee clasp" is when a seated person places hands on both knees and often leans their torso. This is a clear sign they are getting ready to leave but don't want to appear rude. If this happens in the middle of a conversation, as opposed to the end, it doesn't take a genius to figure out this isn't a good sign. If the other person is mirroring your feet and leg position, this shows high comfort and is always a good sign.

UPPER BODY

We expose our ventral (front) side to to those who make us feel good. We immediately turn to the side when someone we dislike approaches. In fact, we use the descriptive phrase of a shunning, "turning our back" on someone, to describe negativity toward that person. As with the feet, watching the torsos of people in a group will give a good indicator who has negative or positive feelings and for whom.

Torso. As discussed earlier, the distance between people relates to their interest and *so does the angle at which they orient their torso.* An *open position*, standing at roughly a 45-degree angle to another is seen as confident, friendly and non-confrontational. Someone who takes a *closed position* and faces the listener directly is seen as aggressive and belligerent.

Closed positions are not only used by people hostile to one another–either physically or psychologically, but also two people sharing an intimate moment. A third party is encouraged to join the group only when the other two assume open positions, creating a triangle. If an interloper is unwelcome, the others will only turn their heads to acknowledge the third person but will remain together in a closed position. Be forewarned and don't intrude.

The torso will also lean away from something perceived as negative. This is an honest limbic demand that cannot be ignored because it requires extra effort and energy to hold the position. The distancing can be abrupt or subtle. Shifting body angles by a few degrees is enough to show negativity.

Torso Shielding. Not only do we turn and lean our torsos away from negative stimuli, but as they contain all of our vital organs, we are limbically conditioned to protect the torso. We may shield our front side subconsciously with our arms or other objects such as backpacks or purses. Women will often hold a cup or glass with 2 hands. Men shield in more subtle ways by reaching to play with a watch, adjusting a shirt sleeve, picking invisible lint off a jacket or holding a briefcase as a barrier with two hands when walking into a meeting. All these behaviors provide the arms with a clever opportunity to shield the body from the stressor.

If you offer someone a refreshment and they place it to the opposite side of their body forming an arm barrier, they are unsure or nervous about the situation. These gestures are used by nearly everyone and we are unaware we do them. Once you know what to look for you will easily be able to spot when someone is uncomfortable.

Torso Splay is when someone "spreads out" over a large area by puffing out their chest or putting their arms on two adjacent chairs. This is normally a sign of comfort but in a serious setting can be a territorial or dominance display. Both these interpretations are commonly recognized so the person *may want you to believe* they are calm and comfortable. Take note when these kinds of gestures are made at inappropriate times because baseline and context may be a tip-off that things are not as they seem.

Shoulder shrugs are of two types. The first is a full shrug that means "I don't know." The second is a partial shrug, or sometimes when only one shoulder shrugs, which means they are not limbically committed to their answer and are possibly being evasive or even deceptive.

As always, these are guidelines and it is only by gauging changes from baseline behavior that we can note when uneasiness arises. Do not form an entire opinion based on a single nonverbal behavior, rather look for "behavior clusters" from the feet to shoulders for a better overall picture of the target's emotional state.

ARMS

Normally, when we are excited or happy arm movements are unrestricted. When threatened, or worried, arm movements are restricted. But man's complex reasoning gives him the ability to alter, limit or stop reflexive movement. Those with an agenda often use the higher brain functions to control reflex action in order to deceive, such as shoplifters who use fewer arm movements (Navarro, p. 112-115). Limbic reactions are automatic but remember <u>body movement closer to the brain is under greater conscious control</u>.

Moving up to the arms we see more signs of complex thought overriding our instinctive reactions.

Arms Crossed: Take careful notice when you observe someone cross their arms and then "abort the landing." They will cross their

Variation of
double arm grip

arms *instinctively* and less than a second later *cognitively* reverse course by putting their arms back at their side, pick something up, groom, or otherwise engage in some affectation to conceal the fact they were about to cross their arms. This should be interpreted as arm crossing behavior.

Crossed arms power pose

As discussed earlier, crossed arms is negative and something to avoid doing yourself; but be aware, your target may also know this.

Crossed arms variations can reveal significantly more information. Crossed arms and clenched fists shows hostility along with defensiveness. The "crossed arms thumbs up" position is a defensive but confident position, or at least an effort to appear that way. Arms crossed higher on the body than normal is a power pose, typically done by police officers, security guards and bouncers. The "double arm grip" is is a pacifying, comforting display which is a form of self-hugging.

The symmetry (or lack thereof) of arm crossing behavior is also a telling indicator. Symmetry shows a defensive and submissive posture. Asymmetrical crossing shows dominance when crossing the arms and moving the outermost arm to touch the face or stroke the neck. The asymmetrical "partial arm cross" is a submissive, low-confidence display when crossing one arm while the other hangs straight down. These nuances of positioning will become more apparent as the Whisperer gains expertise in reading the body language.

Authoritative yet
defensive   vs.

Insecure and
Submissive

Not every instance of crossed arms shows defensiveness or detachment, as popularly interpreted. It is up to you to understand the context in which the behavior takes place and make an accurate assessment. We've already seen that crossed arms can be a pacifying behavior or a power stance. But, crossing arms can also be a mirroring behavior. It can be a sign of self-restraint, anxiety, or maybe the person is just cold! Don't fall prey to the trap of saying, "Aha! Crossed arms… this person is being defensive." You need to understand the context in which the behavior occurs as compared to their baseline to determine what it means.

Watch out for arms that progressively spread over the course of a conversation. This person is becoming increasingly agitated and aggressive. Think about someone arguing over a return at the customer service desk or someone upset about a flight cancellation. As they speak, their arms take an increasingly larger space as their anger grows. When you see this, take immediate steps to remedy the situation.

We've seen in the previous chapter that "arms akimbo" and "hooding" display authority and territorial dominance. When the arms are clasped behind the back ("regal stance") they are projecting higher status indicating the person is not to be touched. It is a way to signal that a handshake would be inappropriate by sending the message, "please do not touch me." Prince Charles uses this stance often. Confident and/or high-status individuals also claim more space with their arms, by draping their arms over the backs of adjacent chairs, as mentioned earlier.

HANDS

Hands and fingers contain the densest clusters of nerve endings in the body, are the richest source of sensory feedback, and have the greatest positioning capability of the body. Our hands provide the primary outlet for our sense of touch, which is the most *active* of the senses. Our other senses: sight, sound, smell and taste are passive; we wait for the light waves and sound waves and odiferous air waves to arrive and send the information to our brain for subsequent processing and interpretation. Contrast that to the sense of touch. It doesn't stand by waiting for passing stimuli to approach; rather, it actively seeks information.

Palms: *Hand movements* are important! From the earliest times, our brains have been wired to notice and assess another's hand movements quickly and to interpret their message (Givens p. 31, 76; Ratey, 162-165). Is a weapon held? Is the hand itself preparing to become a weapon? Therefore, when people want to be seen as unthreatening, they will hold one or both palms upward and outward. This may be a conscious act or sometimes an unconscious limbic reflex to signal they are not a threat. The limbic gesture will be honest and has come to communicate truthfulness.

In chapter 2 we noted that crossed arms can *cause* negative feelings and not just reflect them. Similarly, open palm up gestures cause us to be more direct, forthright and truthful. By consciously making repetitive palm-up gestures, the urge to lie or stretch the truth dwindles. This gesture also puts unconscious pressure on the other person to reciprocate the same level of openness (Pease p. 35-36).

While palm up is submissive and non-threatening, palm down projects immediate authority. An extreme example is the Nazi salute with face down palm, a symbol of domination and oppression during the Third Reich. A more subtle example is hand-in-hand couples. Whomever walks slightly in front with their hand in the outward position is the dominant partner.

Hiding anything is generally thought to be a negative. Hiding hands and palms is no different. Hands hidden in pockets indicate the other is withdrawing and is another culturally recognizable action. Hiding (hands) palms in the back pockets signals low self-esteem.

Briskly rubbing palms together is a positive sign of expectation when the fingers are extended upward or outward. Hands clasped together (loosely or tightly) is a low confidence indicator. A person under low stress will only slightly rub their palms together. If the situation becomes more stressful gentle palm rubbing can turn to a tight brisk stroking of the palms or a more dramatic rubbing with interlaced fingers.

Clenched hands are most often a sign of stress and anxiety and, the higher the hands, the more anxious and negative the attitude. Unlock that position by handing them something or offering a drink to counter the negative attitudes. When the hand grips the wrist, it shows both frustration and a struggle to maintain restraint. The higher the grip, the more frustration (and possibly anger) is being contained. Similar sign, similar solution.

One exception to the hands clenched display is to watch the elbows. If the elbows are splayed out, then this is considered a high confidence behavior. Seated at a table, bring your hands together and interlock your fingers as in a "prayer position." You try it. Set your hands *and elbows* on the table in front of you. This requires a slight forward lean to get your elbows planted firmly. More space means high status behavior, representing confidence and authority. Now slide your elbows off the table and bring them inward until they touch your sides, but keep your hands on the table. This not only looks weaker, it *feels* weaker, too. So when in doubt, *look at the elbows and occupied space.*

Dominant Hand or Digit: When summarizing the points of a discussion people often turn one palm up to present one argument and then turn the other palm up when presenting the other argument. What is less commonly known is that people reserve their dominant hand for their favored point of view. The order of the options, first or second, are not predictive, watch for their dominant hand and you will be able to predict their preference.

*   *   *

An interesting fact: There are no muscles inside the fingers. The finger joints are bent by muscles in the palm and forearm and are connected to the finger bones by tendons. Fingers work by remote control like marionette movements; "pulling strings" is an often-used metaphor.

*   *   *

When a discussion involves more than two options or points of view, people often make each point by touching the index finger of one hand to the fingers of the other hand, one finger per discussion point. Like the dominant hand, people reserve the index finger for their favored or preferred course of action. Whether it comes first in the list or last is irrelevant. When those index fingers touch, you know the outcome the speaker truly espouses. In some instances, I have even seen people skip to their index finger when they arrived at their main point "too early."

Pacifying Behaviors: Hands are instrumental in pacifying behaviors. Touching the neck is a frequent behavior to reduce stress levels. When the nerve endings in this area are stroked, blood pressure and heart rate drops, which helps calm a person down (Moore). This relieves stress but also shows a lower than normal confidence level. Men firmly grasp, cup or stroke the neck area under the chin. They may also stroke the sides or back of the neck. Women "neck pacify" by playing with or fondling a necklace or by covering their *suprasternal notch*, the large visible dip between the neck and the collarbone. These are common actions when anxious, upset, or fearful. Look for them.

Deceptive Indicators: Conventional wisdom tells us that liars have sweaty palms and/or trembling hands. This isn't necessarily true. Sweaty palms *may* indicate stress or possibly a genetic disorder known as "hyperhidrosis". When the limbic brain is stressed, surges of neurotransmitters and hormones (like adrenalin) may cause uncontrollable trembling of the hands. Hand trembling can also be caused by positive emotions. Therefore, these are not reliable indicators of deception. Trembling hands are only relevant as a nonverbal when they represent a sudden change from someone's normal hand movement.

Contrary to popular wisdom, a *good* indicator of deception is when hands are frozen in place and don't move (or move very little). Liars move and gesture less often, consistent with our limbic reactions. This behavior is observed during conversation when a person's arms are animated when telling the truth but immediately become restrained when telling a lie. Keep in mind, however, the behavior is *not definitive*, rather it indicates possible deception. We take a much deeper look at deception cues in chapter 6.

Thumbs Up: The thumbs are a special case which denote superiority and display dominance, assertiveness and sometimes even aggressive attitudes. Lower status individuals rarely use thumb gestures in such dominance displays. Sometimes, the thumb can dramatically change a nonverbal signal into something else entirely. For example, interlacing the fingers is normally a low confidence display unless the thumbs are extended straight up. (Remember the picture of Michelle Obama and the professor? If not, go back and take a second look.) This transforms it into quite an overt high confidence behavior.

When someone's arms are crossed with their thumbs pointing upward, this shows both a negative yet superior attitude. A man's hands all the way in his pockets is a low confidence display; however, when the thumbs protrude from the pockets, it is now more indicative of a confident attitude.

Thumbs protruding from the back pockets show someone hiding their dominant attitude to appear softer. Conversely, when the thumbs are in the pockets and the fingers are dangling outside the pockets, this serves to hide the powerful thumbs and is viewed as a low confidence display. This can look similar to the "thumbs hooked in waistband" where the fingers create a genital framing which is a powerful dominance signal.

As with so much of nonverbal communication, sudden changes in hand motion suggests an abrupt change in someone's thoughts and feelings. This can be seen in both professional and personal contexts. When a decision maker sits in a board room and suddenly shifts his hands from the table to his sides or the arms of his chair, his emotional context has quickly shifted, probably toward the negative. You will see this play out in reverse as well when withdrawn hands are moved into the conversation. This shows a positive psychological shift in thought process. Gradual hand withdrawals (or entrances) are equally worthy of note as they correspond to a gradual shift in thought processes, rather than a more sudden shift.

TIMEOUT: Why are hands hidden? What does it mean when the palms are exposed, up or down? When is dominant hand use and finger sequence significant? What does non-movement say?

(Take another look at the Obama/Putin photo and do your own analysis of the upper body, arms, elbows and hands. There's a lot more to notice on a second look.)

Gestures: While telling a story, gestures improve recall in the listener by as much as 30%, in part by keeping the *listener* more fully engaged and the *speaker* focused on their topic. One needs to be careful not to overdo it because too many gestures can be distracting. High-status individuals and people in authority gesture less, so gesturing too much can undermine your social standing or relative authority.

When speakers use a "closed palm finger pointing" gesture it attempts to force the listeners into submission, which creates negative feelings. When the pointing beats time with the speaker's words it is even more distasteful. When speaking, a better way to proceed is to squeeze your index finger against your thumb in a loose 'OK' gesture and you'll be seen as authoritative but not aggressive.

The volume of data can be overwhelming. Make use of the things you already know, add the ones that are easily remembered because of context or logic, and choose another which might be particularly beneficial for you. And of course, recognizing changes in baseline behavior and looking for clusters are always at the forefront of the Whisperer's mind.

HEAD AND FACE

Most people focus on the face for deciphering nonverbal signals, and it isn't hard to see why. Humans are capable of more than 10,000 different facial expressions that create a language all their own. We can look at a portrait and reliably intuit whether a person is tired, angry, elated, sad, contemptuous, haughty, anxious, frustrated, silly or nearly any other emotion (except for the Mona Lisa). We can look at a stranger and know when they are doubtful, irritated, bored or concerned.

Amazingly these facial expressions are universally recognized by all people across all cultures, regions and borders (Ekman, 2003, p. 1-37). Not only are we able to identify these emotions but this knowledge appears to be instinctively hardwired into our brains. Even babies not only differentiate but show a preference for happy faces over sad ones! (Farroni)

While our faces can be wonderfully expressive in showing how we feel they are less likely to represent our true feelings because we are all able, in varying degrees, to control the limbic response and "put on a chosen face". Therefore this is the last place to look when interpreting someone's nonverbal behavior. *Remember the closer to the brain, the less honest and reliable the nonverbal signals become.* If you interpret by observing upward from the feet, you will form a more accurate picture of the person's emotional and psychological state. If the nonverbal cluster of behaviors validate what you see in the face, this is strong evidence you're witnessing the true sentiment of the other person. If the nonverbal signals are contradictory, the face is likely projecting a calculated message and not true feelings.

WHISPER ALERT: The message of the face is validated or invalidated from the chin to the toes.

Eyes

> *"The soul, fortunately, has an interpreter - often an unconscious but still a faithful interpreter - in the eye."*

-CHARLOTTE BRONTË

Altering our facial expressions to hide our true feelings is not necessarily a nefarious act, but often innocent and even socially expected. If you attend a dinner party where a man makes a disparaging remark about his wife, a typical immediate reaction might be to show obvious contempt. A sneer and a direct look with a narrowing of the eyes would be diminished to subtle lip movement and a sideways glance. To maintain civility, many people are conditioned to override their desire to show disapproval by displaying unoffended or even approval behaviors. When bored with a conversation, instead of yawning, looking at your watch or texting, you feign interest by maintaining eye contact and smiling. These actions are not despicable, but *we need to know if they are genuine.*

Pupil dilation and constriction: One thing that the conscious mind can't control is pupil dilation and constriction. When we see something we like, anything that excites or arouses us, our pupils dilate. When we don't like what we see, creating negative and/or angry feelings, the pupils constrict. As a manager I once had a disagreement with someone on my team. After the smoke cleared, I noticed that every time we spoke her pupils constricted to the size of pin heads. Outwardly, there was no body language indicating stress or anger, but the involuntary pupil constriction made me ask, "Is there anything else we need to do to clear the air? She responded, "No." This exchange was repeated several times. She was always polite and betrayed no outward hostility. Her exit interview, however, was full of invectives about my poor management skills. While not totally surprised, had I looked more closely for constrained limbic responses, I may have changed my questioning approach (see chapter 7), and the relationship may have been repaired. But, of course, I hadn't yet read *The Human Whisperer.*

Increases in pupil size are linked with problem solving, reaching maximum dilation at the point of solution. This is true whether one is solving puzzles and games or formulating a response to an uncomfortable question. Rapid dilation shows excitement to the stimuli *or* stimulation from analyzing how to respond. Squinting and widening of the eyes is also a form of pupil dilation and constriction but because of "executive function" involvement, deception is a possibility. This will be discussed in detail in Chapter 6.

There is no switch, however, to control pupil dilation and constriction. When men view pornographic images, their pupils dilate by nearly a factor of three. For women, the effect is similar when viewing pictures of mothers and babies (Pease, p. 168). Less pronounced changes can be very difficult to detect, particularly in people with brown eyes. Someone with bright blue or green eyes are the best candidates to glean information from pupil dilation; but this signal information is difficult to gather. There are many variables that get in the way, i.e. your angle and proximity to the other person, the lighting, their eye color, etc. Not to mention your focused attention can easily to be seen as a "stare of aggression!"

Squinting is easier to observe. If a client squints when reading a contract they may not like the provisions or wording. If a sports fan strongly squints during the middle of a football game, safe to say the other team just scored or made a good play. Conversely, if the eyes widen, they like what they're seeing.

Blocking: There are many other forms of subconscious eye blocking to reduce the ability of the eyes to take in light. Several examples include moving hands over the eyes, rubbing, squinting and closing the eyes and are indicative of concern, dislike, disagreement or the perception of a threat. These behaviors are hardwired into the limbic brain, as evidenced by babies eye blocking at a loud, sudden sound and even blind children use eye blocking when they hear bad news (Knapp, p. 42-52).

*   *   *

My grandmother lived in a nursing home for about a year. After breakfast the residents were required to adjourn to the community room for low-function games and television. When I found her there, her eyes were always closed and remained closed until she heard my voice. Back in her room she would sit in her chair and we would carry on a lively conversation. Although I noticed the behavior, I never truly understood its significance until later. Looking back now, my heart sinks. Reading this book will have been worth your effort if the one take-away is to look for, and understand, messages sent by your grandparents, which until now you've overlooked. Don't turn off your observational radar just because you're at a family gathering.

*   *   *

Family counseling services work with couples for a myriad of issues. A pastor, fresh from a workshop, related the following incident to illustrate communication. "A deaf couple had sought counseling on resolving several divisive marital issues. During the session their fingers and gestures picked up speed and space, and the pastor was concerned how he might intervene without injury to himself or the couple. Suddenly the wife took her husband's face in her hands, and nose to nose, she shut her eyes." Wow. The people and building survived the explosion! No mixed or missed messages here. The aspiring Whisperer, however, rarely encounters such clear-cut signals.

Looking Away: Gazing away during a conversation, often considered rude and a sign of disinterest or deception, is rather a comfort display. Looking away can enhance clarity of thought when trying to understand a concept or some new information. We may also be processing an emotion or feeling which can range from negative to positive.

For others, avoiding eye contact is a *baseline behavior*. In strongly hierarchical Latin American and African American cultures, eye contact (particularly by the young) is seen as aggressive and confrontational. Many of these children grow up making less eye contact than their peers. In Asian and Middle Eastern cultures, it is rude to make too much eye contact, which is not deemed essential to a successful conversation. And for those on the autism spectrum, making eye contact can be a lifelong difficulty. So don't forget those baselines and jump to erroneous conclusions about eye contact (or lack thereof).

Blink Rate: The most subtle form of eye blocking behavior is the blink rate. Blink rate increases when we are nervous, anxious or troubled and returns to normal when we are relaxed. A slow, extended blink of 2-3 seconds serves the same purpose as rapid blinking which returns to normal when the stressor is removed. Occasionally a "slow blink" shows contempt instead of anxiety, particularly when accompanied by a sneer or other sideways mouth movement. As with nearly all nonverbal behaviors, the context is the determining factor.

Blocking behaviors are not the only nonverbals of the eye. As mentioned earlier "looking at someone sideways" or from the corner of their eye is a sign of uncertainty or suspicion. If the eyes dart from side to side the brain is searching for an escape possibly from insecurity or boredom. As with the feet, the eyes move in the direction the body wants to go. However, as this behavior is well recognized, it is often concealed by anyone with even the most rudimentary understanding of body language. If you're bored by someone, you won't be constantly looking at your watch or at other people in the room because that *would* be socially unacceptable etiquette. *(Unless you're in school or church in which case the behavior is freely practiced!)* *Ironically,* because we know that looking away betrays our thoughts, we look *more* at boring individuals! So if someone is making *a lot* of eye contact as you're relating a riveting story about your grandson's soccer tryout, maybe they would rather be somewhere else!

Always remember that *the mind aligns with conscious behaviors as much as unconscious behaviors align with the mind.* Meaning that if someone is locked into a position and you want to make them more receptive to your ideas, get them to uncross their arms by holding onto something i.e. a pen, a paper, a coffee mug. If their brows are furrowed because they are suspicious or upset with what you're saying, ask them a non-threatening question. It will normally cause their brows to relax or even raise which is a positive physical sign that their thoughts will follow. Changing their defensive and negative behaviors cause them to achieve a more positive mental outlook, if even by a tiny amount, which provides you greater room to maneuver the conversation.

* * *

NLP "Eye Accessing Cues"

In Neuro Linguistic Programming (NLP) there is a theory that the eyes move in specific ways to specific locations during a particular thought process. For example, if someone looks up in response to a question this means that their thought is visual; if side to side, the thought is auditory. Further, if they look up and to the right, they are recalling something visual. If they look up and to the left they are constructing something visual, i.e. a lie. All of these ideas fall under the general term of "eye accessing cues" and have been a subject of great debate.

While I dismiss the specifics of this more-than-questionable theory, there are many adherents who claim that some people's eyes do, in fact, dart around when constructing a lie. In my experience, however, this is neither a universal behavior nor does it even stay consistent for the same person! The only possible way to use this technique is to have extensive baseline experience with the person on whom you are using it, and even then it's a dicey proposition. In my lifetime, the only person on whom I've had genuine success is my 11-year-old daughter, but I suspect it won't last, especially after she reads this book.

There may be something to it but having spent a non-trivial amount of time investigating this avenue of nonverbal behavior, I agree with the overwhelming majority of the scientific community and find these cues to be non-probative. So let's move on. Nothing to see here.

* * *

Mouth

As noted in chapter 2, real smiles use the zygomatic muscles to draw the corner of the mouth up and crinkle the outer edges of the eyes and is synonymous with the term "real smile." A "fake smile" uses the risorius muscle to pull the corners of the mouth sideways but not upward. Both smiles are part of our instinct as even babies reserve their real smile for their mothers, giving fake smiles to other strangers (Darwin, p. 203).

A fake smile does not mean the sentiment behind it is false, but perhaps the emotion itself is incongruent with a genuine smile. While the use of *genuine* smiles to enhance charisma were covered in chapter 2, here is a list of the five most common *fake* smiles:

Tight-lipped smile - Used by women hiding dislike of someone or something and is read as such by other women. Most men are not aware of this signal and are therefore oblivious to it. This picture of Hillary Clinton during her concession speech on election night 2016 is a good example of such a smile.

Twisted smile - It is a signal of sarcasm achieved by executing a fake smile with only one half of the mouth.

Drop-jaw smile - Simulated smile achieved by dropping the lower jaw. It was a favorite of the Joker from Batman.

Sideways smile - This is similar to the twisted smile as it is also a half smile but the difference is that it is more coy and playful. This smile is often used as a flirtatious or seductive smile.

"George W. Bush Grin" - This is a great example of a regional gesture, in this case most commonly seen in the southern United States, where people are expected to always be smiling. As a real smile is impossible to maintain indefinitely, this grin has evolved as a way to show you're doing well. An unsmiling person in Texas would be asked, "what's wrong, sugar?", whereas this grin in New York City would be met with the question, "what's so funny?"

There are other mouth behaviors that don't directly relate to smiling. A tight-lipped smile without the smile is considered a "lip compression." This shows true negative sentiment and can be seen on a spectrum from a partial to full compression where the lips are barely visible or even completely obscured. When someone _purses_ their lips, this is a general sign of disagreement and that they are considering alternative ideas. A sneer is a universal act of contempt. When we lick our lips or run our tongue back and forth across our lips, it is a pacifying behavior. Tongue jutting behavior is used by someone that thinks they've gotten away with something.

Miscellaneous facial behaviors

The tilt of the head up or down is a good indicator of confidence. If the chin, and by extension the head, is pointed downward this is seen as a person lacking confidence. A chin up gesture, as you have already surmised, is a high confidence tell. The exception to this is when the head is lowered and the eyes are raised and looking up. This is a submissive gesture, but not from lack of confidence. It is done in different contexts but in romantic settings is something that is done by women because it is appealing to men.

When you notice a flaring of the nostrils, this is a signal that the person is aroused. It is an intention cue signalling that the person is entering (or about to enter) the flight or fight response. As they prepare to act physically, they will automatically oxygenate which causes the nostrils to flare. Remain alert, as this means the person is about to _act_. Not necessarily in a physical or violent way, but some form of action is imminent.

There is a general rule that lowering (or furrowing) eyebrows shows dominance and aggression and raising the eyebrows shows submission. This is a general rule full of exceptions. Yes, people furrow their eyebrows when they are angry, but they also do it when sad, anxious, concentrating, trying to recall information or just bewildered. You need to determine from context and from the other nonverbal behaviors what is meant by any brow furrowing behavior. Like all facial expressions, it needs to be compared with nonverbals from the rest of the body.

PUTTING IT TO USE

All right, we've covered a lot of nonverbal ground but how can we put it to use? Remember, some nonverbal behaviors are commonly understood which means that interpreting nonverbals *is not a completely intuitive skill.* It requires dedicated and deliberate study to improve your abilities. With more time and practice, the better you will be at deconstructing nonverbal behaviors to decipher the mental state of your target. Practice anytime, wherever you are. While waiting in line at the grocery store, look around at the other people in line. Next time you're at a restaurant, take a few minutes to look around at other tables and focus on their nonverbals. You'll be surprised at your skill improvement after even a short time. These behaviors are recognized often in everyday life by a Whisperer but only occasionally by the casual observer.

Placing behaviors into relevant context aids in understanding what the behaviors mean. If a job interviewee is nervous, it is normal. After their anxiety dissipates and they suddenly became nervous again you need to sort out why. If a robbery victim is shaking and unsteady, it doesn't mean they've fabricated their story, rather, they are exhibiting a normal behavior to a traumatic event. Sometimes a duck is just a duck.

Learn to identify the idiosyncratic behaviors of those people you interact with regularly (baseline). You will notice that certain people exhibit tendencies that run counter to what we've discussed in these pages. Make a mental note of characteristics of friends, coworkers and family members. I once noticed a coworker would chew on a small sprig of her hair when she was stretching the truth. Afterwards I could always tell when she thought something was *really* a good idea or not. She became aware of this habit and would often grab for a bit of hair only to wave off and brush her hair off of her shoulders. It still told me everything I needed to know. Learning the baseline behaviors is even important with people you know well. Learn how they sit, where they place their hands, how much gesturing they do when excited rather than discussing routine information. The better you know someone's baseline the easier it is to determine when they have departed from it.

Accuracy explodes as you _spot clusters of behaviors_ instead of focusing on just one or two actions. The more behaviors you can link, the more accurate you will become. It is a good rule of thumb to give credence to nonverbal behavior when it is spotted in a "cluster of three." A single isolated behavior is not grounds for determining whether someone is suspicious, upset, defensive, etc., especially when observing the upper extremities, head and face.

Most importantly, *be inconspicuous!* The surest way to fail is to be so obvious that you cause the other person to become conscious of their own movements. They should never know you are even looking at their behavior. Stay relaxed, calm and don't allow your observations to obstruct the natural flow of conversation. As much as possible view the behaviors through your peripheral vision and don't overtly stare as you analyze those behaviors. This was my biggest struggle when starting out. It's hard to do at first, but stick with it.

HEALTHY SKEPTICISM--IS THIS FOR REAL?

In discussing the importance of body language–both the signals we convey and how we interpret the signals of others–some have confessed a healthy dose of skepticism whether all of this is real and the behaviors as pronounced as claimed. There are many lab studies that appear to show nonverbals offer little value in determining the mental state of others, specifically regarding deception. While we cover detecting deception in chapter 6, it is important to understand a few things about these types of studies.

Nearly all studies involve a person telling a truth or lie under very controlled conditions and looking to see what nonverbals would be present in such situations. This shows a profound misunderstanding of how nonverbal communication works. As discussed in the beginning of this chapter, nonverbals work because the limbic system (which controls our response to genuine fear) acts independently of our cognitive, higher order processes. Asking a test subject to lie or tell the truth does not instill in them the fear that would be necessary to invoke a limbic response. They have a low level of motivation to be believed. In real-life situations, where consequences may be significant, a limbic response will give away the person's emotional state if someone is observant enough to catch it.

This research is also based on the faulty premise that there are certain behaviors unique to telling the truth or telling a lie. This isn't how nonverbal communication works. These studies do not establish behavioral baselines nor do they give any consideration to evaluating behaviors in context. Training and experience also increase one's ability to detect true and false statements. Artificially motivating people to lie or tell the truth does not identify the ability of appropriately trained people to detect a limbic response in the subject and assess their credibility.

* * *

FORGET-ME-NOTS

- The limbic system's natural "freeze/flight/fight" responses happen outside of conscious control, so the actions initiated by these responses are the truest indicators of a subject's emotional state.
- Low confidence displays indicate stress or anxiety and must be linked to a specific stressor (a question or situation) in order to be useful. So look for *changes* in behavior related to these stressors. (Appendix B provides a reference to these behaviors).
- To be effective in reading body language, you must *baseline, look for behavior clusters, and not get caught doing either of those things!*

* * *

WHAT'S THE CATCH?

Understanding body language allows us a peek at the mental and emotional state of another person, but it is just the first step in reading others. This doesn't tell us another's thoughts, priorities, goals, or how far they will go in pursuit of those goals. To truly understand and connect with others requires additional skills.

We've learned how to use *our* body language to generate charisma. We've learned to assess *others'* body language to understand their mental state. So far, so good. But understanding people beyond the more transient emotional and mental state requires us to make a connection as well.

We all know intelligent people who are knowledgeable about many things including the psychology of "how people think." But, these are often the same people that, when put in a room with others unlike themselves, don't know how to act or what to say. Their interaction generates palpable tension, making others uncomfortable. They may understand people, but cannot connect with them.

Conversely, there are people that "get along with everybody." They can walk into any crowded room *with ease and* strike up a conversation. But it is an empty performance; they don't understand others' motivations or mindset and often seem clueless about why people behave the way they do. Likely, they don't care. While tension-free, any real connection beyond the superficial is impossible.

Understanding without connection forces one into the role of passive observer. Connection without understanding is a superficial, one-dimensional relationship. Both skills are necessary for building rapport and creating genuine bonds, and is a requirement of every Human Whisperer.

In the next two chapters we will deepen our ability to both read and connect with others.

4

Diving below the surface

"Any fool can know. The point is to understand."

– ALBERT EINSTEIN

R eading body language is the first step inside the mind of another person, and it has been fun learning how to read and interpret the emotional states of others through nonverbal behaviors. But this only scratches the surface. In part, we're born with abilities to understand others (nonverbal and verbal), but the most successful among us have cultivated this ability far beyond our inherited skills to gain a deeper knowledge about others' thoughts, feelings and motivations.

As social animals that live in large groups, we *must* be able to communicate with others to survive. The larger our social group, the greater our need (and capacity) to understand one another. This is why the size of the cerebral cortex (which, in part, handles social interaction) of all animals is directly proportional to the size of the social groups they inhabit (Dunbar).

Humans have excelled over all other animals at understanding one another. Not only because of our capacity for written and spoken language, but this understanding is hardwired in a way not seen in other species. Studies designed to compare the ability of chimpanzees and toddlers (with same physical abilities) to find an object based on a researcher's gaze found the toddler to be twice as insightful at a rate of 74% vs. 36%. This experiment required an understanding that where a person is looking is a cue for what they are thinking (Herrmann). We have become the dominant life form on this planet, not solely because of our opposable thumbs or the use of tools, but because of our ability to understand others.

Even though we do a fair job of understanding others, most of us would like to improve. In a 2011 poll people were asked what superpower they would most like to have. Reading minds edged out time travel, flying and invisibility as the #1 response (Marist).

The reason for that ranking is that so often we don't have a clue what others are thinking, and we know how much better we could navigate life if we did.

How do we gain this knowledge?!

HUMAN NATURE'S OBSTACLES

> *"Human nature is not black and white but black and grey."*
>
> -- GRAHAM GREENE

There are many reasons we don't understand others as well as we should, most of which spring from mankind's less-than-noble impulses. However, if you wish to generate charisma, understand, detect deception, guide decisions, and master all the other skillsets of a Whisperer, you must first work to diminish and eliminate the traits which have been the downfall of both great and small. If we are to reach our potential as Whisperers, obstacles such as *overconfidence, lack of self-awareness, hubris and dehumanization* must be overcome.

Overconfidence

As a *species*, we have reason for confidence in our understanding of others, but *individually*, we think we're better at it than we are. In one experiment, people were asked to guess how their friends and coworkers would rate them in traits like intelligence and attractiveness. They were superb at guessing how *the group* would rate them but were terrible at determining *which specific coworkers* found them intelligent and which did not (Kenny, p. 159). In another experiment, test subjects were asked how others would rate a picture of them in terms of attractiveness. Their answers showed no greater positive correlation than random guessing (Eyal). So while we may be good at knowing what people think of us *generally* (giving us a false sense of our abilities), we are bad at knowing what *specific* people think of us.

Not only is our confidence in our abilities to know what others think largely misplaced, but this overconfidence carries over to close friends and spouses as well. Test subjects asked to read strangers were accurate 20% of the time vs. 35% when reading close friends and spouses. Test subjects over-confidently felt they were closer to 100% when reading a familiar group. While these statistics show modest gains when reading someone you know well, of far greater importance is that *your <u>true</u> accuracy in understanding those close to you is far below your <u>perceived</u> accuracy* (Savitsky).

This overconfidence increases in proportion to how long two people have been together. While that may not be very surprising, it may surprise you to know that *the length of the relationship has no bearing on accuracy.* In other words, confidence continues to grow while accuracy remains constant, so being with someone for a long period only increases the illusion of certainty. This is counter-productive, as the more confident we are about our ability, the more likely we are to grossly overestimate how well we understand others:

- Just because you've been part of a family all your life doesn't mean there's nothing left for you to learn about each member
- Your coworker of a decade still has many traits and interests yet to be discovered
- Long-time friends can be a wealth of unsuspected surprises
- Employer and employee–neither are an open book to the other

* * *

The fix for overconfidence is, well, not to be so confident! Remember that others inner thoughts are every bit a mystery. And no matter how long you've known someone, they're still a mystery. Keeping your confidence in check allows you to uncover more about people you *believed* you already knew, because you remain open to the possibility of learning more about them.

Lack of self-awareness

Another reason we don't know what others are thinking is that we aren't very good at knowing our own minds either! Time and again we see the disconnect between how we *think* we would behave and how we *actually* behave.

A famous test called "The Milgram Experiment," measured how far people would go to obey an authority figure if it conflicted with their conscience. Specifically, test subjects were to administer an increasing amount of electrical shock to a person when that person answered a question incorrectly. No actual shock was being administered but actors in the next room would scream in pain when the "shock button" was pressed. Most subjects administered near-lethal shocks at the administrators urging and only a few insisted that the experiment end.

You, like many, may think you would have stood up and said, "No, this is wrong! I won't hurt this person any longer!" This experiment, and variations of it, have been repeated for decades across all cultures and in all cases the majority of people have acted the same way. Most of us would have *actually* pushed the button when in that situation, but most of us *think* we would have been the exception. Therefore, there *is a significant disconnect between what people think about themselves and how they actually behave.*

A few years ago, the ABC television network ran a program called, "What Would You Do?" The hidden-camera show staged conflicts and illegal activities to see if and how bystanders intervened. Variables were introduced, like changing the gender, race, or social status of the participants, to see if those reactions changed. For example, when a white man was seen sawing through a bicycle chain that was securing a bike to a lamp post (in multiple test runs) it took several minutes before someone decided to take action and call 9-1-1. When that white man was replaced by black man, the emergency call was placed much more quickly, in most cases in under a minute. And when that man was replaced by an attractive, well-dressed woman, not only did *no one* call to report a theft in progress, but in one case a good samaritan *actually helped her*, knowing that she was stealing the bicycle! It isn't surprising that we respond differently to situations based on bias colored by our experience. <u>The surprise is that we don't recognize this bias at all!</u> Whether or not we choose to act, we are ignorant as to the all-important *why*.

* * *

This disconnect between thoughts and behavior exists largely because we're only aware of our brain's completed thoughts but are ignorant as to <u>how</u> we arrived at those thoughts. Why do you find someone attractive? If you think it's because of a cute nose or high cheekbone or the shape of the eyes you'd be wrong. Scientist have long known that what we find attractive about someone's face is "bilateral symmetry," meaning the right and left sides of the face are identical. The closer to perfectly symmetrical a face becomes, the more attractive it becomes (Perrett). Try asking a friend to name a very attractive person and then ask *why* they think the person is attractive. You'll hear nearly every answer other than the correct one–symmetry. Why do you like baseball? Apple pie? Long walks along the beach? Reading a good book? I don't know why you like anything–but neither do you!

Being blind to the constructive process that guides our thoughts we are left with the illusion we know more about our minds than we really do. In a simpler, more scientifically rigorous experiment, shoppers were asked to pick the best pair of stockings from a group of four. Respondents, who didn't know each option was identical, were four times as likely to pick the 4th pair and provided many reasons why, except the real one– its position in the row. The ordering created a definite preference, but *subjects remained unaware of the effect of this influence* (Nisbett).

These results, among others, have changed the way researchers now gather information. Psychologists no longer ask people to explain *why* they think something. They now ask *what* they are thinking, because asking why involves nothing but blind guesswork.

This information can help us, too. People often ask one another *why* they believe in "something" or *why* they think a certain way. Knowing that neither you nor anyone else truly knows *why* they think what they do, you can save not only time and energy, but plenty of trips down blind alleys by avoiding the pitfall of trying to find out *why* and focusing more on the *what*.

Hubris

We believe we see the world *as it is*. As we look at a colorful green field covered with wildflowers we forget these colors are not there. They are inside our heads as our brains interpret the light waves bouncing off the objects. But the colors seem to exist *out there* rather than just in our own head. The idea that we perceive absolute reality is called naïve *realism*. If we believe that we see things *as they really are*, and we meet someone who thinks differently, then *they* must be biased, ignorant, or foolish. More than just color, whether we're talking about abortion rights, gun control, capital punishment, or foreign policy, when anyone else sees something differently than we do, naïve realism kicks in. We believe we see how the world really is; therefore, anyone that sees things differently is wrong.

To become more accurate mind readers we need to recognize that our judgments may sometimes be wrong, and they may be wrong more often than we think. If we can truly acquire an intellectual humility that our thoughts and beliefs do *not* reflect absolute truth we will be in a much better position to understand the beliefs of others, even if we disagree. Being genuinely open to new ideas and receptive to new information means that you should be willing to revise even deeply held beliefs in the face of compelling evidence.

"How does being more open-minded help us understand what others believe? Surely, I don't need to entertain the thought that someone else's idea might be correct in order for me to understand it, right?" Well, actually you do. If you give in to intellectual arrogance, you will make less effort to understand competing ideas and viewpoints which, by definition, makes you less likely to understand the minds of others. Further, the more biased or ignorant you believe others are makes it more likely that you overlook their minds altogether, a condition we call dehumanization.

Dehumanization

Failing to recognize the fully human mind of another person is the essence of dehumanization. In a classic example, African slaves in North America between the 17th and 19th centuries were subjected to horrific treatment at the hands of their owners. This behavior was even acceptable amongst people with traditional God-fearing, Christian beliefs because the slaves were not considered people. The justification is, "Treating *people* this way would be wrong, but since these *creatures* are not people, it is acceptable to treat them as property because God has given us dominion over the earth and all the creatures upon it." Anytime one group enslaves another there is a dehumanizing effect at work where the victims are seen as less than a full person.

Dehumanization does *not* require enslavement, or even prejudice and hatred, but can manifest anytime there is a *distance* between two minds that needs bridging. Until the early 1990s (not 1890s – the 1990s!) it was routine for infants to undergo surgery without anaesthesia because doctors believed infants could not experience pain! It took until the 1990s for the medical community's psychological understanding of a patient to catch up with its biological understanding (Anand). Here, it wasn't hatred but rather ignorance that was responsible. History is replete with examples of people failing to realize they are dealing with other fully human minds.

Distance also makes us unaware of other minds. *Physical distance* can stop these triggers from being fired, i.e. "out of sight, out of mind." This makes it easy to dehumanize people in far-flung places on the globe without a second thought. More commonly, however, it is the *psychological distance* between people that causes us to overlook the minds of others. People that are too different, too foreign, too unknown, or just too "other" fail to fire this trigger in our brain and we see them as something other than fully human. *Seeing* another mind does not happen automatically. It takes work to turn on and <u>activate</u>.

There is a way to biologically monitor this process to see exactly when it is happening. A part of the brain, the medial prefrontal cortex (MPFC), engages and activates when we think about what others are thinking. The MPFC helps us make inferences about the minds of others when it is engaged and active (Amodio). If this region fails to engage when thinking about other people it is a strong sign we are overlooking their minds.

Researchers cannot only see *when* it is activated, but by *how much*. This shows that overlooking the minds of others happens on a continuum rather being "on" or "off." The MPFC is engaged more when you are thinking about others who have belief systems more similar to your own. As people become more different from us they become less likely to engage our MPFC. When this part of the brain registers no activity, other people are perceived as mindless–something less than human. Republicans thinking about what Democrats believe activate their MPFC less than when thinking about what fellow Republicans believe. The same is true of Democrats. When thinking about the other party, we don't ascribe the same level of mindfulness that we do with our own (Falk).

Pictures of homeless people triggered the MPFC less than photos of any other reference group. They were rated as more disgusting, less intelligent, less articulate and less emotional than any other group, which means they are seen as more mindless than any other group (Harris). Once a person is seen as mindless, our level of compassion drops, our empathy toward them disappears and negative thoughts about them creep into our consciousness. These feelings quickly transform into contempt and disdain. When this thinking prevails in our minds we see quotes like the following, "Quit feeding stray animals. You know why? Because they breed. You're facilitating the problem if you give an animal or a person ample food supply. They will reproduce, especially ones that don't think too much further than that. And so what you've got to do is you've got to curtail that type of behavior. They don't know any better." This was spoken by South Carolina Lt. Gov. Andre Bauer in 2010 regarding the poor and homeless. He was equating human beings in desperate circumstances to dogs, the very essence of dehumanization. That they "don't think too much farther than that" and "they don't know any better," is dehumanizing because they cast an entire group of people as unthinking creatures that mindlessly follow their basest urges and instincts.

More recently, issues of race have erupted across the United States from Ferguson, Missouri to Baltimore, Maryland. A Justice Department report detailed the racial, ethnic, and gender bias pervasive in the Ferguson police department by looking at email correspondence over several years. One officer from 2008 derived solace from Obama's election by joking "what black man holds a steady job for four years?" (Berman). Wait a second, relax, it's "only a joke," right? And that is how it begins. Subtly, slowly, indirectly. Once these concepts become planted in our minds, however, they can be very difficult to change. What few studies have been done on humor and bias suggests, somewhat intuitively, that racial humor itself will alter one's conception of the targeted group (Greengross). The jokes that get made become part of our deep-rooted belief about people different from ourselves, and foster the dehumanizing thoughts that take root.

Even more recently during the 2016 presidential election, Pres. Donald Trump made statements that were felt by many to be racist, homophobic and xenophobic. As example, he said of illegal immigrants, "They're bringing drugs. They're bringing crime. They're rapists." By definition, yes, every illegal immigrant has broken the law. That does *not* mean they, as a group, are predisposed to committing rape and other violent crime. What little data exists on this issue doesn't support that contention, either. By grouping them together and casting them as violent criminals, however, they are no longer considered mindful people but are instead thought of as a mindless horde of border-crossing rapists.

People dehumanizing others based on party affiliation is an all-too-common occurrence in modern politics, and of course, isn't limited to one side of the political debate. After Pres. Trump won the election, celebrities, social media personalities, and many rank-and-file members of the Democratic party vilified Trump voters as white national-ists and racists. As an example, one article titled, "There's No Such Thing as a Good Trump Voter" asserts that, "People voted for a racist who promised racist outcomes. They don't deserve your empathy." The article goes on to say that, in part, "your frustra-tion at being labeled a racist doesn't justify or mitigate the moral weight of your political choice." (Bouie)

Liberal-minded citizens tend to take umbrage when people are defined by unfair stereotypes that paint an entire group with cherry-picked exceptions. Yet that is exactly what some liberals were doing when describing the "average Trump voter." They were defining these people by Pres. Trump's most extreme rhetoric. They were perceived as mindless racists blindly following their outspoken leader. (The data doesn't support this narrative, of course, as Pres. Trump won key states by winning over people that voted for Pres. Obama in both 2008 and 2012).

This political division exemplifies the obstacles we face when understanding one another because it is based more on emotion than logic. Once we become emotionally invested in one side or the other, we put all of our psychological weight behind support-ing that position, and reflexively dig in regardless of all evidence to the contrary. This conviction causes us to stumble over *all* of the obstacles: overconfidence, lack of self-awareness, hubris, and dehumanization.

*   *   *

When we dehumanize we conclude that "they" do not have our level of mindfulness and we make assumptions, such as that we have more *free will* than they do (Pronin). As fully actualized human beings, *we* can see all the options and make fully informed deci-sions. "We" have a richer choice of life options, from careers to life partners to where to live. "They" do not have the capability of exercising the same amount of free will because they cannot escape their inevitable situations. "They" are slaves to their baser instincts and urges and are not capable of behaving freely. This is when we fall into the trap of seeing others as lesser minds.

This "lesser minds" effect also creates the tendency to assume other minds are less sophisticated and more superficial than our own. Groups that do not fully trigger our MPFC, like terrorists, hurricane victims and political opponents were rated as less able to feel complex emotions like shame, pride, embarrassment and guilt than members of one's own group (Leyens).

This is a trap we must avoid.

How can we fight this tendency to see others this way? First, we need to be conscientious in detecting when we're overlooking the minds of others. We need to be socially adept enough to proceed on the assumption that others' minds are as rich, complex and full of contradictions as our own. Not just *thinking* it, but *knowing* it to be true, we can start to humanize those groups whose minds we have overlooked.

Taken as a whole, our natural tendencies move us further from understanding one another because of:

- Overconfidence - Remember we aren't as good at understanding others as we think.
- Lack of self-awareness - It isn't possible to truly understand *why* people think the way they do
- Hubris - We think *we* have a cornerstone on truth, which, of course, we don't.
- Dehumanization - Overlooking others' minds prevents any real understanding between people.

The key to overcoming all of these is *to be aware of these pitfalls*. Once you become conscious of these behaviors you will be amazed at how often you find yourself, and others, thinking along these lines. Only now you can take a step back, realize what's happening and adjust your thought processes accordingly.

Your clarity of thought and ability to "get inside someone's head" is directly proportional to how well you avoid these traps.

THE TOOLBOX OF INFERENCE

If we can overcome those obstacles, we are better positioned to gain a deeper understanding of others' thoughts and motivations. *The problem now is that the methods we use to understand others are largely based on inference.* These indirect methods, learned from the earliest ages, are used throughout our lifetimes because they *can work reasonably well* at times. While these tools give us *some* information, we need to understand why inference through self, others and actions are insufficient to attain greater insight.

Understanding through self

Our first attempt to understand others is to intuit what *we* would think if we were in another person's shoes. That *should* give us a good idea of what someone is thinking, but as we cannot completely step out of our own mind, we are subject to common pitfalls. Most see the term _egocentrism_ as simply a preoccupation with self, but it's more than that. It is the _inability_ to see a situation from another person's point of view. It's the fly in the ointment that prevents us from successfully using ourselves as a guide to what others are thinking. Social psychologist Jean Piaget postulated in his _Theory of Cognitive Development_ that egocentrism was a natural part of childhood development which progressively diminished into adulthood.

Young children assume other people experience the world exactly as they do. Adults don't _outgrow_ egocentrism; rather, these tendencies are _overcome_ by critical and reflective thinking.

In one test an experimenter asked test subjects to pick up the smallest item in a group of objects. The test was designed so that the subject could see additional objects that could _not_ be seen by the experimenter. Children most often selected an object that was hidden from the experimenter while adults selected the smallest object _that the experimenter could see._ The children assumed other people experienced the world exactly as they did while the adult's critical thinking evoked a response from the perspective of the experimenter. These results are expected, but by watching eye movements to discern patterns of thought, however, the surprising factor was that both groups _made identical initial assessments._ It was only the adults that _overcame_ their hardwired egocentrism, but it was not a natural behavior (Epley, p. 87-9).

We first see things from our own perspective, reflexively and instinctively. No matter how hard we try to see things from another perspective, we can only overcome this egocentrism in momentary bursts.

WHISPER ALERT: You can't stand in every pair of shoes.

The consequences of this egocentrism are:

**Exaggerated mental states.** After 9/11, most people reported being more distressed than others around them, particularly pronounced in New York and Washington, DC, where the trauma was most closely felt (Smith, p.11). Similar results are found in studying responses to other major national events like the Kennedy assassination or the Boston marathon bombing. During stress we are not only less aware of others' emotions, but assume that our feelings are more profound. Here, egocentrism manifests as a misperception of our emotional state relative to others.

**Exaggerated importance.** In a household there is bias for both partners to overestimate the amount of work they contribute. This overclaiming also holds true for negative things like causing fights. Study subjects assigned themselves a disproportionate share of the credit for the work and the blame for the fights! They also assumed the other would take too much credit for the good and too little credit for the bad! (Kruger)

In professional working groups, the larger the size of the group, the greater the individual assessment of their contribution. By the time a group reached a size of eight people, the members collectively claimed 140% of the work! (Epley, p.94-5) It takes *conscious effort* to guard against egocentrism.

So when others don't appreciate all you do, you may not be doing as much as you think! Be sensitive to the recognition that they, too, may do (or think they do) a lot more than you realize, and respond accordingly. Guard against exaggerating your contribution to the world, for better *and* for worse.

Interpreting events. Ask a parent if the world has become more dangerous over the years and nearly all say, "yes, of course it has." Ask them to name *when* this happened and they will give you a date close to the birth of their first child (Eibach). My parents still enjoy saying, "When we were young, we never locked our doors!" The world is actually *less* dangerous now than in the past, but the lens through which we view it has changed (Pinker). *We see the world as more dangerous reflecting our concern for family safety rather than an unbiased interpretation.* These interpretations cause us to assume that changes in ourselves reflect changes in the world.

False-consensus effect. We read the same books, see the same news stories, and live in like-minded communities, so we all see things the same way, right? "Our thoughts, decisions and actions are normal, therefore all reasonable people must feel, decide and act the way we do." This is a form of cognitive bias that assumes consensus around each individual's conclusions (Wojcieszak). When it is shown that there is no consensus, people immediately assume those who disagree are defective or wrong (Dean).

Curse of Knowledge. When someone with knowledge in one area has difficulty understanding the perspective of another without that expertise, it is called the "curse of knowledge." That lack of perspective creates a situation where real communication and dialogue becomes difficult or even impossible. A simple example is when a local gives a tourist directions by saying "turn left at the road where the farmhouse used to be." They have fallen prey to the curse of knowledge.

A fun study examining the curse of knowledge used tapping. The "tapper" would "tap out a song" and the listener would try to determine the song. The tappers guessed that the listeners would be right 50% of the time, but in fact the listeners got less than 3%

correct. Why the the large disparity? The tappers could hear the melody in their head and assumed the listeners could somehow pick up on this (Gilovich p. 636-65). This is fun to try yourself. Pick up a pencil and tap out "Happy Birthday" or "Jingle Bells" (or even the listener's favorite song) on a table and see how often others can identify the tune.

The less you know. When others' minds are unknown to us, the mind we imagine is increasingly based on our own. During a brain scan, test subjects were asked to comparatively think about 3 minds: their mind, another's mind, and the mind of God. The functional Magnetic Resonance Imaging scanner (fMRI) shows increased brain activity when comparing their own minds to the mind of another. The big surprise was that *there was no difference in overall neural activity between people reasoning about their own beliefs and God's beliefs.* It is as though the subjects' beliefs and God's beliefs were the same (Ross, Lelkes, & Russell).

If people believe exactly as God instructs them to believe, this would account for the results. However, when beliefs were artificially manipulated, their assessment of God's beliefs moved in lockstep with their own, whereas estimates of other people's beliefs remained unaffected. This is a startling discovery. "If God is a moral compass, that compass seems to point believers in whatever direction they are already facing" (Epley, p.110-11).

This is a powerful example that *the less we know about the mind of another, the more we use our own mind to fill in the blanks.* If the mind of God is completely unknowable then it only makes sense that a subject would use their own mind to try to make sense of it. This happens to a lesser extent with other people but is still a valid principle. The more different the person, the more we use our own mind as a template, which too often leads to failure.

When we use our minds (inference through self) to understand others, ask:

- Do I see the issue from my frame of reference without considering the other's circumstances?
- Is heightened stress magnifying egocentric tendencies?
- Is the natural tendency to exaggerate one's contribution at play here?
- Is my/their world view or interpretation a logical extension of current circumstances?
- Am I the only reasonable and normal person in the room? *–different is not right or wrong!*
- Is my knowledge a barrier to understanding?
- We think alike, right? *–This may be a red flag for knowing too little.*

TIMEOUT: Identify a circumstance when an interference of egocentrism was at play in preventing a connection. Note the specific egocentric intrusions which you must consciously work to diminish.

Understanding others by imagining ourselves in a similar situation is only helpful in simple situations. We can't just "try harder" to understand how others see the world because we remain ignorant of our biases. So we take the next logical step. We look at *others* who are like the person we are trying to understand, for guiding principles which may yield a better understanding of the one.

Once "they" become a group, egocentrism fades away and we use stereotypes to help us understand the minds of others. While sometimes useful, stereotypes can lead to predictable mistakes.

Understanding through others (stereotypes)

Using a stereotype is not a bad thing when gaining preliminary insight about others. Using them to paint broad generalizations, however, is as disastrous because stereotypes are never wholly accurate. The important question isn't why stereotypes are somewhat accurate. The better question is, what keeps them from being highly accurate? Turns out, there's more than one answer to this question.

Too little information. Stereotypes are most off the mark because we see only the tiniest sample of the world's people, listen only to media with which we agree, and we talk to a philosophically homogenous group of friends. We only get a fraction of the information necessary to form a complete assessment.

The more direct experience we have with the members of a given group, the more accurate our stereotypes become. Direct contact doesn't mean stories cherry picked from the news or anecdotes passed around Facebook. The more people from a certain group you *interact* with, the better situated you will be to make general observations about that group at large.

When seeing a computer repair man wearing glasses, a pocket protector, and out-of-fashion clothing, one may think "geek" or "nerd." Given the stereotypes associated with those words, one thinks "loner" "void of female friends" "spends all his free time playing video games." In reality, perhaps none of those things are true.

Globally, we hear how Iraqis, Syrians, or better-yet, "middle-easterners" think. Those propagating these stereotypes may have never met someone from this group or may have had only one isolated experience with this ethnicity.

Within a country, most stereotypes relate to minority groups and are inaccurate. It is majority-group stereotypes that tend to be more accurate because more data can be collected (Ryan).

Stereotypes are not always centered around cultural and racial lines. Whenever you see someone from a group to which _you don't belong_, you judge them through the lens of whatever stereotype you have of that group. Typical groups:

- Renters and owners
- College or trade
- Married/unmarried
- Strong vocabulary
- Trendy or conservative dress

- Tattoos or piercings
- Democrat or Republican
- Food or fancy fare
- Social clubs member or loner
- All the different faith groups

All of these groupings color our _assumptions_, which we elevate to stereotypical status.

Different by definition. _Stereotypes can get the direction of differences right but the magnitude of those differences wrong._ We don't define groups by characteristics they share with other groups (like having ten fingers, liking pizza, and feeling utter contempt for people that take up two parking spaces) but by what makes us _different_ from most others, e.g., a stamp collecting banjo player that enjoys macrame and brewing his own beer. _Groups only emerge when we detect differences between them._ A group defined by characteristics shared by everyone is, by definition, no group at all.

The largest study of human mating habits was published in 1989 using over 10,000 men and women across more than thirty countries. This study has been cited ad nauseam with the finding that men rated "good looks" as more important than women did, while women rated "earning potential" as more important than men. This has falsely led people to conclude men are hyper-focused on women's physical attributes while women are just as focused on the money.

It was only noted at the end of the study that "both sexes ranked the characteristics 'kind', 'understanding', and 'intelligent' higher than earning power and attractiveness across all samples." (Buss) So neither attractiveness nor earning power were near the top of either sex's list. Meaning that men and women are more similar when selecting a mate than the study would suggest. This drives home the point that _noting_ differences is one thing but _defining_ groups by their differences can become problematic by painting a skewed picture of that group.

In political polls, the habitual assumption is that "their" side is too extreme but "our" side is the moderate voice of reason. This misperception fosters a further increase in partisanship because of the perceived partisanship on the other side. As I sit and watch the 2016 U.S. Presidential election unfold, the partisanship displayed by all parties provides a true barometer of just how large the gap is between perceived and real differences.

When you only hear about the differences between Republicans and Democrats it becomes easy to forget that the ideas uniting them far outweigh those that divide them. The fringes of both parties aside, most would agree that:

- Representative democracy is the best form of government, warts and all
- The Constitution and Bill of Rights are the key documents that define our ideological bedrock
- A free society is comprised of citizens that are free, not because of their wealth or social status, but simply because they exist
- We shouldn't be overtaxed for unnecessary and frivolous programs
- We should have the world's greatest military force, not necessarily in size but in effectiveness
- We must have a safety net in place for people that genuinely need help
- Education and innovation are vital foundational elements that propel us forward

The differences we perceive come more from the rhetoric than the policies. Of course they disagree on what exactly defines "overtaxed" and "frivolous" and how much to spend on goals like the world's most effective military and our nation's schools. But given the size of America's GDP, they make a hue and cry over *relatively* small changes in taxation, or adding and cutting various programs.

The true secret to overcoming stereotypical thinking is to realize the other side may not have completely opposing interests. Conflict is created by the differences we imagine rather than the nuanced and more moderate differences that actually exist.

Stereotypes as self-fulfilling prophecy. Political correctness aside, you won't be surprised to find African American students perform well below other groups in both math and verbal tests. Why? Explanations range from family values, poverty levels, innate abilities and testing bias, but none of them can fully explain the gap between Black and White test scores (Jencks).

A partial explanation is the existence of the stereotype that Blacks don't perform as well on standardized tests. When Black students were asked for their race on the first or last page of a math exam, students answering the question on the first page did markedly worse than their counterparts who answered the question at the end. Being asked about race brought the test performance stereotype to the forefront of their mind and affected performance as dictated by the stereotype (Steele).

This process also works in reverse. When Asian students were asked to note their race on the first page of the exam, their results were *better* than the control group. These results have been named the "stereotype threat" and the "stereotype boost", respectively.

A similar example is the self-fulfilling prophecy of declining mental abilities of the elderly. In China, where the elderly are revered as wise and learned, decline is far slower than in places like the United States. In one long-term study it was revealed that:

- 56% of people with negative aging stereotypes had cardiovascular events before 70.
- 18% of people with positive aging stereotypes had cardiovascular events before 70.

The cultural stereotype about aging can have a tangible impact on our mental and physical abilities as we age (Levy, 1994). In yet another study elderly people seeing the words 'wise', 'sage', and 'learned' on a computer screen did better in mental acuity testing than those that saw 'senile', 'confused', and 'demented' (Levy, 2009).

They can just be wrong. While stereotypes can often provide some useful information, at other times they lead us *further* from truth. German researchers divided participants from different countries into pairs. Participants were given 100 pennies and asked to give some amount to the partner, or perhaps keep it all to themselves, without knowing what the other person had done. Six rounds were played with players from each country. The only information players had was the nationality of their partner in each round. The size of transfers depended on how cooperative participants expected *other* nationalities to be, and that's where stereotypes come into the picture. Post-experiment questionnaires showed "strong expectations" about other countries. The most cooperation was expected from the Japanese (which correlates to their group-oriented culture), followed by the Americans, Germans, Mexicans, Indians, and finally the Israelis.

The point of the experiment was to test how closely the cooperative stereotype matched the actual cooperation. The result showed a negative correlation! Japan, with the highest expected cooperation level showed the lowest actual cooperation. Israelis showed the highest transfer level among all the nations, with Mexico close behind (Brake).

Besides experimental data, real stereotypes can be just as wrong. The Irish have a worldwide reputation for being drunkards. But in 2014, it was found that Ireland didn't even rank in the top 20 countries in average alcohol consumption! (Witherington) As it turns out, the British have the best teeth in the world, the Dutch aren't a bunch of potheads–they have one of the *lowest* usage rates of marijuana throughout Europe, and French people don't hate Americans–only nine other countries on Earth have more favorable views of America, like South Korea and Israel.

Whisper Alert: Stereotypes help define differences between groups, but skews the degree to which differences exist.

Getting over stereotypes. Clear signs of stereotypical thinking were found by a control group viewing a 15-second video interview of a white or black student discussing campus life. After viewing a full 12 minute segment, however, no stereotypical thinking was found. So while stereotypes are quick to proliferate through a society, the speed with which we drop a stereotype when dealing with a specific member of the target group is heartening (Kunda). So, always look at members of the target group as individuals. Recognize they are as different from one another as you are from the groups to which you belong.

* * *

When you know little, or nothing, about a person you fill in the blanks with who a person *is* (their group) but when you learn more, this is quickly supplanted by what a person *does*, which contains its own pitfalls.

Understanding through action (correspondence bias)

"If you don't understand the motive, don't judge the means!"

– STEPHEN MAGNUS

That one's actions directly correspond to one's thoughts and feelings is known as *correspondence bias*. You might think it easy to infer a person's thoughts and motivations based on their actions but this isn't the case. Why? Because we must also consider the *context* in which the behavior occurs.

When dealing with someone who is rude or obnoxious we assume that is "how they are." We don't think about the things that may color these negative behaviors, e.g. they are dealing with a sick loved one or they are going through a messy divorce, or maybe they're just having a bad day. As we cannot fully view the context, we only focus on the behavior to help us determine "who this person is."

When thinking about our own behaviors we understand the context. We know that sometimes none of the available choices are ideal but we understand the larger context in which the decision is made. Those on the outside looking in only see the direct effect of our action and may wrongly conclude the decision is our preferred choice.

An illuminating but tragic example is domestic abuse. How often have we heard, "if she *really* wanted to leave, she would, right? Why would someone stay in a situation that was genuinely abusive?!?" This is correspondence bias in action. Looking at the behavior of "not leaving," it is incorrectly inferred that the situation can't really be that dire.

So why would someone stay? If we can get out of our own heads and dig below the action itself to find the more substantive context, we will be in a much better place to understand her state of mind. (I know that men can be trapped in abusive relationships as well and for many of the same reasons, but for our purposes we will focus on the more (stereo)typical case.) In domestic cases there are many reasons a woman stays in an abusive relationship.

Let's start with the obvious–fear of her partner's actions. If she is being abused, then she might be made to believe that he will hurt her, kill her, or spread horrible rumors about her to friends, family and coworkers. Children make it even more difficult as the fear exists that he might take or harm the children.

The psychological effects of abuse are less obvious but more powerful–in fact, it is the psychological context that often proves the greatest barrier to escape. Systematic abuse can cause a feeling of paralysis and indecision. It can affect self-esteem to where she thinks her life is worth nothing, and she doesn't *deserve* better. He may also have convinced her she wouldn't be able to get along in life without him. Other factors could include:

- Having grown up in an abusive household makes this seem normal
- Being emotionally attached to her abuser and remaining hopeful he will change
- Traditional gender roles reinforcing the notion that she needs to be the one to maintain the relationship and keep everything together
- The fear he will turn the children against her
- Economic dependence on her partner

Any of these could be reason enough to stay when you really want to leave, but in most cases the true cause is a combination of factors.

This focus on actions is particularly pronounced in two cases: first, when you do not have direct experience with the situation, and second, when you are interacting with someone you don't know well. In the domestic abuse example, that she does not leave does *not* mean it is her preference to stay. The people that have the hardest time understanding this are the ones to whom domestic abuse is most foreign.

Overcoming this bias is even more difficult if the person is a stranger. If someone you don't know is rude to you, you are likely to conclude "this is not a nice person." Someone you know well, however, gets the benefit of the doubt and you are more likely to infer that she is just having a bad day. Because you have seen your friend in many situations, you have a much better read on her typical disposition and can adjust your thoughts accordingly. When your only experience with someone is negative, it becomes easy to fall into the trap of assuming her current behavior defines who she is as a person.

Whisper Alert: Connect their frame of reference with their action...and add in context.

It is important to identify when you are inferring thoughts from actions. When you find this happening, step back and realize that you need to gain a broader perspective to understand another's true motivations. This is a difficult thing to do, but the more willing you are to gain that broader context, the easier time you will have understanding others.

*   *   *

These tools are inexact shortcuts into the minds of others. <u>Egocentrism</u> *overestimates* the extent to which others' minds are like our own. <u>Stereotyping</u> *exaggerates* the differences between groups at the expense of their similarities. <u>Correspondence bias</u> *oversimplifies* assumptions about the minds of others, largely owing to lack of context and familiarity.

All of these solutions attempt to achieve understanding through *inference:* using various pieces of information to make a determination about what someone thinks. Attempts to understand others that are *indirect*, second-hand and require too much guesswork are not reliable tools.

The better solution is to gather another's perspective *directly*. This requires engaging people and asking insightful questions and listening to the answers, rather than just guessing about their thoughts and motivations. Only by developing a natural curiosity of others can you form a deeper understanding of them.

It is this understanding that forms the basis of the persuasion techniques covered in subsequent chapters.

TRUE UNDERSTANDING IS JUST A QUESTION AWAY

"The best way to resolve any problem in the human world is for all sides to sit down and talk."

--DALAI LAMA

Children ask questions incessantly, sometimes to the chagrin of everyone within ear shot. As we get older, we lose that inquisitiveness. In a recent poll it was found that 70-80% of children's interactions with others were based on questions. For adults, it dropped to 15-25% (Pohlmann). Not only do adults ask fewer questions, but the questions they do ask are overwhelmingly requests for favors. As a general rule, strive to turn half of your conversation into questions about someone else. Since the average person doesn't ask enough questions, you will easily stand out and be seen in a more positive light.

"Half of the conversation" means after you've communicated an idea, not necessarily "every other sentence." Before moving to a new topic, or even a new point, force yourself to ask a question. If you're talking about your day, conclude by saying, "Tell me about the most interesting part of your day." If you're telling a story about how you dealt with a situation, finish by asking, "how would you have handled that?" If you shared a story about the crazy day you had, ask, "does that remind you of anything that's happened to you?" When outlining tasks for people that work for you, ask, "Does this make sense to you?"

Make asking questions your default setting and you will naturally have a better understanding of everyone you come into contact with.

* * *

The Curious Case of the African Well

United States aid workers were visiting a small village in sub-saharan Africa. They noticed that the women were walking over a mile to fill up their containers only to walk a mile back. The workers built a well in the middle of the village so that fresh water would be more readily available. After the time and expense of building the well, they noticed that the women were continuing to use their original water source over a mile away.

After questioning the women about their behavior, the answer caught the aid workers off guard. The women said that going to get water each day was their one opportunity to get away from the village, get some peace from their children and husbands, and talk to one another about their lives. Not only did the women not mind traveling to get water, it was a welcome escape from the rest of their duties and obligations! The new well was considered a threat to this routine and went unused.

If the aid workers had bothered to question the women beforehand, a lot of frustration could have been spared. This is just one example of how asking questions and actively getting others' perspectives could have avoided an unnecessary misunderstanding.

*   *   *

This process needs to run in both directions to be most effective. If you want others to be more transparent in disclosing their thoughts and feelings, then you must reciprocate. Not only for their benefit, but for yours. Studies have shown that being more open with people makes you feel better understood, happier and more satisfied with life (Human). This concept works so well that when researchers need to create a genuine bond between people in a laboratory setting, they will have them disclose private thoughts and feelings to one another (Aron). Not only will it make *you* feel better, but it will generate positive feelings for *others* who will now be more open to you, which increases rapport and your ability to generate influence.

This phenomenon has tangible benefits besides just "hard-to-quantify feelings." Preliminary research suggests that doctors who are more transparent and openly admit their mistakes find a *reduction* in litigation (Kachalia). Transparency allows caregivers to do what they were trained to do in the first place–take care of patients and ensure the same mistakes don't happen again. Transparency isn't just beneficial in the medical profession. By opening yourself up to others you can foster transformative, reciprocative relationships.

Good questions are more powerful than answers. They can challenge our thinking in constructive ways. They can force us out of narrow viewpoints to reframe problems in ways that generate potential solutions. Get in the habit of asking questions and you will always be in position to understand the thoughts, feelings and motivations of others without falling into the common traps which result from guesswork.

Genuine interest

> "It is the individual who is not interested in his fellow men who has the greatest difficulties in life and provides the greatest injury to others. It is from among such individuals that all human failures spring."

--ALFRED ADLER

What is the difference between people that can successfully engage others and those that can't? Genuine interest–which cannot be faked. When you're speaking with someone for the first time, the conversation quickly burns out under the weight of useless, but polite, questions like, "What do you find to be the quickest route to work?" or "Do you like hockey? You do? Well, not me…" These types of exchanges are all too common with people that have no genuine interest in one another.

Throughout our lives, the conversations that stand out the most are the ones where someone was genuinely interested in what we had to say about… well, anything. Become that person who creates the remembered conversations. The only way to learn about a person is to have a natural curiosity in finding out about their lives and how they think. You will never reach your potential as a Human Whisperer unless you can cultivate this curiosity. With nothing more than questions, genuine interest (genuine presence), and curiosity, people will tell you everything about themselves. From that you can gain real insight into their mind.

WHISPER ALERT: Curiosity didn't kill the cat and it won't kill you!

If you have an interest and curiosity, what will you do? You will engage; *you ask questions.*

Your questions will be based on the context and subject matter of the conversation. Whom you are speaking with, in what capacity, the occasion or event, and your specific preferences–all determine the appropriate questions and so demand a degree of common sense.

Sometimes you want to ask the *unexpected* question. Years ago, while attending a rooftop cocktail party in Washington, DC, I observed the host was wearing a tuxedo with giant clown shoes. Instead of going for the obvious, "what's the deal with those shoes?" I went the other way with, "Gee, why mess up those beautiful shoes with such a hideous tux?" It got a chuckle and broke the ice. Mission accomplished.

Getting started

There are times, even with sincere interest, that the right question escapes you and you struggle with what to ask. This is especially true if you aren't used to flexing your question-asking muscles, or if you're dealing with someone that is a *complete* mystery, or you're uncomfortable with conversation in general. Until you get used to it, what follows is a list of fallback questions that work in both business and personal contexts and with slight wording changes can be adapted to nearly any environment.

Some books and articles provide dozens or hundreds of possible questions to keep a conversation lively. Rather than providing a laundry list of impossible-to-remember questions, this is a narrow group. Each question is designed to provide a deeper under-standing of the person or business. Besides a couple of general questions, I've chosen a few situations where there is more uncertainty in what to ask: first meetings; when some-one tells you about a problem; and when you're trying to find out more about a person. Don't just think of these as fallback questions, they are all great ways to get people talk-ing. I've used these questions successfully in a variety of situations and hopefully they will work for you, too. Above all, please remember *these are not to be used sequentially!* Each question acts as a springboard into a deeper and more specific conversation. Pick out just two or three to remember and use them often!

*   *   *

And if the wording of a question isn't to your liking, change it to suit how you speak. Write in the margins. Tailor these questions for situations you typically encounter.

General Questions

"What do you think about...?" The need to be heard is a powerfully motivating force. It is a simple truth that we care most about the people who really listen to us. This question is direct and can be used in nearly any situation – when someone is dis-cussing a personal or business crisis, after you've shared your views, or when soliciting 3rd party input in a conversation, etc. It is an open ended question that will allow the person to start truly expressing themselves. More than any other question listed, this one *requires* you to be a great listener. Allowing your focus to drift or answering a text while someone is answering this question is the surest way to destroy any rapport you may have developed.

"Tell me about your plans." Questions can be turned into statements. This is an-other open ended question that allows you to showcase the greatest trait of a great questioner–curiosity. Develop your natural curiosity and you will be more focused and attentive to their answers. In a business context, you might try a variation like, "Tell me about your company's short and long-term goals" or "What are your biggest priorities this year?" You will achieve a greater understanding of their commitments and will learn their specific approaches to attaining goals and what motivates them–all impor-tant to the Human Whisperer.

First Meetings

From your perspective, what is the most valuable way to spend our time together? This is a personal favorite as it saves wasted time. Particularly in preliminary meet-ings with potential clients and business partners, this question cuts to the core of what they want and what is most important to discuss. In fact, this is one of the first questions I ask in every meeting. Not only will you get valuable information on their thought processes, but it also lets them know that you are listening to their needs and will respond accordingly. Too many salespeople prattle on about their goods and services without first asking, "How can I make our time the most valuable to you?" Ask this, then listen. They will tell you their mindset, allowing you to edit your pitch accordingly.

What would your closest friends say they like most about you? As noted earlier, we aren't very good at knowing what people think of us, but it doesn't matter. Asking someone this question will often result in an answer formulated solely for the questioner. This question is targeting what *they* think their greatest strengths are by couching the question through the eyes of their close friends. This also avoids the overly modest answer. Their response tells you what attribute about themselves they hold in the highest regard and is *valuable information.*

With a slight wording change this question is just as effective in business, "What would your best customers say if asked why they do business with you?" Again, they enjoy a freedom to honestly tell you the finer points of their business of which *they* are most proud without false modesty.

Responding to problems and issues

How is this affecting other aspects of your life/business? If someone is telling you about a personal or business problem, this is a great question to use to broaden the nature of the discussion. Sometimes people get locked into discussing a single topic and have difficulty seeing it in a larger perspective. This question provides a great segue to change the topic, provided you can ask timely follow-up questions related to their answer. This also shows a keen interest in the other party and allows you to find out what other things in their life (or business) hold a high priority. Knowing an individual's values is essential in understanding the other person.

If left unresolved, how will your life/business be affected? This question moves the inquiry from the current situation to the future. In business, this can be a great question to provide an opening to discuss how you are situated to help mitigate the effects of this issue and moves the discussion toward finding a solution. Or, this question can show that when forecasting our present troubles into the future, things are not as dire as they seem today. It helps provide perspective.

Discovering motivations, interests, and goals

[Past] **What has brought you the most fulfillment in your life?** This is a backward looking, open-ended question that will get people talking. The older the person, the more detailed and interesting the answers are likely to be. You can ask this of a younger person and change "fulfillment" to "enjoyment" or "satisfaction" to generate more stimulating conversation.

[Present] **What are you most (passionate about/interested in) right now?** The focus is on the here and now. The wording shows interest and curiosity in a way that the question, "so… what kind of stuff do you like?" doesn't. Also watch *how* they answer this question. If their eyes light up and they show that passion with their response, it is genuine. Even people that are not normally demonstrative will rise above their "animation baseline" when discussing something they love to talk about.

[Future] **You've accomplished a lot. Where do you go from here?** This question is effective not only because it allows someone to talk about their goals, but also because it starts off with a compliment. For this question, look not at *how*, but at *how quickly* they can answer this question. This will tell you if they are forward looking and how much they have been thinking about the future.

Many questions will accomplish the goals of determining a person's motivations, interests and goals. Another favorite is, **"If you knew you couldn't fail, what would you choose to do?"** This initiates a fun exchange and almost always moves the conversation to unexpected places.

For the curious, these questions are a valuable resource. Remember just a couple and use them when you can't think of anything more fitting.

WHISPER ALERT: A skillful questioner becomes a great Whisperer.

"The Failsafe"

A simple, but effective, strategy to keep people talking is to echo back the last word or two of the last thing they said. If someone says, "Both at work and at home this has been a tough week." Maintaining your sincerity, curiosity and interest level, say, "tough week?" This lets them know that you're interested in finding out more and allows them freedom to discuss whatever is on their mind. (How many times, however, has this initial declaration been met with, "Me too! Let me tell you about mine!" Which says "not interested" and "don't care.")

To nonverbally project your interest it's also a good idea to subtly furrow your brow and tilt your head as you ask the question. If you find this happening automatically, it's a good indicator of your sincerity. If not, it's fine to control this behavior consciously, but put in the hard work to force yourself to *become* curious. Taking interest in others and being curious about what they have to say becomes easier the more you do it. Getting that inertia moving is the hardest part of the process.

If this technique is used too often or insincerely, it can become transparent and can easily tear down any rapport you've built. Instead of just echoing the last couple of words say, "What do you mean by [fill in the last couple of words]?" This helps provide variation so that as you move back and forth between different forms of questions it won't be as obvious.

* * *

FORGET-ME-NOTS

- The very nature of human beings creates barriers that inhibit our ability to understand others, most notably:
    - Overconfidence, when we assume we already know what others are thinking
    - Dehumanization, where we overlook the minds of others by elevating the importance of our own mind.
- The ways we go about understanding others are largely based on inference:
    - Using stereotypes to compare groups exaggerates the differences
    - Judging others by their actions fails to account for the context and the available alternatives
- To understand others, the direct approach is best; _ask questions, engage, and become interested in the world outside your own doorstep._

* * *

Acknowledging the limits of our insight forces us to directly interact with others to acquire true understanding of thought and motivation. Engaging others by asking sincere questions gives us the clarity we need to move even deeper. Once we use our interest and curiosity to _understand_ others, we must use that as a springboard to more deeply _relate_ to them. We need to put ourselves in the right frame of mind to get into rapport with others, which in turn facilitates a genuine connection.

5

Generating rapport

"The life I touch for good or ill will touch another life, and in turn another, until who knows where the trembling stops or in what far place my touch will be felt."

-Frederick Buechner, The Hungering Dark

WHAT'S THE POINT?

Connecting means relating to someone in a non-superficial way. People who are passionate about the same things and are able to share that passion are connected. When one's problem is solved, or even alleviated by another, that, too, creates a connection. Just spending time with people creates connections. These emotional bonds last well beyond any single conversation and can even happen with people you've just met.

"If I learn how to read people and influence them, what's the point of making a 'deeper connection'. Who cares?" Creating connections is about more than just becoming a Human Whisperer–it is about developing relationships. It isn't about the angle or how you can leverage others to your advantage. It's about striving to make every interaction meaningful, in some way.

As a member of the human race, we are duty-bound to be of service to our fellow man. Acting to strengthen our relationships, even with casual acquaintances, is a goal unto itself.

On a daily basis, we give up opportunities to make a connection. In trains, subways, buses, waiting rooms, and airplanes we are inches away from several people but instead of engaging with others, we stick our head in our phone, tablet, or newspaper. This does not mean talk to everyone you meet, but social isolation is a bigger risk factor for cardiac arrest than smoking or obesity! (Holt-Lunstad) Yet, we refuse to turn an isolating experience into a social one by interacting with the person sitting next to us.

Experiments show people rate solitude as what *would* make them happiest, but when they tried speaking with someone next to them, it was *actually* rated the more pleasurable experience by a large margin. This was true whether the initiator was outgoing, shy, introverted or extroverted (Epley, p. 58). So not only can you improve the disposition and outlook of *others*, reaching out and connecting will also improve *your* physical and psychological well-being.

Make it a habit to engage those around you–it benefits everyone. The biggest impediment to overcoming isolation is inertia (and our handheld devices). If isolating yourself has become your default, it can be a tough habit to break. Once you start actively engaging others around you it becomes increasingly easier to do.

Of course, this has an added benefit for aspiring Whisperers. Connecting with others while using the techniques from chapter two will put you on the path to becoming the charismatic person others want to be around. And yes, your effectiveness in wielding the techniques of influence and persuasion (described in later chapters) will become fully actualized. If you understand people well, but remain isolated in life, it benefits no one.

SINCERITY

When connecting with people, *sincerity* trumps everything. This is no mystery, and is in fact, self-evident. We still need to hear it because it is easy to forget. Be open, honest and genuine in your desire to deepen your relationships, and it will happen naturally.

There is a wealth of advice from everyone on what to do, what to say, and how to say it, in order to connect with people. So much of that advice is targeted to specific personality types. Four universal ways to demonstrate your sincerity is to show your interest *in them*, show that you are interested *in their interests*, be of service, and be open with your imperfections. These concepts were chosen because they're simple and everyone can use them, whether you're shy, outgoing, loud, quiet, nervous, confident, contemplative, or if you tend to say whatever comes to mind.

More questions! (Take an interest in the person)

Understanding others by asking questions is one thing, but creating a lasting connection is quite another. One simple way of fostering that connection is to make sure your questions aren't just about "digging for information." Generate the curiosity to ask all manner of questions.

"Well, what kinds of questions should I ask?"

That depends on you. We all have our own sense of humor and conversational rhythms. Questions that I would feel comfortable asking may not work for you.

Here's a quick tip: when someone asks you an interesting or funny question, re-member it! Tuck it away in your conversational toolbox and get ready to use it when you're trying to make a connection with someone (we're not talking about pick-up lines). Even people that don't consider themselves funny can generate an amusing, fun, or thought-provoking moment. There are countless potential questions out there. In an effort to spur your own ideas, here are a couple of generic ones that might be fun to try out:

- *What is really popular right now, but will embarrass everyone involved with it in 10 years' time?*
- *If you got arrested, what would your friends and family think you'd done?*
- *What will people be nostalgic for in 30 years?*
- *If you were mistakenly put in an insane asylum, how would you convince them you were sane and not just pretending to be sane to get out?*
- And my personal favorite–*Toilet paper: are you a crumpler or folder?*

* * *

The best questions, though, will be based on observation or context. Back in 1994, I met a real cute girl at a recording studio where a mutual friend's band needed people to make up the audience for a "live track". When she was alone, I began making my way toward her and noticed another couple on the dance floor amorously engaged. It looked like they were trying to swallow each other whole. As I walked up to her I no-ticed she was eyeing this couple too, so I said, "Doesn't that just make you sick!?!" She laughed out loud and said, "YES, it does!" That girl is now my wife, who later confessed that my little question immediately put me on her radar. She explained that *what* I said, and *how* I said it, projected humor and confidence (neither of which I actually felt in the moment).

Never underestimate the power of a well-timed question to create a connection.

Aside from better *understanding* others (and obtaining a spouse), questions allow you to achieve a deeper *connection* by:

- **Making people feel important.** Everyone feels more important and special when they are asked questions. It allows them to be seen as someone with expertise, knowledge and experience that the questioner does not have.
- **Immediately getting one's attention.** People don't listen to what you _tell_ them, they listen to what you _ask_ them. In any group situation where you are vying for

someone's attention, the quickest path to success is to ask them questions. They will instinctively engage you with an answer.

- *Demonstrating your interest in others.* Sincere questions show you are interested in the other person and that you truly care about what they have to say. This eliminates questions such as "What about this weather?"
- *Subtly taking control of the conversation.* Whoever asks the questions is in control. You can use thoughtful questions to steer the discussion in any direction, but you must remain <u>present</u>.
- *Entertaining others.* Funny and/or interesting questions can both amuse and fascinate, which has formed the basis for more than a few relationships.
- *Getting people talking...about themselves.* The only thing people love more than talking is talking about themselves. Once they start talking, it takes little effort on your part to keep them going.
- *Indirectly showing your knowledge.* Well-worded questions are a great way to show you possess a depth of knowledge in a subject without overtly showing off.
- *Covering up any unwanted lull in a conversation.* When you're unsure what to say, ask a question! It is a great way to keep the conversation moving without blurting out some nonsensical gibberish like, "I love lamp." (Brick Tamland, Anchorman)

This doesn't mean that you should only ask questions which may give the impression you have no thoughts of your own. Remember you're engaging in a dialogue with someone and questions should only be part of that equation.

When answering questions, appeal to *their* curiosity. Don't tell them everything you know about a given topic, just what they need to know to keep the conversation moving. Be aware that no one is as interested in your stories as you are, but if you add a "dangler," a thought they can choose to follow, you can gauge their reciprocal interest. "Work was interesting today. The lunch thief won't steal any more lunches after today!" The response to this question, or lack thereof, will be telling in either case.

Don't over-use danglers to overtly invite a follow-up question. This is how some people communicate by default and as we all know, it can get irritating quickly. Make the sentence sound like a completed thought and be fully prepared to move on. If they do ask a follow-up question, you can assume they're at least interested enough to hear a little bit more or willing to engage.

Engage (Take an interest in their interests)

It is your initial questions which kick off a good discussion, but it is genuine interest that keeps you in the conversation. Everyone knows more about *some* topic than you do.

Make it your mission to find out what someone knows more about, and learn *just one or two* things about it that you didn't know before. Even if it's something you don't care about, you'll be amazed at the breadth and depth of knowledge gained from generating sincere interest in the experience of others. From what *not* to do when brewing your own beer, to why PE ratios are no longer a reliable stock indicator, to a detailed discussion on the glue used to hold the backs and fronts of playing cards together–being interested in what others have to say can open your eyes to a larger world and make you a more well-rounded person. (And yes, these unrelated topics are among the three most recent conversations I've had with people where they got to explain things of interest to them.)

Your genuine interest fuels *their* passion about whatever it is they're talking about. It is those animated parts of a conversation that are most memorable, for both of you. You don't need to be outwardly demonstrative to internalize their passion, but let that emotion carry you to find out as much as you can about the topic in question. If you truly have that interest, they will know it, and you will form a connection based on nothing but curiosity, interest and a willingness to listen and learn.

<u>Great relationships begin with great conversations</u>. Too many equate a great conversation with showing off how much they know. Rein in your natural tendency to impress others and do something that will seem unnatural to most of you–*let them impress you!* As Dale Carnegie once said, *"You can make more friends in two months by becoming interested in other people than you can in two years by trying to get other people interested in you."* Listen to their stories and experiences without feeling the need to interject, even if your comments are related.

Achieving their goals (Be of service)

Often, these discussions result in learning that a person is trying to accomplish an objective, reach a goal, or fulfill a dream. Help them do it! Give them some advice you've learned along the way that might make achieving their dreams easier. Or maybe put them in touch with someone in a position to help them. The more people you are in contact with, the easier it will be to connect others together.

Give them *<u>encouragement</u>* by letting them know you believe they can reach their goal. Just expressing a little faith in a fellow human being can have a profound impact not only on their current pursuits, but for the rest of their life! This support shouldn't be too general, as in, "I know you can do it!" These are the kinds of phrases people hear so often they tend to tune them out. You can say the same thing in a way that they *will* hear by being just a tad more specific, "Seeing your passion and how knowledgeable you are about this, I'm sure you can open your own restaurant!" This even works well with people you've just met.

An even better way to help someone reach their dreams is to _hold them accountable_. Tell them you're going to check in on them at regular intervals to find out how it's going. This is such a small thing but keeps people motivated and focused on their goals, and they will remember that you helped them succeed. (No one wants to confess '0' progress.) "Checking in" doesn't necessarily need to be done in person, or even over the phone (although these are the most impactful ways to communicate). A text or email may be all that is required, depending on the frequency and purpose for checking in. And, checking in is easy if you've connected them with a connection of yours!

Connecting through vulnerability ("I'm not perfect.")

There are two common, but related, misconceptions about vulnerability. The first misconception is that being vulnerable means expressing your deepest thoughts and feelings, exposing your most intimate secrets. The second is that you should be cautious showing your vulnerabilities, reserving it for your very closest confidantes.

The first misconception is too confined, because being vulnerable also means exposing your flaws, foibles, eccentricities and failings, all without shame or remorse. Showing that you're human and you make mistakes is a different type of vulnerability but is no less important to let others see. Once you accept this broader definition, the second misconception fades away too. You should let _everyone_ see your vulnerabilities. And, as we will see later, this makes you "likeable" too!

Relationships are deepened when you openly show that you can make mistakes just like anyone else. It implicitly shows that you don't think you're better than anyone else. Granted, your deepest secrets should be reserved for those closest to you, but there is a lot of room to demonstrate your vulnerabilities to everyone else. What follows are a few easy ways to accomplish this.

Say you're sorry. It is amazing how difficult this one can be for some people. The inability to sincerely apologize is an enormous character flaw. Own up to situations where you've said the wrong thing, did the wrong thing, showed a temporary lapse in judgement, or just downright "messed up." The people to whom you apologize will appreciate and respect that you've owned up to your mistake. It can also neutralize their anger and frustration at the situation. Get into the habit of apologizing, when appropriate, if you don't already do so. (Some people "over-apologize" which is a different problem altogether. It comes across as both insincere and insecure. So if you're someone who apologizes all the time, work on doing it less.)

Ask for advice. This one has a twofold impact. First, it shows that you don't have all the answers and aren't afraid to ask others for their opinion (vulnerability). It also shows confidence because only a self-assured person would ask for someone else's thoughts without fear of being thought of as less intelligent. Second, the person you're asking will feel good that you think enough of them to ask their opinion in the first place. It is an indirect compliment that works better than any direct compliment could.

Talk about feelings instead of just thoughts. This one is more targeted to men as women tend to have less problem in this area. When discussing ideas or important issues, letting people know how it makes you *feel* is a type of vulnerability and can deepen the connection between people. At least once in a conversation, move from an idea to a feeling. It doesn't need to be a particularly overpowering feeling like love, hate, anger or despondency.

(For example, as I sit here typing, the news is alight with coverage of the Manchester bombing in the UK. It makes me *feel* powerless to help. And I don't understand why there seems to be no boundary that hatred can't cross. I don't *feel* equipped to understand the nature of that hatred or how to even begin thinking about countering it. Today, I *feel* very small.)

Be open about your failures. Most of us don't openly admit to failures, but we should. Discussing a situation where you said or did the wrong thing, or had an "epic fail," these stories lighten the mood and cast you as more approachable. Don't be afraid to embrace an opportunity to share these stories. Too many people think they will come off looking diminished in the eyes of others, but they invariably come off looking more confident.

On a related note, when speaking to people about an embarrassing or painful situation, watch for facial reactions that coincide with the emotion you're conveying in the story. Whether pain, or embarrassment, anyone wincing or making other supportive faces is said to be "easily empathetically embarrassed." This doesn't mean the subject embarrasses easily, but it does mean they are displaying a high level of empathy, which is accompanied by a release of oxytocin, which modulates trust and generosity. All of which are good signs when looking for an emotional connection. And later, when using techniques of influence, it is those people with the greatest amount of empathy that are most likely to accede to a request.

Self-deprecating compliments. Rather than just a vanilla complement like, "that's a lovely dress," use comparative statements so that it makes a far greater impact and shows a little vulnerability. Something like, "you know, the dress is great, and it just highlights your sense of fashion! Consistently putting a great look together is something I'm still working on." This type of statement works because you don't come across as someone that thinks they're the greatest at everything, because you're openly admitting that they are *better* at something than you are. Also, in this case, you're not only complimenting the dress, but also the fashion sense of the wearer. This is a much deeper compliment and will leave a longer-lasting impression on the recipient. (Be careful not to over-do the self-deprecation, or you may look as if you are fishing for compliments.) Everybody is better at *something* than you. When you see an example of it, let that person know.

*   *   *

Connections can be strengthened by asking questions, becoming interested in *the other person*, helping them achieve success through encouragement and accountability, and finally showing your vulnerability. This must be genuine and done *for real!* These are simple, honest, and do-able things to deepen all your relationships. Not only will they feel more invested in the relationship, but so will you.

> **TIMEOUT:**   Sometime in the next month, deepen a relationship with just one person. Be sincere in your desire and then:
>
> 1. Ask them questions about their primary interest(s), and if you don't know what it is, find out!
> 2. Learn at least one thing about this topic you didn't know before, but preferably two or three.
> 3. Make one self-deprecating compliment that highlights one of their strengths.

FAKING IT

"Sincerity - if you can fake that, you've got it made."

- GEORGE BURNS

For everyone, there are times we can't motivate ourselves to generate interest in others. Once in a while, we need to fake it. By faking it, we don't mean the *desire* to create a connection is fake. Rather, the mind's *current ability* to create that connection is compromised. Whether through fatigue, preoccupation with other thoughts, or maybe we're just distracted by the spinach in someone's teeth, we can't get into the right mind-set to effectively make a genuine connection.

Even when conditions are right, sometimes we just can't "get in synch" with the other person. Maybe we are too dissimilar, are on "different wavelengths", or maybe just started out on the wrong foot. For these situations, too, we occasionally need to rely on other tools.

When learning to fake a connection, why not learn from the best...psychics. Ahh, the word itself conjures up images from crystal ball reading carnival workers to the darkened rooms of tarot readers all the way up to charlatans like John Edward, who despicably extorts grieving people with the promise of speaking to departed loved ones.

Their approach is largely summed up in a single phrase: "cold reading," which is a psychological strategy used to create the appearance that you deeply understand and can relate to another person, even when you know nothing about them. Cold reading is not just one thing, it is a set of techniques used to achieve a specific objective. And unlike those that speak with the dead, our purpose isn't fraud, but rather appropriating their techniques to create rapport and deepen connections. (Not all psychics are frauds, but the line can get blurry. A palm reader at a state fair is clearly there to entertain, but someone asking for your life savings in order to speak to your departed child is entirely on the other side of that line.)

A good way to understand cold reading is to think about a horoscope. Some people believe wholeheartedly in its ability to reveal relevant information for people sharing their zodiac sign. Others think that the information is so general, it could apply to anyone. This is an example of cold reading, but only on the most superficial level. Good cold readers don't stick with vague information, they tell you specific information about your life, people you've met and places you've been with remarkable accuracy.

Cold readers build rapport by giving character readings and facts about a person's life. Once rapport has been established they *extract* information (while seemingly *providing* it), and provide predictions about the future. Our approach won't cover all of these techniques, rather, we will focus only on the rapport building elements.

Psychics use oracles to presumably uncover truths about the "sitter," which is another term for the client. These oracles range from tarot cards, crystal balls, the palm of the hand, tea leaves, runes, chicken bones, or any other implement or tool that purports to divine the

otherwise unseeable. We use none of those things. We are not pretending to tap into any spiritual or otherworldly connections. Our conversation should appear as though it is *our insight and perception alone* that reveals the inner workings of our subject. Even people that completely reject the notion of psychic mysticism are susceptible to cold reading because we aren't pretending to tap into those mystical energies. We are just having a conversation where we *appear* to understand our subject in ways that seem impossible. We are using the tools of the psychic without the "psychic slant."

*   *   *

We can also use *targeted guessing* to figure out information about people, such as, "what is the typical profile of a person that reads a book like this?" Well, look no further, because I've created an extensive profile of my readership based on the types of people that would read a book like this. Since you're in that demographic, please assess how close I've come in describing *you*:

*   *   *

You, dear reader of The Human Whisperer, are a person prone to bouts of self-examination. Your ability to appear socially engaged convinces others you are genuinely interested but you are all too aware it is sometimes a façade.

This means you will often be at a gathering and find yourself playing a part. While on the outside you'll be talkative and funny, you're actually detached to the point that you find yourself watching everything going on around you and feeling like a spectator. You play conversations back in your head and wonder what that person really meant when he said such-and-such — conversations other people wouldn't think twice about.

You deal with this situation through self-control. You show a calm, self-assured stability. You protect yourself by keeping people at bay to avoid disappointment until you decide they are allowed over that magic line into your vulnerable space. However, once across that line, an emotional dependency kicks in which leaves you feeling very hurt or rejected if it appears that they have betrayed that status.

You are creative, and have explored different avenues to utilize it. It may not be that you paint, but your creativity shows itself in more subtle ways, and you will certainly find yourself having vivid, well-formed ideas which others find provocative or hard to grasp. You set high standards for yourself and others. You often don't get things done, because you are frustrated by the idea of mediocrity but are wearied by the idea of starting something fresh.

Once your brain is engaged you find yourself sailing. You've considered writing a novel, songs, even the odd poem. However fear of achieving your lofty expectation stops you. Because of these expectations for yourself and others, you are currently fighting against restraints upon your desire to express yourself more freely.

Your relationship with your parents is or has been under some strain. You wish to remain fond of them but recent issues are causing frustration. They are unaware of your thoughts, partly because of your ability to play a part to hide that you are feeling like something of an outsider. Now you are embracing that outsider role to the point of consciously avoiding being part of a group or clique. You have a cynicism towards those who prefer to be part of these groups and you feel a pang of disappointment when you see your 'close' friends seeming to follow that route. Deep down it feels like rejection.

For all that introspection, you develop a dry sense of humor that makes connections quickly. You often rehearse jokes or amusing voices to yourself in order to 'spontaneously' impress others.

You're naturally a little disorganized. A look around your living space would show a box of photos from before the rise of digital cameras and camera/phones, out-of-date medicines, broken items not thrown out, and notes to yourself which are significantly out of date.

You procrastinate and have given up dreams a little easily and let your mind flit elsewhere. You sometimes question whether you're talented enough to achieve your dreams. But those instances are countered by that other voice that says, "I'd rather dream big and fail, rather than settle for the little others are content with."

Conclusion: People who read books like "The Human Whisperer" present something of a conundrum, which won't surprise you. You are bright, and open to life's possibilities – more so than the average person. You'd do well to be less self-absorbed, as it tends to distance you a little, and to relinquish some of the control you exercise when you present that stylized version of yourself to others. There is a darkness or vulnerability you feel you should hide (which is related to a neediness you don't like), which you should overcome in order to let people in a little more.

*   *   *

So how did I do? Of course, not everything will be 100% right for every person, but on a scale of 1-10, how closely did you see yourself in this profile? Please think about it before moving on…(dog-ear the page… we'll come back to it).

*   *   *

As some may have guessed, this profile is **not** targeted to this books' demographic. This is an edited version of a cold reading experiment conducted by UK performer Derren Brown in which he gave this "custom profile" out to several groups of college students claiming that each profile was individually crafted. It was only later they found out they all received an identical profile. Before revealing this, however, the average student rated the profiles' accuracy at over 90% (Lonegunman). (Hopefully, you rated it nearly as highly.) This type of profile is so successful because there are a number of cold reading techniques in use, so let's unpack some of this information by first looking at character readings.

Character readings

A character reading is an opportunity to express your understanding of someone's personality traits in a way that convinces them you possess real insight. People will stop speaking and immediately pay attention to what you're saying, because one thing people will always listen to others talk about is *them!* Feeling understood is a great way to strengthen bonds between people, even when you don't *really* understand them.

Phineas Taylor (P.T.) Barnum

Barnum statements

The term "Barnum statement" is a reference to P.T. Barnum, a showman and businessman of the 1800's famous for finding and perpetuating fantastic hoaxes and starting the famous *Barnum & Bailey Circus*. Like the circus' motto, "Something for everyone!" Barnum statements are generalities that most everyone would agree applies to them. At first blush they may sound like they describe your subject, but they actually describe *everybody*. Doing a Google search for Barnum statements will show you plenty but here are a few examples:

- "You have an unexpressed need for people to like and respect you."
- "Some of your hopes and aspirations can be quite unrealistic."
- "While you have personality weaknesses, your strengths have more than compensated for them."
- "You have a lot of unrealized potential that is held back by your career choices."
- "You can be quite critical of yourself."

While Barnum statements can be used effectively, they are best used sparingly amongst other types of character statements. However, there are two techniques that can dramatically increase the impact of Barnum statements: "countering" and "forking."

<u>Countering</u> is when you openly admit that the statement applies to most everyone but then counter that fact by claiming that it is *truer* for the subject than for the average person. People will readily agree with this assessment, as it sounds like you know how your subject differs from everyone else. It's a highly effective way to strengthen a run-of-the-mill Barnum statement:

> *"When I look at you it's clear that you have a lot of unrealized potential that has been held back by your career choices. <u>Yes, most people could probably say that, but this has affected you far more than most.</u>"*

<u>Forking</u> is when you gauge their reaction to your initial statement and either strengthen the idea or pivot away from it 180 degrees and say the *opposite* of what you were just saying. If you say, "You can be quite critical of yourself…" and you see a nod of *agreement*, strengthen that initial statement by saying:

> *"…and you beat yourself up over things that other people would never even think about. Being your own worst enemy has affected your confidence and held you back on multiple occasions."*

If, however, you see a look of confusion or disagreement, such as someone shaking their head to your initial statement, you will immediately pivot:

> *"…but you've been able to largely overcome these negative feelings and accept who you are and who you are not. You know how destructive being overly self-critical can be and you've been able to grow beyond that and find contentment in the gifts you have."*

Countering and forking should be used whenever you employ Barnum statements. Without these techniques, they can be especially transparent, particularly amongst savvy, modern subjects.

"Everything" statements

Many people think that Barnum statements are the primary tool of the cold reader but this isn't true. Character readings often employ more advanced ideas like the everything statement. This is where you credit someone with a certain trait and then you credit them with the opposite trait too! It's difficult to find disagreement with these types of statements because people tend to exhibit *every* characteristic at various times, hence the term "everything" statement. We are not static creatures that only behave in one way:

"You are someone who tends to be charitable and compassionate, but as we're speaking, I also sense a selfish streak that comes out a little more often than maybe you'd like it to."

"When you take a mind to it, you can liven up any party, but more often than not, you tend to be subdued and introspective."

If spoken sincerely, these statements sound profound but upon closer examination, don't really say anything other than, "sometimes you're kind, sometimes you're selfish" and "sometimes you're outgoing, and sometimes you're not." These thoughts and moods strike all of us at one time or another so they are going to be true for nearly everyone.

Make sure you only apply these statements to moods and characteristics, and not something that is quantifiable, like money:

"Sometimes you find yourself quite well off and you lavish yourself with expensive gifts. But at other times, you're poor as a church mouse and don't know how you're going to stay afloat."

This is **_not_** a good use of the technique. Instead, focus on traits like generosity/greed, shyness/extroversion, friendly/disagreeable, hardworking/lethargic, neat/messy, etc. Think about the times in people's lives they're most likely to manifest each characteristic and then apply that to the everything statement.

Phases of life

These statements are based on common life stages that we all pass through. As most of us go through similar experiences at certain times of our life, we can use these rites of passage to our advantage. Someone in their 40's and 50's think about their dreams of youth:

"More so than others [countering statement], you often think about the dreams of your younger self. Your schemes and plans were so important and thoughtfully laid out. There's more than a little part of you that wants to just get out of the rat race and start over, only this time you'll have the benefit of a lifetime of experience."

Whereas maybe someone in their 20's is working to get established and make a name for themselves:

"You seem to exude an underlying frustration that your talents and abilities are being wasted. You feel like you're on a leash preventing you from showing what you can do. You don't think you know everything, and are willing to learn new things, but others, too inflexible, don't appreciate your contributions."

"The road not taken"

These are statements that appeal to the notion that we are all drawn to the choices we **didn't** take. It's normal to think about how different your life would have been had you turned left instead of right. These universal thoughts provide the basis for "the road not taken" technique. However a person's life has turned out, think about the inverse of that life arc, and connect the dots. For example, career driven globetrotters think wistfully about a quieter, more fulfilling domestic existence:

"Your career success has paid off both financially and in terms of prestige, which is a testament to your hard work and dedication. But these rewards come at a price. Though you don't advertise this, I get the feeling your home life is not as stable as you'd like it to be. Your allegiance to your career has created, not a void, but a sense of incompleteness. Speaking with you it's evident that you often think about how to foster a more fulfilling domestic life. It's clear this has been a source of internal conflict."

What about an office worker or laborer doing the 9-to-5 grind? Same thing:

"You've worked hard to create a stable environment for yourself and your family, and that's a credit to your determination and drive. But this secure existence comes at a price. Though you don't talk about it, and though you wouldn't necessarily give up the life you've built, you feel a sense of incompleteness. To create this life, you've had to let go of certain talents and abilities that fueled the dreams of your younger self. You often wonder how far those gifts could have taken you, if only you'd chosen a different life. But you didn't, and I think I know why. Fear of failure was only part of the reason, but it was also your desire to live in the here and now and build a life you could be proud of. And that's exactly what you've done, though it remains a source of conflict within you."

These statements don't work solely with our career choices. If someone lives in the country, you could talk about how they sometimes yearn for the excitement and faster pace of the city. Conversely, tell a city dweller how you know that they sometimes long for a more peaceful, freer existence. Any choice where someone might think about "what if...?" is perfect fodder for *the road not taken*.

TIMEOUT: These themes are universal. How many movies can you think of with these story lines?

Facts and stats

To really cement the idea that you've made a connection, as you're providing a character reading, throw in a few facts that make it appear that you really understand your subject, when of course, you don't!

These are simply groups of information that are very *likely* to apply to specific people. We're playing the numbers game here, and if skillfully played, will be right far more often than not.

Psychics have the advantage here because they can access more guesswork than someone appearing to do this purely by perception and intuition. A psychic might say:

"I'm getting the sense of a career in transition. This is either yours or perhaps someone whose path is linked to yours in some way?"

A psychic might pivot to the second sentence if they don't get a nod or some other nonverbal acceptance of the premise. The second sentence is broad enough that it could mean someone you work with, work for, someone who works for you, or even someone you know socially that is going through a big transition. Everyone knows someone going through a big transition of some kind, so this works great for the psychic. However, there would be no reasonable way for *us* to divine that information through our perception, no matter how insightful we appear to be.

We need to stick to the facts that reinforce our character reading by providing concrete examples of what we're saying. So, unlike the psychic, certain doors are closed to us, but the remaining options are good ones.

Targeted Trivia

In the 1992 movie *Leap of Faith*, Steve Martin played a faith healing con man that used cold reading techniques that got him both into, and out of, trouble along the way. In an early scene in the movie, he was arrested and placed in the back of a police car. By using his powers of observation and encyclopedic knowledge of statistics, he was able to divine the officer's marital status, religious affiliation, the name of his child, and other facts that reinforced the idea that he was truly gifted.

Fortunately, we don't need to be as talented as a fictional con man to achieve similar results. "Targeted trivia" is when we use a fact that applies to almost everyone, but is presented in a way that demonstrates apparent insight. This isn't to be used *instead of* character readings but as complement to them (Rowland, pp. 53-55):

In most homes you will find:

- A haphazard, unsorted box of photos
- Books and "stuff" for an interest or hobby which is no longer pursued
- A calendar hanging from a prior year
- An old key no longer needed, or whose use has been forgotten
- A broken watch or clock

Most men:

- Tried learning a musical instrument as a child but gave it up
- Wore a moustache or beard at one point even if they've been clean shaven for years
- Have one old suit hanging in their closet which no longer fits
- Keep one tool that is broken, unfixable, but hasn't been thrown out
- Keep a computer, or other electronic device, that doesn't work but haven't thrown that out, either

Most women:

- Own, or have owned, an item of clothing which they bought but never wore
- Wore their hair long as a child, then adopted a shorter haircut into adulthood
- Have at least one earring, the mate of which is lost

Most people:

- Have, or had, a scar on a knee
- Have been involved in some sort of childhood water accident
- Have experienced a horrible sunburn (highly reliable if subject is fair skinned)

These are just the basic facts. In order to use them properly, don't just blurt out, "Somewhere in your house is an unsorted box of photos." These facts must be woven into the presentational embroidery of the larger conversation. Using the photo example, here's one possible way of using it:

"Throughout our conversation, it's clear that you have a well-developed sense of compartmentalizing, and creating definite boundaries between what is and isn't important to you. The important things are given an elevated status in terms of your time and attention. In fact, before digital cameras and camera phones were ubiquitous, you are exactly the type of person that had her important photos neatly arranged into attractive photo albums, whereas the others were just haphazardly flung into a box, where they are probably still sitting!"

The key is not to overdo it. Don't use more than one (or *maybe* two) of these in a given conversation. <u>*Used sparingly*</u>, when peppering one of these statements into a character reading, it can dramatically enhance the perception that you are in tune with your subject. Cultural and regional differences result in some of these being more relevant to you than others. The idea isn't to master the list, but pick out one or two that you'd be able to work into a conversation. It's impossible to overstate how strong a simple thing like this can be. Throwing in just a single bit of targeted trivia causes your subsequent observations to carry more weight.

Context

This one requires the most thought but if you are observant to the time of year and social context, you'll be able to describe them in great detail. End-of-year holidays like Christmas and New Years are wonderful examples of how context can help round out a conversation. Our moods tend to change during the holidays, so we either feel better or worse than we do during the rest of the year. For people that welcome this time of year, it's a time for positive nostalgia. Remembering good times and old friends. Maybe even reconnecting with a couple of them. For others, it can be a time of sadness, depression, and anxiety. This most often manifests as *negative nostalgia*. Thinking back to how things used to be so much better than they are today. Remembering strong friendships and not having any current friends that compare.

When speaking with someone during this time of year, notice their disposition based on both what they say, how they say it, and their overall body language. If they seem a bit down:

You try to hide it, but I can tell you seem a bit down right now. Though I don't know you well, I strongly suspect that doesn't represent your typical state of mind and you are normally a person that lives on a more positive note.

There are plenty of time-of-year contexts if you apply just a little thought:

- Single people feel lonely and isolated around not only end-of-year holidays, but Valentine's Day too.
- Sports fans feel optimistic and hopeful for their teams' success at the start of each season; the day after their team loses or wins will also find them depressed or elated, respectively. During football season, every Monday you can tell the biggest sports fans by watching their demeanor (and you can also determine pretty easily whether they won or lost).
- Seasonal workers are employed all over beach towns in the Eastern United States, like Myrtle Beach, South Carolina and Rehoboth Beach in Delaware. They are happier and more energetic at the start of the season than at the end. Most of these seasonal workers live elsewhere and move to these cities to coincide with beach season.
- Retail salespeople face extra workloads during peak shopping times, Labor Day through the run-up to Christmas, so they're feeling unappreciated, overworked, and overwhelmed.
- People that tend to overspend during these periods will tighten their collective belts and feel more financial pressure in subsequent months, like January and February, as credit card bills come due.

Subtly using just a little of this information can go a long way to rounding out a successful conversation, but as with the other facts and stats, don't overdo it.

Now that you've seen some of the basic techniques of cold readers, you will be able to apply them to conversations where you aren't able to generate legitimate rapport for whatever reason. <u>This isn't used to artificially manipulate others; rather, it is a temporary tool to bridge the gap until you get in sync and create a real connection.</u>

TIMEOUT: Go back and re-read the extended cold reading profile from the beginning of this section and look for all of these techniques: Barnum, "everything", phases of life, and "road not taken" statements. On a second read-through, you will be better at understanding how they work, and you'll be better protected from less scrupulous individuals that try to use these techniques against you.

If you want to look at cold reading in more detail, I highly recommend Ian Rowland's The Full Facts Book of Cold Reading. This book breaks down how cold reading works in a systematic way and explores these (and many other) techniques in use by cold readers and psychics.

* * *

FORGET-ME-NOTS

- Asking questions is about more than just getting information, it creates connections through sincere interest.
- Use your newfound knowledge of your subject and the rapport you generate to be of service and help *them* achieve a goal.
- When you can't seem to get in sync, you can always pepper some *cold reading* into an otherwise lifeless conversation until you genuinely generate that rapport.

* * *

THE FLY IN THE OINTMENT

A potential problem with trying to understand and connect with others is that others' words are often unclear leaving room for misinterpretation. If you are present (meaning you stay in the moment and listen to what the person is saying) you are less likely to make mistakes of this type. Any ambiguous responses demand appropriate follow-up questions until you really understand. Many people don't ask enough questions for fear they will appear less knowledgeable, or that they "just don't get it." To the contrary, asking good questions can subtly let people know you *do* understand the nature of the issues involved *and* are interested enough to find out more.

A bigger problem is that people tend to omit, distort, or alter facts they would rather not share. Being charismatic and well-liked (and these are NOT the same thing) are both effective tools to short-circuit this issue. (Besides general principles of charisma we've already discussed, we will also discuss how to become more well-liked in chapter 10.)

There are still times when someone might not be forthcoming. Even worse, sometimes people may actively try to deceive you. This may be true for reasons other than malice. Sometimes people don't want others to know they are sensitive about a certain issue. Other times they may feel outnumbered by the group and fear being shunned or somehow ostracized because they feel differently.

For these situations, it is important to cultivate the ability to spot both verbal and nonverbal deception. But remember that the more rapport you can generate with someone, the less likely they are to alter uncomfortable information.

6

Detecting deception

"We swallow greedily any lie that flatters us, but we sip only little by little at a truth we find bitter."

--Denis Diderot

We learn to lie before we can speak. Six-month-old babies fake crying and laughter to get what they want. Young children lie to stay "out of trouble."[2] As we get older, we still lie, but for a variety of reasons, not always for pure self-interest:

- To avoid hurting others' feelings – "You look fantastic!", "I didn't even notice the stain!", "That dress looks great on you.", "It's not you, it's me."
- To manipulate people – "I can get you a boatload of money on your trade-in. Just come into the dealership and let's talk about it.", "If you loved me you would trust me."
- As a method of conflict avoidance – "It's nothing personal. Nobody got a bonus this year."
- To help people – "Billy was hanging out here with me the whole night. Honest."
- To preserve our autonomy – "Mom, I'm just going over to my friend's house. No one else will be there."
- As a mechanism of pure self-interest – "My manager will probably chew me out for this, but I want to give you the best deal.", "I wrote these reports by myself because I know you wanted it done right.", "I've got the money, but my funds are all tied up right now in escrow or stocks or something."

---

2 Lying is even hardwired into other social species. Koko, the sign language speaking gorilla, ripped a sink off the wall after getting angry. When questioned about it, Koko used sign language to blame her kitten by saying, "cat did it." Certain types of shoreline birds fake injuries to lure would-be attackers away from their young (Slater). If other animals can engage in deceptive behavior then perhaps lying isn't the sole purview of our higher order brain functions; rather, it is a fundamental survival tool required of social species.

- Even as an act of aggression – "Everyone thinks you're an idiot. Even your close friends said so, but I promised I wouldn't say anything."

Lies can be broken into roughly two groups, prosocial and antisocial. Prosocial lies (more commonly called "little white lies") are intended to benefit people. They are told to strengthen relationships and create tighter social bonds. Antisocial lies are destructive, self-interested and weaken bonds between people. Though some dismiss all lies as destructive, there is evidence to show that antisocial liars become more isolated in their social groups while prosocial liars form stronger links with others in their social network. Telling prosocial lies is an important developmental skill that can strengthen social bonds (Palermo).

Even if some lies serve a constructive purpose we still need to separate truth from fiction. As we attempt to read, connect with, and persuade others, our chance of success plummets if we aren't hearing the truth.

The good news is that becoming more charismatic, well-liked, and able to generate rapport gives us our best defense against deception–by fostering an environment where lies are less likely to be told. The bad news is lying cannot be eliminated no matter how charismatic or well-liked we are. Therefore, you need to be armed with the tools to know when someone is lying.

Other books covering this subject talk about the standard verbal and nonverbal indicators of deception. While interesting to read, this information alone does not assure success. Why? Because these books and articles are addressing behaviors only observed in "high stakes" lies, i.e., assault, fraud, arson, embezzlement, theft, murder, robbery. These are lies, which, if discovered will bring about dire consequences for the liar. Sometimes we even see high stakes lies in our own lives – "Did you have an affair?" "No!"

For most of us, though, the more typical cases are "low stakes" lies. These are lies that, if discovered, may bring about some mild social tension or discomfort, but won't result in any serious repercussions. Simple examples include "You are such a good artist!" or "I love what you've done with the place!" or "I totally forgot about meeting you for lunch!"

Remember our old friend the limbic system that controls fear and our freeze/flight/fight response? High stakes lies are serious enough to trigger a limbic response which more readily results in "nonverbal leakage" (and no that's not a medical condition). Low stakes lies are not serious enough to engage the limbic system, so nonverbal behaviors will not be visible.

In the *next* chapter, we look at *how to structure questions properly* so others are more likely to tell the truth and when they don't, how to best reveal these deceptive behaviors that would normally remain hidden. This chapter, however, first lays out the most common deceptive behaviors, breaking them into three main areas: nonverbal, verbal, and paralinguistic.

A WORD OF WARNING

Reading a person's mental and emotional state via body language (chapter 3) is far easier than trying to discern a lie. Lies are difficult to detect because we use them early and often as a tool for social survival. Given our extensive experience with lying, it is not surprising we get away with it far more often than we get caught.

If spotting a lie was as easy as looking behind someone's back, then everyone could do it.

There is no movement, expression or gesture that guarantees that someone is lying. There are no *unique* behaviors associated with either truth or deception. *All* behaviors are used when lying and telling the truth. Our goal is to spot "behavior clusters" to make a reasonable assessment of what is true and what is false. Remember, *none of these behaviors are determinative.* Their presence only makes it more (or less) likely that a statement is false.

Psychologist Paul Ekman listed the most common mistakes when attempting to detect deception. Any of them can completely foil our ability at spotting a lie, but taken together they create a murderer's row of obstacles, which we need to guard against at all times.

Confirmation bias. If I have determined a fact as true, then any denial of that fact is perceived as a lie and any supporting evidence for that fact is seen as true. I *believe* I'm missing $20 from my wallet. Only my 11-year-old daughter had access to it and her denial that she took the money is presumptively seen as a lie. The stronger my (erroneous) belief that the money is missing results in the enhanced belief that the child is lying. The bill may have been hidden behind a receipt or perhaps I had less money than I thought; in either case, my level of conviction in a mistaken belief results in disbelieving the truth.

Signs interpreted as deceit do not always indicate deception. It is easy to misinterpret nonverbal signals as deceptive as they are often just manifestations of discomfort and anxiety. If a person is under stress, it is nearly impossible to separate those signals from signs of genuine deceit.

Signs interpreted as truthful do not always indicate truth. There are several reasons you might not observe deceit signals in someone who is lying. First, they may be superb at lying. Accomplished liars are good at masking both the verbal and nonverbal evidence of a lie. Or, you may be focused on the wrong signals and ignoring others.

Another possibility is that some people are incapable of manifesting normal deceit signals. Psychopaths nearly always present with symptoms of a damaged amygdala which controls the freeze/flight/fight response. This prevents them from feeling fear or anxiety about the consequences of being found out. They are naturally gifted liars because there is no difference in their truthful and deceptive responses.

Overconfidence in one's ability to spot a lie. Many people think they are good at spotting lies–they've been watching too many crime dramas. One team of researchers put this to the test by analyzing hundreds of "truth-telling" experiments over several decades and concluded that people were accurate 54% of the time where a random guess would yield a result of 50% (Bond). Just a few percentage points above a coin flip is not good odds in spotting a liar. In fact, even the best "human lie detectors" rarely do better than 60% (Ekman & O'Sullivan). The more confident we are in our abilities, the lower our success rate. When assessing truth, use the information that follows as a guidepost and not as proof that someone is lying. By exercising a little humility and understanding the limits of these techniques, you will achieve far more success than you would otherwise.

TIMEOUT: Don't always believe your eyes and ears. Don't be overconfident. Guard against common pitfalls, but if something strikes you as "off", trust your instincts! Think of a time you gratefully did and sadly did not trust your instincts.

HIGH STAKES VS. LOW STAKES LIES

Popular wisdom tells us that when lying, nonverbal behavior is hardest to mask because it happens outside of our conscious control. These nonverbal behaviors arise as a byproduct of our limbic system's response to fear. Many books, articles, and websites talk about the reliability of these signs, but their claims are suspect if they make no distinction between *high stakes* and *low stakes* lies.

Again, *nonverbal deception cues appear more consistently in high stakes lies.* Denials to the questions, "Are you having an affair?", "Have you been drinking tonight, sir?", "Have you ever hit your wife?", "Did you start the fire?" will likely generate a limbic response revealing many of the nonverbal indicators of lying (if in fact the answer is a lie).

Low stakes lies do NOT usually generate nonverbal deception cues because these lies do not create the fear and anxiety necessary to generate a limbic response. Therefore, when answering questions like, "How does this dress look on me?", "I made this fruitcake myself. Do you like it?", "Ancient Egyptian and Star Wars fusion, how do you like our new living room design?", you are unlikely to notice any nonverbal signals.

You must be aware of whether you are asking a high stakes or low stakes question. *If it is a low stakes question, then focus on the verbal/paralinguistic channels or change the question to "increase the stakes,"* which is discussed later in this chapter.

For both high stakes and low stakes inquiries, first establish a comfortable environment. This allows the person to relax and gives you a chance to establish a baseline from which to recognize behavior change. This is especially critical when testing nonverbal deception cues. Keep variables to a minimum; don't change your demeanor from calming to threatening by demanding answers and being rude or unpleasant. This results in low comfort displays that are impossible to sort out from true deception and would invalidate any changes in the original baseline behavior.

NONVERBAL INDICATORS

Posture

If you have created a calm, relaxed atmosphere for a conversation, it will be reflected in the posture of your target. Remembering the discussion from Chapter 3, you know are looking for an open, easy-going demeanor with a frontal or slightly angled alignment. Studying their posture alone can show their levels of confidence and emotional involvement.

A closed, retreated posture is a good sign they are not yet comfortable so keep the conversation light and flowing until they relax. Other indicators include a sideways alignment where they are facing away from you, or to the extreme side.

An occasional forward lean is a good indicator of interest. A permanent forward lean possibly accompanied by a stern look is a sign of hostility and must be overcome before assessing other nonverbal cues. Once the favorable signs are apparent, you are ready to continue with the process.

If their posture and overall body language becomes frozen and static in response to a specific question, this is an indicator of lowered confidence. It doesn't indicate deception; rather, that they don't like the question and are deciding how to answer, truthfully or otherwise.

Hands

This is where an observer will focus their attention and for good reason. The hands are used to perform many of the low confidence and pacifying behaviors we looked at in chapter 3.

Low confidence indicators are used instinctively in response to sudden stress or anxiety. They include hand wringing; tugging the nose or earlobes; scratching the neck, forearm, or leg; wiping sweat; blocking the eyes; the collar pull, which helps ease pressure and heat because of stress or irritation; covering the mouth, with one finger or the whole hand (something done almost reflexively when telling a lie); resting their head on their palm; and repetitive hand behaviors like drumming fingers.

In addition to repetitive movements, *pacifying* behaviors are used to dissipate and displace anxiety and help the subject remain calm. They include adjustment of clothing, jewelry, or accessories; picking at (real or imagined) lint or threads; dusting clothing; cleaning or inspecting fingernails; tidying up the surroundings; and focusing attention on hair or beard. These could be characterized as grooming and light housekeeping.

Some of these behaviors go beyond the psychological and into the biochemical. When we lie, catecholamine is released increasing our blood pressure and moving blood flow to our vital organs which takes it away from the surface of the face causing a tickling or itching in the nose and face. This may account for the desire to scratch facial features and tug at clothing to relieve the symptoms. This same phenomena accounts for people being suddenly cold in a room where they had been comfortable.

Scratching and tugging can be telling indicators *before or after* a question is answered. By intentionally avoiding scratching or rubbing, it is only delayed, but the need to scratch that itch remains. Therefore, maintain an awareness of this possible deception cue even after receiving an answer. But, sometimes an itch is just an itch (maybe their shampoo wasn't working so well that day) so look for confirming clusters.

Feet and Legs

As we learned in chapter 3, we have the least conscious control over our feet and legs and so is a great place to look for signs of deception. When we lie, we are focused on what to say, maintaining appropriate levels of eye contact, and controlling hand movement to put forth the best approximation of truth. Our feet and legs are a forgotten part of the prefrontal cortex equation.

Some people claim you can gauge deception by how much people move their feet while answering a question. The simple fact is that both honest and dishonest people twitch and jiggle their feet and legs but the key factor is *to note when the behavior changes*. Repetitive leg movements that are not in response to a question helps reduce anxiety, it is not an indicator of deception.

The key for nonverbals of the legs are to *note changes that occur on cue to something that is said or asked*. Sudden change shows a spike in anxiety level. A shift from jiggling to kicking is a good sign they have seen or heard something negative. Kicking is a subconscious way to combat something unpleasant (i.e. the fight response) and since it is an automatic limbic response, most people are unaware they are even doing it. A shift from jiggling to freezing (i.e. the movement suddenly stops) shows stress, or that they feel threatened. Similarly, when the toes turn inward or the feet become interlocked, it shows insecurity and anxiousness. Remember, this doesn't directly translate to deception, but subjects *are generally* more likely to lie about something that causes them stress. If you ask a question and receive an answer that reveals no changes in leg movement, this indicates the question and subsequent answer caused no stress and is more likely to be truthful.

Any of these leg change behaviors can mean stress and/or deception:

- If the legs are stationary and then suddenly move or bounce in response to a question
- If the legs are in motion and then suddenly stop. This one is so easy to spot it is often detected by the subject as well! To cover this up, they will start moving their leg(s) again, which makes it even more obvious. Sometimes the pause is brief but if it comes as a direct response to a question, interpret it as a full stop.
- If the speed or amplitude of leg motion changes. This one is slightly harder to detect but should be considered an indicator if the change comes as a direct response to a question.
- If the direction of their feet changes, even slightly, away from you and/or toward the exit. This is also a stalling tactic completed by changing posture or shifting in the chair. If it occurs at a "point of denial" deception should be considered.

After collecting any available clues in the feet and legs, you are ready to move your observations upward.

Head and face

Located so close to the limbic system, the head and face cues for anxiety can be very difficult to separate from deception. As an added difficulty, our faces house the largest number of idiosyncratic movements, twitches, and expressions compared to the rest of the body. Each person makes "a face" for different reasons, with varied timing, and in different degrees. As we saw in chapter 3, the face is under the most conscious control so nonverbal leakage is even less likely to occur in the face than anywhere else in the body. So we look for clusters.

Stress will dry the throat so note throat clearing immediately before, or after answering a question. Hard swallows also happen due to a dry throat so you need to be observant enough to catch it. However, overt observation will destroy your ability to get any kind of reliable read on their behavioral cues, so remain subtle!

Any facial expression that lasts too long is not normal. The best example of this is smiling. Numerous studies have shown that when people lie, they smile less than normal. However, when they do smile, the smile comes quicker and lasts longer because it was *created* by their conscious mind – unlike a genuine expression. When a liar is thinking about what to say, he doesn't spend enough mental cycles on all the variables to determine how to look, and it shows. A similar issue is *eye contact.*

* * *

Oh, those lying eyes!

The golden rule of detecting deception: No eye contact means the subject is lying! Right? WRONG!!

Shy or nervous people may meet our gaze less than 20% of the time and often appear untrustworthy. During conversations it is common to look the other person in the eyes around 60-70% of the time. This means that even in everyday exchanges, people look away 30-40% of the time. In addition, less eye contact may mean they are thinking about the question. Or perhaps the questioner has created a hostile environment so someone might look away to reduce stress.

Conversely many cultural groups see eye contact with an authority figure as a sign of disrespect.

In fact, habitual liars typically engage in more eye contact than normal! They know that looking someone in the eye is perceived as a sign of truthfulness. So if someone makes too much eye contact, that would be a reason to doubt them.

This cue will mislead more often than not. Leave it on the cutting room floor.

* * *

WHISPER ALERT:: Look for sudden changes in nonverbal behaviors, particularly in response to questions.

VERBAL INDICATORS

With high stakes lies, nonverbal cues are more numerous and more reliable because these are instinctive and bypass our cognitive processes. It is more difficult to detect high stakes lies on the verbal channel because the *first* instinct of the high stakes liar is to *plan the verbal deception.* The high stakes liar knows if he doesn't at least get the *words* right, the consequences could be dire.

For low stakes lies, however, the situation is different. Nonverbal cues are few. Remember that low stakes lies don't create a primal, limbic, fear response so nonverbal leakage is minimal. The *verbal channel* gives us a *relatively* better chance at detecting low stakes lies because the higher order processes at work on formulating a verbal response are the same regardless of the stakes involved. The verbal messages are not easier to decipher; rather, they become easier by comparison because the nonverbal indicators disappear.

* * *

A person has two choices in response to a question or giving a message: truth or lie. Outright lying is the least palatable option, so the deceiver will use *evasion, denial and qualifiers* when avoiding the truth.

Evasion

Answer a question with a question. This old chestnut has been around for a long time. It avoids an outright lie by turning the tables on the questioner. It is also one of the most transparent of all evasive answers and its overuse has eroded its effectiveness. At the right time, however, a well-placed evasive statement can still be effective.

> Q: *"Did you steal $20 from your mother's purse?"*
> A: *"Why do you think I would do something like that?"*

Answer a different question. Robert McNamara, John F. Kennedy's Secretary of Defense, once quipped, "Never answer the question that is asked of you. Answer the question you wish had been asked of you." This technique is a particular favorite of politicians and anyone having to face the public, like at a press conference. It is also used to great effect in one-on-one situations. Expert practitioners of this technique can even make it sound like they are answering the question.

> Q: *"Did you steal $20 from your mother's purse?"*
> A: *"If I had $20 more dollars I would have been able to buy those new shoes I've been wanting."*

Change of subject. Another classic technique is to completely change the subject. The difference between "answering a question with a question" which is designed to change the subject, is that the response from the deceiver has nothing to do with the original topic.

> Q: *"Did you steal $20 from my purse?"*
> A1: *"Speaking of which, that is the most beautiful bag I've ever seen. Where did you get it?"* (Flattery)
> A2: *"At what point in your life did you become so suspicious?"* (Combative)

112

A3: "I can't even think because I'm so hungry. What's for dinner?" (Blatantly ignoring the question)

Rely on implication. This is a classic evasion tactic which is technically truthful but deceives the questioner into making erroneous assumptions. This type of evasion is commonly called a *lie of omission*. It is used any time you do not correct a misconception, or where you consciously create a misconception yourself. Understandably this is popular because at no point is an outright falsehood uttered. Rather, the deceiver is planting the seed of misconception by omitting certain details and congratulating himself that he didn't lie.

Q: "When is the last time you saw Bill?"
A1: "I drove him home after school on Friday. I got to his house right around 3:40." (Evasive)
A2: "On Friday. I dropped him off at his house, which was right around 3:40. That's the last time I saw him." (Direct, therefore more likely to be truthful)

Q: "Did you steal $20 from your mother's purse?"
A: "How could I? I don't even know where Mom's purse is." (The implication is that the whereabouts of the purse were unknown at the time of the theft, but the verb tense [don't/didn't] plants a clever seed to be inferred incorrectly by the listener.)

Lying by referral. This allows someone to support a previous lie with the truth. If a lie can be maintained with a truth, it creates less stress and anxiety in the mind of the speaker. But it requires an initial lie and so becomes an evasive answer. This is used less often than other evasive answers and is truly a testament to higher order reasoning.

Q: "Did you steal $20 from your mother's purse?"
A: "I already told Mom that I didn't take her money." (True statement supporting a previous lie)

WHISPER ALERT - All evasions are different ways to not answer the question. Train yourself to spot them, and so force the subject into the truth or an outright denial.

Denials

The guilty will not confess and the deceiver will not admit deception. When asked point blank about an activity or action, the *manner* in which a denial is made can be an indicator of deception.

Specific Denial. Truthful people use broader language when making a denial. Deceptive people often deny some narrow aspect of the question which allows enough wiggle room to mislead the questioner. In the philosophical denial below the added word "your" would be slipped in as if that were the exact question. Smooth move!

Q: "Did you take the cookies?"
A1: "I didn't take any cookies <u>from the cabinet.</u>" (Specific)
A2: "I didn't take any cookies." (Non-specific, so more likely to be truthful)
A3: "I didn't take any of your cookies." (Philosophical - After all, who can "own" a cookie?)

Lack of specific denial. Sometimes the denial moves in the opposite direction from the previous example. Sometimes, the denial is *so* broad it becomes more of a general statement and moves away from an actual denial. Common phrases are "I didn't do anything" and "I wouldn't do something like that." The word *anything* is a psychological ploy to mute what would otherwise be a bare faced lie. This makes the lie somehow less egregious to the teller, so watch out for it.

Q: "Did you tear down the poster off of the school wall?"
A: "I didn't do anything."

Buried denial. If the denial itself is buried in a long, narrative response, deception is indicated. Honest people want you to know straight away the truthful nature of the situation. Deceptive people need time to "work up to the lie." This often takes the form of a long winded explanation where a simple answer would be more appropriate. <u>It is an important cue when the denial is a small percentage of the statement.</u>

Q: "Did you tell the board members I wasn't to be trusted with the money?"
A: "First of all, it was just a couple of the board members. A few of us went out for cocktails after the meeting last week. In fact, we even ordered some appetizers. We happened to get those sushi rolls you really like. Anyway, we were talking about the last treasurer and how she often delayed paying the expense reports. Guess it was a type of power trip for her. But anyway, no I didn't say that about you. Hey, is that a new dress?" (Buried denial with a change of subject)

Qualifiers

There are many qualifiers used when telling a lie. In most cases, they are words or statements that preface a denial, or are words used to mask the truth. The qualifiers seem to make telling a lie less offensive to the teller. Outside of standard evasive techniques, qualifiers are the most common verbal indicator of deception.

Generalization Qualifiers. These are words or phrases that seek to generalize a specific question into more general patterns of behavior. As with many qualifiers, this allows the thinnest veneer of truth to remain intact. The most common generalization qualifiers are: "As a rule…", "Generally…", "Typically…", "Normally…", and "As a matter of habit…"

Q: "Where did you go after you left the bar?"
A: "Typically, I just come straight home from there."

Oath Qualifiers. This is tough to analyze unless you have a good baseline on the subject you're testing. Some people use oaths a lot whereas some people almost never use them. Studies have shown that liars use these far more frequently than people telling the truth. If you hear someone use an oath declaration once or twice in a conversation you can disregard it. If, however, they use them throughout a conversation, it should cast doubt on the veracity of their story. The most common oath qualifiers are: "As God is my witness…", "I swear…", "Honestly…", "On my mother's grave…", "I swear on a stack of Bibles…", and "My hand to God…"

Memory and Knowledge Qualifiers. Phrases that allow any deception to be blamed on faulty memory and lack of knowledge. A few of the most often used are: "To the best of my knowledge…", "As far as I recall…", and "Not that I'm aware of." (These are also good to keep you free of perjury charges.) Truthful people stick to the simple phrase, "I don't know." Keep in mind there are situations where a knowledge qualifier is appropriate.

Q: "Has any employee viewed pornography at your workplace in the last year?"
A: "Not that I'm aware of." (Appropriate. In fact, a "no" response would be suspicious.)

Q: "Have you viewed pornography at work in the last year?"
A: "Not that I recall." (This is suspicious.)

Qualifiers against belief. These qualifiers are commonly used before telling an elaborate, highly suspect, and over complicated story meant to confuse and deflect. The phrases to look out for here are: "You aren't going to believe this but…", "This is going to sound crazy but…", and "What I'm about to tell you is incredible but…"

Truthful people use these phrases before telling a funny or interesting story. Only when you hear them as a direct result of a question, however, should it be viewed as suspicious behavior.

Exclusion Qualifiers. These are similar to generalization qualifiers, but act inversely. Instead of speaking about what *normally* happens you speak about what *rarely* happens. Like generalization qualifiers, they are used to withhold information while still answering truthfully. Common words that show exclusion qualifiers are: "hardly ever", "not often", "rarely", and "not really."

Q: *"Did you get drunk last night?"*
A: *"I hardly ever drink."*

Implied Action Qualifiers. These qualifiers hope to trick the listener into inferring something that did not happen by focusing on thoughts or motivations. This allows the liar some wiggle room in answering, as they're talking about a *feeling*, not about what they *actually did.* Common phrases which will preface the action or deed are: "I wanted to...", "I thought about...", "We started to..."

Q: *"Were you home all night last night?"*
A: *"I thought about going out, but I just wanted to stay in."*

Estimation Qualifiers. These phrases show you aren't 100% sure of the exact answer. Similar to memory qualifiers, these need to be examined in context. An estimation qualifier is entirely appropriate when dealing with a range of numbers or time. However, when you are asking a definitive yes/no question and hear an estimation qualifier, deception is indicated. Common phrases to look out for are: "I would have to say..." and "My answer would be..."

Q: *"What time did you pick up your friend?"*
A: *"I would have to say around 9:30"* (This is appropriate given the context)

Q: *"Did you have any friends over after we left the house?"*
A: *"I would have to say no."* (Deception indicated)

Perception Qualifiers. Truth tellers make every effort to ensure people understand the situation by explaining completely, staying focused on the issue, and "telling it like it is." Liars try to manage the perceptions of others by creating the impression of being candid and truthful through declaration. The more of these statements they make, the less likely they are to be telling the truth. Common statements are: "To be perfectly honest...", "Frankly,...", "To tell you the truth...", "Honestly...", and "I wouldn't lie about this..."

Word Choice

Some specific word choices can signify a move away from a truthful answer. A liar processes a lot of verbal and nonverbal behaviors, so word choice gets very little of a liar's attention, to our benefit. However, it is the easiest to miss and the hardest to practice. Attention to specific words people use enhances your ability to separate truth from fiction. (Another advantage is that word choice deception also applies to *written* statements.)

Verb Tense Changes. Deception is indicated when the verb tense changes during a story. When someone speaks truthfully about the past, they are recalling those events and will speak in the past tense. Liars alter the truth by manufacturing events *in the present tense.* Listen carefully for verb tense changes to find out which parts of a story are made up (Dulaney). Look at the example of a store clerk suspected of theft. His shift from past to present tense shows when the crime probably occurred.

"I <u>locked</u> the door and <u>closed</u> the cash register at about midnight. I <u>took</u> the cash drawer to the back and __count__ the receipts. I __see__ a dozen $100 dollar bills. I __place__ the bills in the night deposit bag. I <u>sealed</u> the bag, <u>dropped</u> it in the drop box, and <u>went</u> home."

Passive Voice. Those engaged in deception use passive voice more often than people who are telling the truth (Rudacille). For those who may have forgotten, the subject performs the action in active voice, but in passive voice the target of the action becomes the subject *or eliminated altogether.*

"Mark stole money from Wendy when she was in the hospital." (Active)
"When Wendy was in the hospital she had money stolen from her by Mark." (Passive)

In the first example, Mark, as the subject, is the focus of the sentence and the one performing the action. In the next example, Wendy, the target of the action, is promoted to subject, and so the focus shifts away from Mark and onto Wendy.

When people speak they most often use active voice as it is more precise and easier to understand. Passive voice is more wordy and awkward. When lying, people shift into passive voice to psychologically distance themselves from the action and move the focus onto someone or something else. As with verb tense changes, notice when there is a shift in voice from active to passive. It is at this point in the story that deception is most likely.

Not every instance of passive voice is an attempt at deception. It is also used to distance one's self from any event or situation that is traumatic or emotionally difficult. Context can help determine whether they are trying to distance themselves as the *cause* of the action or because of emotional difficulty.

Prepositional Phrases. People less frequently use prepositions or prepositional phrases while lying because forming them requires more processing than simpler sentences. The lying brain needs all its power to figure out the lie itself (Lieberman, 1998). On the other hand, the truth teller uses *more* prepositional phrases to amplify information which he is eager for you to understand. The liar uses *fewer* because they are too busy keeping their facts straight to worry about complex grammar structure.

Articles. When introducing a noun (person, place, thing) and carrying it through a story, articles "the" "a" and "an" are used. After the noun has been introduced with an indefinite article "a" as a modifier, the definite article "the" is used as the modifier. Any deviation from this ingrained nuance suggests deception or that some of the story remains untold. Further questioning is warranted.

> *"A man walked up to me and pulled out a gun.*
> *He pointed the gun at my head and forced me into the truck."*

References to the gun are accurate. The first time it is mentioned it is referred to as "a gun." Subsequently it is referred to as "the gun." The problem with this statement is the phrase "the truck" instead of "a truck." Either part of the story is missing (maybe they were both previously in the truck, for example) or part of the story is fabricated.

We are not consciously aware of the significance of article usage because this nuance is learned and ingrained within our speech patterns from an early age; it is not a "taught" pattern. As an experiment, tell a friend or family member, "I was talking to *a* man…" and wait for them to ask a follow up question. It will be something like, "OK, what happened next?" or "What did he say?" Try the same thing another time but change the article, "I was talking to *the* man…" and wait for the response. It will be something like, "what man?" A few trials will yield the same results. Why? Because "*the* man" *hasn't yet been introduced into the story*. When this occurs now in your observations, the otherwise subtle change in article usage will strike your ear like dissonance in a harmony.

Possessive Pronoun "My." People drop the possessive pronoun "my" when talking about an object from which they are seeking psychological distance. This is true of both criminal behavior and anything that might get someone into trouble (Sapir). During an espionage investigation, an interviewee stated, "I took <u>my</u> radio, <u>my</u> tape player, <u>my</u> tapes, and <u>the</u> palm pilot out of <u>my</u> trunk." Because there was intent to put distance between the interviewee and palm pilot, the interviewer used a presumptive question to elicit a full confession about how the interviewee had downloaded classified material onto the palm pilot (Schafer, 2010).

Interjections. The common interjections "oh" and "well", used separately or together, signal a thought process. For the liar, these words are used to buy time to construct an answer. For the truthful, these words are spoken quickly, in an almost staccato manner. Of course, if the event occurred in the past and the subject is trying to remember, slow and drawn out interjections are not indicative of deception but is a struggle to recall the information.

> Q: *"Where did you go after you left the house?"*
> A: *"Oh! Well, first we went to the park and then we…"* (truthful interjection)

> Q: *"Where did you go after you left the house?"*
> A: *"Ohh….Well…. first we…went to the park…and then we…"* (false interjection)

Non-contracted Denial. To emphasize their denial, liars often avoid using contractions, "I did *not* steal the money." Truthful people use contracted statements without the need to emphasize any particular word, "I didn't steal the money." As with all of these verbal cues, failure to use a contraction isn't evidence of a lie, but it is worth some follow-up questions. The most famous use of a non-contracted denial was made by Bill Clinton during the Monica Lewinsky scandal, "I did *not* have sexual relations with that woman, Ms. Lewinsky."

Text Bridges. These are words allowing liars to skip any information they wish to withhold. Words associated with text bridging are "then", "so", "after", "when", and "next." When you hear these words be aware of missing elements in the story. Following is a written statement from a student refuting an allegation she stole $20 from her professor's office:

> *"I arrived at 7:45 a.m. with Jenna. I came into the room, put my bag at my desk and Jenna and I went to the little snack area to get some coffee. I returned to the classroom and sat at my desk. At 8:50 we went on a break. Jenna and I went to the bathroom.* **After that,** *I came back to the classroom and Jenna stayed in the bathroom. She came back to the classroom soon after. We sat at our desk and waited for our class to continue."*

The phrase "after that" allowed her to bridge over the time between when she left the bathroom and when she arrived back in the classroom (Schafer, 2011). When pressed on it, she admitted that she took the money after she left the restroom and before returning to class. These phrases are another form of lying by omission and if you're unaware of them, they can be difficult to spot.

Convincing Statements. These are the most deceptive phrases. When asked a direct question, instead of an outright denial, the speaker will provide reasons why they are innocent without directly making a denial. So many phrases fall under this category they cannot be listed exhaustively. Here are a few examples to highlight the concept: "That's illegal and I'm not the kind of person to do that.", "Ask anybody, they'll tell you I wouldn't do this", "Look at my record", "Are you suggesting that I would burn down my own house for the insurance?"

These statements are deceptive because honest people say the same things. The key difference is an honest person only makes a statement like this once and *includes an explicit denial.* A deceptive person won't make an explicit denial and uses *several convincing statements* strung together.

<u>Evasion, *denials, qualifiers, and word choice are all strong indicators that you're not hearing the truth.*</u>

Misdirection

Anytime the subject is working to alter your perception or move you away from your question is considered a misdirection tactic. Remember that truthful people try to make you understand, but liars try to alter your perception of the truth and themselves. When you hear a misdirection statement, remember that while it may or may not represent truth, there is an agenda being pushed forward.

Overly specific answers. When discussing specific denials, we looked at one type of overly specific answer allowing for wiggle room in denying a narrow aspect of the assertion, i.e. "I didn't take the money *from the bread box.*" In this context, however, we mean answers that are longer than they should be given the question. This type of answer means the speaker is trying to create a "halo" effect to influence your opinion of them.

If you ask someone how long they've worked somewhere and their answer begins with "two years now..." and then continues on with several caveats about how they took a break for a month back in March and took two weeks off a year and a half ago to visit the Grand Canyon, and then continues on with previous jobs they've held, it qualifies as an overly specific answer.

Inappropriate Politeness. Watch for "spikes of politeness" in response to a certain question or line of inquiry, such as, "no, sir, I did not see who did it" or "those are really nice shoes, by the way." This is designed to promote their likeability. Some people naturally speak this way. The key here is "inappropriate" level of politeness in relation to their baseline.

Inappropriate lack of concern. This is more commonly seen in high stakes situations when the facts don't support the narrative. If someone senses you don't believe them because the facts are not on their side, they work to downplay the severity and importance of the accusation. Phrases like "this isn't really such a big deal" and "People shouldn't get so worked up over nothing" are examples of this ploy.

This is also used to assuage one's guilt. If you suspect your spouse is cheating, talk about a cheating spouse at your place of employment and look at the reaction. If they downplay the severity of the event with a phrase similar to those above, this is a misdirection cue. Follow up.

Procedural Complaints. These are questions that relate to the situation and environment but are unrelated to the matter at hand. These questions serve as delaying tactics to forestall an upcoming question or to give the speaker time to think of an answer to the previous question. Common complaints are: "How long is this going to take?", "Has the meeting been properly opened?", "Why talk to me about this?", "It's hot/cold in here. Can we fix the temperature?", "Before I talk anymore about this, I need something to eat/drink."

Spontaneous Negation. Answers to open-ended questions should not include actions that were not taken. Their inclusion indicates a likelihood of deception.

Q: *"Where did you go today?"*
A: *"I went to McDonalds, then the mall, then Costco, but I didn't go to the bar."*

The negation is often more subtle and can also be used in a closed yes/no question. Here is an exchange between an investigator and rape suspect:

Q: *"Did you want to kiss her?"*
A: *"I...I...I didn't feel...I didn't remember feeling any attraction toward her, so..."*

The response contains two spontaneous negations, "I didn't feel" and "I didn't remember". Neither of which answer the question, rather they provide a means of avoiding the question while denying any culpability.

In one study, people were asked to lie or tell the truth about a videotaped shoplifting event. Spontaneous negations were found in 60% of the results, and of those, 90% were found in the untruthful statements. This is a telling result and one which shows that a spontaneous negation is strongly associated with deception (Schafer, 2010, Psychological Narrative Analysis, p. 98).

Rehearsed responses. If a meeting is scheduled where questions need to be answered, people with nothing to hide do not memorize or meticulously rehearse their answers. "Meeting" could be as serious as a criminal interrogation, or as mundane as a conversation with the boss, principal, or neighbor regarding a broken window. Those with something to hide rehearse what they are going to say beforehand (except in formal situations like a deposition when a rehearsed response is expected).

Two indicators of a rehearsed response are non-contracted denials (discussed earlier) and listing. This is a list of reasons removing suspicion from the accused but is a strong sign that the answer was premeditated and rehearsed. Sometimes the listing response contains delimiters, i.e. "Number 1... number 2..." or "A...B...C..."

Q. *"How do I know you didn't hit her?"*

A. *"Number 1, we weren't even arguing, so why would I hit her? Number 2, I wasn't even home. Number 3, that's the mother of my kids. Number 4, her sister was there."*

Verbal attacks. This is more common in high stakes situations where the person being questioned is on the defensive and lashes out at a perceived (or real) accusation. This is part of the fight response discussed in chapter 3. It is used when the stakes are high enough to cause a limbic arousal and when the freeze and flight options have failed.

Lashing out does not mean one is deceptive, but rather feeling defensive and attacked. If this behavior is not justified, closer scrutiny of the subject's motives are necessary.

PARALINGUISTIC BEHAVIOR

Paralinguistic behavior relates to the vocal signals that lie beyond speech itself. Paralinguistics is *how* something is said (emphasis, rate, pitch volume, fluency) and not *what* is said. As the paralinguistic channel (and nonverbal behavior) is under less conscious control than the verbal channel, it is a great place to look for signs of deception.

Early Response. An answer starting before the question is completed is an early response. This behavior is common both when people lie and tell the truth. The truthful person responds early because they are eager to get their side of the story out, often early in the conversation. If and when they step on the end of the question with their answer, they repeat their response again as soon as the question ends to make sure they have been heard.

The deceptive person responds early because it helps them combat nervous tension, but usually near the end of the conversation when there is a need to relieve the building anxiety and stress. They are focusing so hard on the message itself as soon as they understand the nature of the question (a bit delayed) they answer reflexively. They are relieved to have answered successfully so when the question ends, they don't repeat the answer.

Erasure Behavior. Deceptive subjects laugh, smile, cough, and clear their throats as erasure cues. These behaviors indicate deception when they occur immediately after a significant denial, as demonstrated by an actual interview with a bank employee (Inbau, p.120).

Q: *"Did you steal that customer's $4,600?"*
A: *"No." [laugh]*
Q: *"Do you know who did steal it?"*
A: *"I don't even know that it was stolen." [laugh]*
Q: *"Do you think a bank employee did steal this money?"*
A: *"That's hard to say, you know. The customer may have just made a mistake on his deposit slip, you know?" [clears throat]*
Q: *"How do you think the results of our investigation will come out on you?"*
A: *"Well, I hope it will come out, you know, okay...because I know I didn't take that money." [laugh]*

Response Length. Open-ended questions, where one is asked to provide an account or explanation, can reveal deception based on the length of the reply. As truthful people need to be understood, they offer longer, more complete responses *and stay on topic.* Deceptive people, hoping to manage the situation, offer as little information as possible so as not to further incriminate themselves, but responses lengthen if they ramble and *drift off topic*, especially at the point in the story that the subject does *not* wish to discuss.

Close-ended questions, that ask for a direct answer, reverses the pattern. In these cases the truthful answer is short and direct. The deceptive answer is one that seeks to offer qualifiers and caveats and is drawn out when you would only expect a one or two-word answer.

Rate, Pitch and Volume. Taken as a group, these indicators are useful when you observe changes in response to questions. While an open ended account is being related, watch for *decreases* in rate, pitch and volume when looking for deception. This can mean that the speaker is editing information or is processing a fabricated response. In response to a direct question, however, sudden increases in rate and pitch or decreases in volume is considered a deception cue unless the response relates an emotional account.

Response Continuity. Truthful responses are free flowing and spontaneous but still maintain continuity within each sentence. Common in deceptive answers is a lack of continuity, also called "stop and start" behavior. The speaker begins in one direction but abruptly stops and starts over again in a different direction. This signals anxiety and the sudden switch to a different place in the story is a way to deal with the stress.

> Q: *"Alec told us that this entire plan was your idea."*
> A: *"Man, he's a liar. Only thing I ever… [pause]…he doesn't know what he's talking about. He's the… [pause]…I had nothing to do with it."*

In this interview the suspect stopped on two occasions. We don't know what he was going to say but we can make a good guess. In the first case, he was about to admit to his part in the plan but then realized that was not a good idea. The second stoppage happens as he is about to explain this plan was Alec's idea. After he realizes this statement won't help his situation either, abruptly changes again.

Response Latency. Of all the paralinguistic deception cues, this one is most telling. Response latency measures the elapsed time between the end of a question and the beginning of the answer. An NSA study found that the average latency of truthful answers was .5 seconds, whereas deceptive answers averaged 1.5 seconds (Inbau, p.118).

It is imperative to establish a latency baseline during the early part of a conversation. As some people naturally have longer pauses, even before answering truthfully, you need to know what is typical before making assumptions about the subject's truthfulness.

Why does a deceptive answer come more slowly? When someone lies, they are thinking about so many things: "What am I going to say to get out of this situation?", "What does the other person know that would cause me to be found out?", "What can I say that can't be easily verified?", "How will I answer any potential follow-up questions?", etc. Dishonesty forces the brain to work harder, and this extra effort is revealed by studies showing an increase in prefrontal cortex activity when people lie (Curley). This part of the brain deals with planning, problem solving, and attention, which are key components of deception. All this extra effort comes at a cost and leaks out unintentionally as response latency.

Deceptive people are often aware of the delay caused by their deception and so resort to a variety of tactics to disguise it. Hearing any of these responses should be equated to a latent response:

- Failing to answer - thinking about the answer with so much effort it is never verbalized
- Repeating the question or asking you to repeat the question (this one is seen often!)

- Non-answer statements - "I'm glad you asked that", "That's a good question", "I knew you were going to ask that"
- Failure to understand a simple question - when a simple question is countered with statements like, "What do you mean?", "I don't understand what you're asking", and "I'm not sure I follow you."
- Asking you to clarify a word or phrase - this can allow for wiggle room in a specific denial, but is also a stalling tactic to buy more time to think of an answer, i.e. "What do you mean by 'take'?"

Depending on the context, sometimes a latent response is what you would expect. A delayed response would be appropriate to the question, "what did you have for breakfast exactly 3 weeks ago?" A delayed response would *not* be appropriate to the question, "did you steal breakfast from the diner exactly 3 weeks ago?"

WHISPER ALERT: Don't dismiss a suspicious cue, look for relevant signal clusters.

LET'S SIMPLIFY

Nonverbal, verbal and paralinguistic channels contain a dizzying amount of information that without a disheartening amount of practice and experience it's impossible to keep it all straight. Familiarity with the information allows you to notice some of these cues. Appendix B lists these cues for quick reference. For our everyday needs, though, former FBI agent Joe Navarro has come up with a streamlined method, the "Four Domain Model" of detecting deception (Schafer & Navarro). It uses the most common, and reliable, deception cues and categorizes them into "domains", making it easier to spot behavior clusters rather than focusing on individual cues. The domains are *Comfort/Discomfort, Emphasis, Perception Management,* and *Synchrony.*

Comfort/Discomfort

People that have done wrong or are trying to hide something carry signs of tension and distress throughout their body. Instead of focusing on the myriad *nonverbal* signals, <u>first target your energy on signs of comfort and discomfort.</u>

Key comfort signals:

- *Mirroring* is a reliable sign of comfort and typically occurs at later stages of a conversation (Knapp)

- A *relaxed posture* is another positive signal. Sometimes people will clear obstacles that partially block their view so they can maintain that relaxed posture.
- *Genuine smiles* require true positive emotions. Not a guarantee but always a good sign.

Key discomfort signals:

- *Too much movement.* Fidgeting and persistent posture readjustment, tapping or drumming or constant foot movement.
- *Too Little Movement.* Being frozen in place with little or no movement is another sign of discomfort, even if the person appears otherwise comfortable.
- *Desire to leave* is another clear sign of discomfort. Either by expressly verbalizing this desire or by nonverbal behaviors such as looking at their watch or phone or pointing their feet toward the exit.
- *Distancing.* Leaning away and using physical barriers like a briefcase or purse are examples of distancing behavior.
- *Blocking behavior* includes rubbing the neck/head, eye blocking, and even creating a wall between people with body parts like shoulders and arms.

Perception Management

Liars seek to mold your perception to fit their narrative and this is reflected in a disproportionate percentage of their responses. Instead of focusing on the myriad *verbal signals,* target your energy on statements and phrases that attempt to alter your perception.

Convincing statements and perception qualifiers are the two categories of verbal responses most tied to altering perception. *Convincing statements* never address the issue at hand, but rather seek to place the speaker in a favorable light. Here are a couple new examples: "You know I'd never do something like that!" and "I've spent my life helping people, why would I hurt someone?" *Perception qualifiers* also attempt to affect perception by explaining how truthful the speaker is and how truthfully they are answering. As discussed earlier, common phrases include, "to tell you the truth…" and "to be honest…"

Knowing an open, relaxed posture is a sign of comfort, some people feign these signals while delivering convincing statements and/or perception qualifiers. Stretching out, extending the arms and taking up more space than normal might be evidence of someone trying to manage your perception of their comfort level. Yawning, slow blinking, eye rolling, looking at one's fingers/hands, and looking around the room to appear disinterested are additional examples. Look for signs of feigned comfort when the conversation is serious and you expect more active involvement from the subject.

Emphasis

When speaking, people incorporate their entire body for emphasis. Feet and legs engage in "gravity defying" behavior, by rising up on the balls of the feet or making a sudden gesture with the legs. Hands gesture in concert with what is being said. Vocal inflections and accentuations emphasize the speaker's points. *When it's genuine, adding verbal and nonverbal emphasis is universal.* <u>*When it's insincere, verbal and nonverbal emphasis do not correspond naturally.*</u>

Liars rarely emphasize, and when they do, they do it incorrectly (Liebermann, 1998). (How do you emphasize incorrectly?!?) Signs of manufactured emphasis are:

- Unusual movements that are too large or too small for the corresponding speech
- An unnatural delay between the speech and point of emphasis
- Emphasizing unimportant minutiae of a story
- Emphasizing negation over action
  - "I did **not** start the fire!" - Focus on *negation* indicates a deceptive response
  - "I didn't **start the fire**!" - Focus on *action* indicates a truthful response
- Thoughtful displays like stroking the chin or cheek shows focus on *what* to say instead of emphasizing the point they are making

Liars expend their mental energy figuring out *what to say*, but they don't think about *how to say it*. When lying, people are not aware how deeply inflection and emphasis color the conversation, so how words are presented isn't consciously considered. Even when emphasis is present, it shows up as an insincere and delayed display. Liars focus on the words themselves.

Synchrony

Truthful people don't need to consciously synchronize their verbal and nonverbal messages. It comes out naturally with words and gestures confirming each other. *Verbalizing* "yes" or "no" should evoke a corresponding, non-delayed *nonverbal* head movement. <u>A red flag is thrown when verbal and nonverbal elements are out of sync.</u>

Lying uses different areas of the brain and so the verbal and nonverbal channels are, literally, not on the same wavelength. When synchrony is absent someone might say, "No, I didn't do it", while nodding their head up and down. Asking, "would you lie about this?", generates another up and down and head movement while they say "no." As unbelievable as it sounds, you see this frequently when someone lies. Remember emphasis and movement levels of liars are diminished, so the head movement may be small but still perceptible.

Unpracticed liars are oblivious to the need of synchrony, so it is a strong indicator of deception. When they notice the error in their behavior, there are two ways they try to conceal the mistake. First, when making the wrong head movement, they will suddenly reverse the indicator from a head nod to shaking their head, or vice versa. This makes the lack of synchrony even more blatant.

Second, after they realize this asynchrony, head movements are then delayed because the brain must process the verbal and nonverbal cues sequentially. While *message synchrony* is restored, it comes at the expense of a delayed response, so *timing synchrony* is lost.

Truthful people exhibit synchrony in both message and timing.

*   *   *

FORGET-ME-NOTS

- Nonverbal indicators of deception only manifest *if the limbic system has been activated.* This only happens with high stakes (and sometimes medium stakes) lies. Low stakes lies will not elicit nonverbal deception cues.
- Verbal indicators are processed by the higher order brain functions. Therefore, they tend to manifest across all types of lies but are more subject to thoughtful manipulation by a skilled liar. (A summary of verbal and nonverbal deception cues can be found in Appendix C).
- When starting out, keep it simple by focusing on the "four domain model:"
  - Discomfort: does the level of comfort change in response to a question?
  - Perception management: look for words or phrases that try to alter your perception.
  - Emphasis: do the verbal and nonverbal <u>emphases</u> correspond?
  - Synchrony: do the verbal and nonverbal <u>messages</u> correspond?

*   *   *

WHAT NOW?

We have gained an impressive array of knowledge about deception itself, but remember that knowing when someone is lying is not the same as learning the truth. Detecting deception is a passive activity reliant on observation. Getting the truth is an active pursuit that requires you engage people *in the right way.*

We must act preemptively by using strategies to reduce the chance someone will lie. Where that isn't possible, we use different techniques to unmask the deceptive behaviors we've looked at in this chapter. Knowing what questions to ask and *how* to ask them will uncover the deception cues covered here. Looking past the lies and unearthing the truth is another tool a Whisperer uses to better understand people.

7

From lies to truth

"Truth will ultimately prevail where there is pains to bring it to light."

--GEORGE WASHINGTON

In chapters 4 and 5 we discussed asking questions to better understand others and form deeper connections. Because others sometimes mislead, we need strategies to learn the truth. Detecting deception is one thing. *Uncovering the truth is another matter altogether.*

There is a 3-phase approach to getting at the truth in any situation. First, we employ behaviors aimed at *preventing* lies from being told. Second, we borrow both *interview* and *interrogation* techniques from the criminal interrogator and alter their methods for everyday situations. This allows us to elicit those deceptive behaviors discussed in the previous chapter.

"AN OUNCE OF PREVENTION..."

Preventing lies is better than *detecting* lies. Remember that using the techniques outlined in chapter 2 makes you more charismatic, allowing you to generate rapport with people in a way that reduces the likelihood of deception.

During any interaction, good indicators to determine if rapport has been established are *mirroring* gestures reflected back to you like head tilt, posture, and hand/arm placement. Body language that shows *openness,* rather than low confidence displays or shielding postures, is an equally good sign. If they occasionally take a deep breath, they are not completely comfortable even if they appear to be otherwise.

* * *

<u>Low stakes lies</u> are the easiest to prevent. These are the prosocial, "little white lies" that we tell one another to maintain harmony in our social groups where the lie protects

the feelings of the questioner, "Do you like this outfit?" -OR- "I rearranged the furniture while you were gone. What do you think?" Friends and family overwhelmingly respond positively, but falsely, to these types of questions as they want to reinforce social bonds. There are a handful of strategies you can use to overcome these natural tendencies, but only use these techniques when you need to know their *true feelings*.

Temper your enthusiasm. Your own excitement when asking for feedback can cause others to downplay their true feelings. "I think this is the perfect outfit for tonight! What do you think?" will result in agreement. To get someone's true opinion, downplay your opinion to the point of being noncommittal. Look quizzically at the outfit and say, "hmm… I'm not sure about this outfit for tonight. What do you think?" If they know you aren't sold on the idea, they are now in a position to offer their true opinion.

Appeal to flattery. Let someone know they are *better* at something than you and ask their opinion. *"You are better than I am with creative strategies. Tell me, what do you think of this sales pitch for my new client?"* This gives them license to provide their true thoughts because if their opinion differs from yours, it's due to their knowledge in this area and not a personal criticism.

Reverse the guilt. People tell lies to keep from feeling bad about hurting you. Reverse this process by making them feel guilty if they *don't* tell the truth. Let them know withholding the truth is more harmful, so it's in everyone's best interest to be honest. Ask, *"I know you don't want to hurt my feelings, but it will hurt more if you're not completely honest; If not for you, I wouldn't know where to turn; I'm counting on you to tell me the truth, because no one else will."*

Overcome apathy. Less often, but no less important, are situations where strangers with no vested interest tell a "fuzzy lie" because it is the most expedient solution, "Yep, your car will be ready by Tuesday morning." While he hopes to be done by Tuesday, he knows there are several jobs ahead of yours and doesn't *really* know when it will be ready, and isn't inclined to figure it out.

You need to infuse the situation with enough gravitas so he is *motivated to think* about exactly when it will be done. He will move from a fuzzy lie to a closer approximation of the truth. Your motivator might sound like, *"My mother is going into surgery on Tuesday and I'm the one that is driving her to the hospital. If there's a chance the car won't be ready by then you need to let me know now."* I'm not advocating lying, this is just an example. Our lives contain enough drama, you should be able to pull from your own experiences to add immediacy to the situation.

All these methods of questioning build rapport by linking the status and importance of the other person contingent on their honest response. Rapport is especially relevant in low stakes lies because they are meant to protect the feelings of others and do not normally elicit behavioral cues of deception.

* * *

Somewhere between, *"Do you like the peach cobbler?"* and *"Did you kill him?"* are a host of <u>medium stakes</u> questions. These are generally harder to counteract with the strategies listed above. Answers to these questions don't rise to the level of a felony but are more serious than a "little white lie." Medium stakes lies will elicit behavior clues of deception because they engage the self-preservation response of the limbic system. Their assertion of innocence, if not real, *needs* to be believed.

Some examples of medium stakes situations are if you suspect:

- A coworker has badmouthed you to the boss
- An employee was drinking during work hours
- A car repair estimate contains inflated prices and items that don't need repair
- Your spouse or significant other of cheating

It starts with a suspicion. You believe someone may be lying to you but you need to be certain. It may be something they said (evasion, qualifiers), the way they said it (inappropriate emphasis), body language, or some other deception cue from chapter 6. (Throughout this chapter the term "suspect" refers to someone about whom you harbor a suspicion of deceptive behavior, not a person under legal investigation for criminal activity.)

THE CONVERSATION

To get the truth in these situations, we must adapt tactics from the world of law enforcement. The first step is investigating and interviewing witnesses. In our frame of reference, instead of *interviews*, think of them as *conversations*.

The conversation should be casual, and above all, non-accusatory. If the interviewee suspects you're looking for signs of deceit, it limits your ability to ferret out the truth. The purpose is solely to gather information and make a preliminary determination whether you think someone is involved in duplicitous behavior. No one should know your suspicions.

*   *   *

Columbo and Sherlock Holmes were masters of this investigative technique. Distinctive personas aside, you want to melt into the background, *don't skulk about in a rumpled raincoat or don a fox and hound cap and tweed jacket!* Like them, however, <u>you will use the *conversation* and your *questions* to *elicit* the signals of deceit we learned about in the last chapter.</u>

The situation determines how many people to speak with, perhaps as few as one. Conversing with as many people as possible gives you a broader base of information on which to formulate a preliminary theory. Get as much input as you can from anyone even marginally involved to figure out logical explanations, extenuating circumstances, mistaken conclusions, etc. Resist any inclination during information gathering to prematurely reveal suspicions you may harbor.

Before you begin, make sure you have established rapport with the person. Ensure they are relaxed, calm and have a positive mental attitude. If they feel cornered, defensive or upset at the outset of the conversation, it severely hampers your ability to get the truth.

Open vs. closed questions

Open-ended questions are general requests for information requiring more than short one or two-word answers and don't have a definite yes/no answer. They often start with the phrase, "tell me about…" and is a way to get someone talking about a specific topic.

Open questions produce a flow of information, especially important during the early phases of the conversation. Answers to open questions are more likely to be edited accounts which contain *omissions* rather than *lies*. These statements can be evaluated for *editing* by looking for text bridges and indications of rehearsed responses.

This is a good starting point because it is easier to get the truth from an initial omission than from someone who is fully committed to a lie.

On the other hand, closed questions have one or two word responses and can be more readily evaluated for deception cues. These are better used later in the conversation.

Simple examples of open vs. closed questions are:

- "Tell me about your trip." vs. "Did you have a nice time on your trip?"
- "How did the two of you meet?" vs. "Did you two meet at work?"
- "What do you like about those types of movies?" vs. "What was the leads name of the action movie we saw last week?"
- "Why is the 2016 Presidential election making everyone so angry?" vs. "Is the 2016 Presidential election making you angry?"

Opening question

The first question you ask should be a broad, open ended question that doesn't accuse the person of any wrongdoing. Give them a full opportunity to answer the question without interruption, which breaks the flow of ideas and restricts your ability to evaluate the story for edited information. At no point do you want to betray yourself with eye rolling, smirking or any other sign that indicates you don't believe what you're hearing. You want them to be as comfortable as possible in relaying their story. *If the answer contains an edited account of the events, deception is indicated.* Consider the scenario *"tell me all about your trip."* What follows are the key things to look for while someone is answering a broad, open question.

Proportional level of detail. Truthful accounts nearly always contain three parts–an intro, the main event, and an epilogue. Truthful stories have a level of detail that moves relatively quickly from the intro to the main event, and then the epilogue may be shorter or longer depending on its *relative importance* as compared to the main event. Made up stories omit one or more of these sections and/or vary wildly in detail. A suspicious answer to the question that omits the main event might sound like this:

> *"Good trip. Woke up late so had to scramble to get to the airport. Of course, I was in long-term parking and had to wait forever for the shuttle. By the time I got through the security checkpoint I thought I was going to miss the flight. I made the flight, but it was a close call. Anyway, got there and had a great time. On the way back I didn't have any complications. The lady next to me snored the entire time, but if that's the worst that happens on a flight, it can't be too bad."*

In this example, the entire story is *getting to* the destination and *getting back* from the trip. Almost none of the story detailed the main event which is what happened at the destination itself. This indicates a calculated omission.

Out of sequence information. Truthful stories jump around from event to event in an unsequenced way. Recall of the major events stimulates recall of minor events which are not sequenced properly. A perfect chronology which moves from beginning to end shows a rehearsed and constructed story. In a formal environment like a courtroom, however, it is reasonable that even truthful people will rehearse exactly what they are going to say. So in these settings, rehearsed answers with exact sequencing do not indicate deception. Here is an example of a truthful, out-of-sequence informal recollection:

> *"We went to Madison Square Garden to see the concert. Oh, but before that we had dinner near Times Square where we saw the world's worst jugglers. Anyway after the show, we just walked around marvelling how nothing ever closes on our way back to the hotel. Oh, but before we got back to the room, we managed to walk by Rockefeller Center."*

Lack of emotion and emphasis. Note how expressive the thoughts and emotions are while the story is being told. *Absence of emotion and lack of emphasis* are indicators that the story has been rehearsed and is now being recited. Also, making up facts on the spur of the moment may cause cognitive overload which prevents proper display of emotions and emphasis. In either case, it is a strong sign of an evasive, and possibly deceptive, answer.

Text bridging. Most verbal and nonverbal deception cues are more easily observed with closed questions, but text bridging is a notable exception. These are textual clues that the speaker is skipping parts of the story. Hearing these doesn't immediately point to evasion or deception, but these are parts of the story you want to revisit later for closer examination. When you hear words and phrases like, "next", "eventually", "then", "later", and "after that" make a mental note of what occurred before and after the text bridge.

Implied action phrases. Remember, these phrases focus on the motivation of the speaker, not on the action, but they want you to *infer* that the action happened. This is another group of verbal deception cues commonly seen in open-ended answers. "*We wanted* to just head back to the hotel," often this means what *didn't* happen. The speaker hopes this is missed in the volume of the story *and* <u>they didn't have to actually lie</u>.

Scenario:

Suppose you suspect your boyfriend cheated on you while he was away. Before moving to the closed questions, you might add another open ended question, such as, "*What was the most interesting thing that happened while you were away?*" If you want to make this sound like a *knowing* question where you already have the answer, pause ever-so slightly *before and after* the word "interesting" and make the first few words sound like a question on their own. "*What was the most...interesting(?)...thing that happened while you were away?*" This is *not* an overt accusation, but it needs to be <u>said neutrally</u> in an off-handed manner so an innocent person would interpret it as an innocent question, and only a guilty person would get nervous and perceive it as accusatory in any way.

Any information seeking responses like, "*Why do you want to know?*" or "*What did you hear?*" means they think you're asking a leading question. An innocent person doesn't care why you're asking. Only the person who thinks you may know something you're not supposed to know will ask these types of questions.

This also provides your first key opportunity to assess deceptive cues we looked at in the last chapter. Look for both verbal and nonverbal deception cues. You will be surprised how often you will spot a *behavioral cluster* at this early stage of the conversation, particularly if they think you suspect something.

WHISPER ALERT: Start with open questions before moving to closed questions.

Closed question follow-up

So far you've asked open-ended questions and gotten responses. To this point you have said little, but you should have a good idea if your suspect is truthful, and if not, which parts of the story have been edited, omitted, or falsified. These are the areas to focus on in the follow-up questions. Remain calm lest your subject becomes suspicious!

Focused question sequence. The next step is to ask a series of closed questions but still in a casual, non-accusatory, non-threatening way. This has two benefits. First, you can more readily see the signs of verbal and nonverbal deceptiveness discussed in the last chapter. Second, if someone is making up answers, they will become *increasingly* bothered by the need to construct lie after lie and attempt to end the conversation and/or change topics. The suspect may become defensive and ask questions of his own, "why do you want to know all this?", "what is this about?"

Your questions should focus on the fuzziest parts of the open-ended story, which is a logical reason to ask for clarification or more detail. You will either get appropriate responses as you go deeper into the story or you may witness signs of deception and/or low confidence behaviors (rubbing palms together, eye blocking, crossing arms). When you see signs of deception, never telegraph your suspicions, verbally or otherwise. From their perspective, you're just having a pleasant conversation.

Part of the reason investigators write responses is to create a several second gap between each answer and the next question. This gives ample time to watch for nonverbal cues of discomfort. It would look odd to do this during a casual conversation. The best thing we can do to create a delay is look contemplatively after each answer as though contemplating or lost in a short reverie, nod slowly, and then ask an appropriate follow-up. Keep an unrushed yet steady pace from open through closed questions.

Fake a fact. Somewhere in this group of closed questions, you may optionally add a fake question. Something that sounds so reasonable that a liar would be compelled to play along with your made-up story. This is a great way to figure out if they are telling the truth. Don't overuse this technique because if they realize what you're doing, it will not only fail to work, but may cause feelings of resentment. A good rule of thumb is *once* per conversation, no more.

Let's say you suspect a friend pretended to be in New York City to avoid your anniversary party. After he's back in town, you say to him, "You missed a great party. Tell me all about your trip to New York." If your open question revealed text bridging and/or a lack of appropriate level of detail, ask a series of closed questions with a faked fact in the mix:

Q: *"Where did you go the day you arrived?"*
A: *[pause] "The Metropolitan Museum of Art."*
Q: *"A wonderful Museum! What exhibits did you see?"*
A: *[longer pause] "I can't really remember. We were in and out of there pretty fast."*
Q: *"Oh, Where else did you go?"*

A: "Uhh, the 9/11 Memorial"

Q: "Must have been an emotional visit. What surprised you most about the site?"

A: "Umm.. just everything. It was quite a place."

Q: "I read in the paper that they were closing down most of the memorial this weekend to do some upgrades and repairs. Did you get caught up in all that?" (Fake fact)

A: "Yeah, there was a bunch of work going on but we were still able to see some of the exhibits."

Q: "Where did you go for dinner?"

A: "Just some place near the memorial, I don't even remember the name" (starting to short circuit any additional questions)

In this scenario, you have enough information to go straight to the admission. In other scenarios involving someone's risky behavior or the smooth operation of a business or a threat to family unity, the questioning cannot end here without total confidence in a suspect's honesty. Further questioning will most likely be required and greater skill of the questioner will be necessary.

TIMEOUT: What might be some open and closed question follow-ups for situations I routinely experience or may encounter?

Adapted techniques

Additional law enforcement techniques adapted for casual conversations can be used alongside both open and closed questions. Each serves a different purpose but used in context, and at the right time, each can produce reliable indicators of guilt. *These questions are your greatest asset to elicit deception cues if someone is lying.* When using these techniques, make sure you are locked in on their verbal and nonverbal responses and look for any of the deception cues from chapter 6.

Presumptive question. These are closed questions *implying the speaker already knows the answer* when they do not. The purpose is to dissuade the subject from lying, and if asked persuasively enough, can cause an indirect admission.

If you suspect your child was drinking and driving, instead of asking, *"were you drinking and driving?"* change the question to, *"who else was drinking with you before you drove home?"* The automatic implication is that you already *know* they were drinking and driving, but now just want to find out who else was there. This forces the subject to figure out what you may know. Their hesitation caused by their uncertainty gives you the opportunity to evaluate for possible deception cues.

An innocent person would know how to answer immediately, *"I wasn't drinking!"* or *"What are you talking about?!?"* The guilty person will exhibit the "freeze" as their brains are overloaded trying to process not only what you know, but how they should answer next.

Presumptive questions need to be asked in a calm, neutral, non-accusatory way so that any deceptive cues can be directly linked to the question and not the manner in which it was asked.

If you want to suggest more strongly that you *know* something you don't, you can preface a presumptive question with the phrase, *"Think very carefully before you answer this question..."* This creates the strong inference you already know the answer. This technique should be used sparingly as it is no longer a casual, neutral question, but is flirting on the brink of being an outright accusation.

Bait question. One of the most powerful techniques in use by investigators is the bait question. As with all interview questions, it is non-accusatory but *presents plausible evidence* that would implicate the subject. Its intention is to persuade the subject to change, or consider changing, some earlier part of their story and should only be used after a denial of motive or opportunity.

It should be spoken as a sincere, reasonable inquiry, "is there any reason why..." As with all of these techniques, using any of them more than once per conversation will render the technique transparent and ineffective.

If Janet claimed to be home all night, you could use a bait question, "Janet, is there any reason you can think of why one of our neighbors said they saw you pulling out of the driveway last night?" If innocent, Janet will be unphased. She will deny strongly deny the possibility and assume the neighbor was mistaken.

If lying, she is now in a bind and has to gauge the possibility that someone saw her. She must decide whether to continue to lie or acknowledge she left. If she acknowledges leaving, she must also consider what explanation she should provide as to why. All of this cognitive processing will create a noticeable delay in her response. The nature of the denial may also change at this point. *"Oh, I remember now, yes I left for a few minutes to go to the store but I wasn't gone more than 15 minutes."*

The fewer specifics you provide in the bait question the better. If you're too specific, you could be wrong about one or more facts and the subject will know you are bluffing. "Is there any reason Mrs. Jones would say she saw you leave the house at 10:30 and not come back until early in the morning?" This is an exaggerated example of a very poor bait question. Too many specifics. Departure time, arrival time, naming a specific neighbor. Maybe Janet knows that Mrs. Jones is on vacation or maybe those weren't the times she left and came back. Compare that statement with the original bait question to see how vague it is. The less specific the question, the greater the effect in the mind of the listener, as they now have no idea how much you know.

Parallel scenario. This is an open question that introduces a specific scenario you suspect is happening. If you suspect Rhonda is clocking out for a coworker that is leaving early, you might bring her into your office and ask, *"Rhonda, it's come to my attention that someone in the customer service department may be punching out for someone else. Do you have any thoughts on how to approach the person and deal with the situation?"*

If innocent, she will be glad you are seeking her advice and will freely offer suggestions. She may also ask who is under suspicion and will assist in whatever way she can. A guilty person in this situation will first seek to assure the questioner she would never do anything like that. She will also have little or no input on how to handle the situation and will express no curiosity over who has been doing this.

Suspicion scenario. Similar to the parallel scenario, this is another open question that uses general language implying that the guilty party has been discovered. The question should be structured such that it will immediately <u>make a guilty person nervous</u> and, at the same time, <u>arouse the curiosity of the innocent</u>. In our time clock caper, the question might change to, *"Rhonda, I don't understand why some people will clock out for someone else and not think they'll be found out!"* Or if you suspect someone has bad mouthed you to the boss say to them, *"It's surprising that someone will bad mouth you to the boss and not think it will get back to you. Don't you think?"*

Watch immediately for the freeze response, followed by one or more nonverbal discomfort cues and/or pacifying behaviors. The guilty also seek to quickly change the subject. The innocent person is intrigued by the statement and wants more information about why you're saying this or who you're talking about with a request for more details. They also betray no signs of defensiveness or discomfort.

Either response tips the balance of suspicion. Having the indicators of truth and deception in your toolbox gives you the edge when determining the likelihood someone is lying.

Note: All the adapted questioning techniques (presumptive and bait questions, parallel and suspicion scenarios) rely on the subject believing the questioner is privy to significant evidence and/or information. These same techniques can be used whether or not you *actually* have proof, but hard-clad evidence is better! Lacking this, determine the plausibility of your suspicions.

WHISPER ALERT: Channel Columbo--downplay questions as the consequences increase. This keeps truthful and deceptive cues tied specifically to the question and not the delivery.

If you conclude after your conversation...your investigation...that it is likely you are being deceived, it is time for confrontation. So far, all of your questions have been neutral with possibly only hints of your suspicions. This changes now.

THE CONFRONTATION

In law enforcement, the interview phase is about gathering information; whereas the interrogation phase is about securing an admission. For us, this parallels the conversation and confrontation phases but lacks the animated intensity and more formalized structure.

If you have already established the *likelihood* of guilt in the conversation why continue to the confrontation? Because all verbal and nonverbal indicators of guilt are just that–*indicators*. There is no way to know for certain without hearing directly from the suspect. The confrontation phase is the place to learn the unequivocal truth and hopefully elicit an admission.

Unlike the conversation, the confrontation is accusatory. You assert your suspicion and switch to statements rather than questions. Whereas the conversation requires more listening and observing, the confrontation requires more speaking and persuading. We are not looking for signs of deception anymore. We are focused solely on an admission.

The principal parts of the confrontation are the initial accusation, theme development and the closing question.

Initial accusation

The "initial accusation" is where you first make your suspicions known in a direct manner, which comprises three elements: accusation statement, pause, and transition. Collectively, these provide the suspect the first opportunity to admit guilt.

Accusation statement. You know the who; you know the what. This is the first *direct, accusatory* statement showing your conviction the suspect is guilty. You need to say this in a slow, confident and deliberate manner. Don't use a preface that weakens the conviction of this statement like, "I think that…" or "I believe you did…"

Delivery of this statement should contain emphasis but not strong emotion. Don't use an angry, sad, or judgemental tone. *"After speaking with you, (and others,) it's clear **you** are the one that has been taking money from the cash drawer."*

In a law enforcement setting, the stronger the evidence (real or imagined), the greater the chance for a confession. Interrogators often bring case file folders, DVDs and other video media, briefcases, and even USB drives into the interrogation room to convince the suspect that there is physical evidence against him.

In less formal settings, we can't produce such voluminous displays of evidence, but we can still plant the seed we have proof to back up our claims. You can edit the confrontation statement to allude to some unnamed evidence <u>on your phone</u>. This will get the suspect's mind questioning what it could be. Is it an email, video, text message, what is it?

With cell phone in hand, *"After speaking with you, and others, and reviewing all the facts (look casually toward your cell phone) it is clear that **you** have been drinking on the job."* Then set the phone face down on the table and don't mention it again (until later, if need be). If they are guilty, this simple addition to the confrontation statement will set them on their heels and their mind will be occupied with thoughts about what you know and *how much* you know.

Pause statement. This directly follows the accusation statement and allows you to observe if the suspect exhibits an initial "freeze" reaction to your accusation. The pause may include a statement that you want to settle the matter, "Let's sit down together so we can get this straightened out, OK?" This statement creates a pause for the subject to consider if coming clean would be a better choice than outright denial.

Besides the standard nonverbal indicators of guilt, the guilty suspect will calmly *ask clarifying questions* like, "what did you say?" or "what do you mean?" (Guilty people are more passive and even fall asleep in police interrogation rooms!) Innocent people don't ask clarifying questions because they have nothing to clarify–they didn't do it. They do not try to hide their anger and irritation and always issue a clear and sincere denial.

Transition statement. This is where you must provide a real, or *perceived*, benefit to telling the truth. The statement must reinforce the certainty of the accusation statement without appearing too eager to get an admission. You must convince the suspect you have all the information you need, but you want to hear their side of the story. *"As I said there is no doubt you have been drinking at work. The reason I wanted to sit down with you was to get your side of the story.* **Why** *people do what they do is as important as* **what** *they do."* This statement creates a pause for the subject to consider if guilt and ill-will can be alleviated by explaining their actions.

The accusation, pause and transition statements together create the "initial accusation." These statements should be punctuated by breathing spaces where necessary for the subject to digest the revelations while considering a response. They are broken down here to illustrate the purpose of each part so you can adapt them to fit your conversational style. Taken together, here is one possible initial accusation:

> *"After speaking with you, and others, and reviewing all the facts at hand (look casually toward your cell phone) it is clear that you have been drinking on the job... Let's just sit down together so we can get this straightened out, OK?... There is no doubt about this... but the reason I wanted to sit down with you was to get your side of the story. Why people do what they do is more important than what they do."*

At this point, if luck is with you, you'll get an admission! If you hear, "How did you know?" Under no circumstances do you use the self-congratulatory, "You just told me." It's time for them to explain and you to listen.

If, on the other hand, no admission is forthcoming, it's time to develop a theme which allows them to justify their behavior.

TIMEOUT: In what areas of my life and situations encountered would I be persuading another to be truthful? What transition statements would have helped resolutions for situations I have experienced in the past?

The Justification

All people need to explain questionable behavior to achieve cognitive harmony and to show others they are not a bad person. Now is the time to reinforce the subject's need to justify their actions. By developing a justification, it becomes easier for the subject to latch onto reasonable explanations for their behavior.

All situations do not work equally well with every justification. Pick one or two and stick with them. Focus your message, but if it isn't well received, choose a different justification and work on that. The average criminal interrogation is 2-4 hours long. In casual situations, this isn't typical, however it shows sometimes you need to keep moving forward before declaring a stalemate.

Many people have difficulty using these techniques because they originate from law enforcement settings and are strong tools to get an admission of guilt. Also, it requires a certain level of moral flexibility as you won't believe everything you are saying. The point is, you want *them* to believe in the justification you are offering. If they come to accept one or more of these rationalizations, they will admit to the behavior. Anything that gets them to admit responsibility while relieving their emotional guilt is ideal. The rule of thumb: *anything that would not cause an innocent person to confess is permissible.*

The scripts that follow are simple examples of these justifications. In real situations, it requires repeating one's self and moving between themes until you come upon something that resonates with the accused. You need to keep talking until they realize admitting guilt is the best option. Notice how these justifications contain no questions. The time for questions is over; it's time for persuading.

Justification #1 – We're all the same – "Anyone else would have done the same thing." This powerful justification is an appeal to the nature of man, that anyone in a similar situation would have acted in exactly the same way. Recap the suspect's life circumstances and the details of the offense and let them know that anyone in their shoes would have done the same.

"Listen, if even half of what you've told me about your neighbor is true, you're a saint to have put up with it for this long. Chopping down your tree last year, stealing your wi-fi,

and not picking up after his dog. Then almost hitting your child after driving too fast through the neighborhood was the last straw. I get it. I would have slashed his tires, too. In fact, I would have done a lot more than that! This just shows how over the line he was! But now that you've had a chance to calm down, you need to come clean about what really happened."

Justification #2 – Downplay the moral severity – "It's really not a big deal." Diminishing the seriousness of the behavior is another strong technique to elicit an admission. Make sure they know you aren't judging them and don't feel what they did was egregious. You can also talk about how you've seen and heard of worse situations. If you suspect an employee stole computer equipment you might say,

"I understand. Those computers were 2 months away from being upgraded. We know what happens then–they get thrown out. So all you really did was save them from the trash a little early. But we still need to know exactly how many computers we're talking about for inventory purposes. Give us the whole story so we can just move on from here."

Justification #3 – The ethical motivation – "You did it for the right reasons." When someone lies about some action or behavior, they also misrepresent the true motive behind it. Tap into this need for "motive purification." Convince them you know the intent behind the action was pure and the guilty party will more likely admit to the action.

"As a real estate agent you have a duty to be honest. And although didn't disclose every defect as required, you didn't do it for you. The sellers are under a mountain of debt and have even more medical expenses coming in. You're helping them get their lives back on track, this wasn't for self-interest. I get it. What you did was done for the benefit of others, and you shouldn't be vilified for it."

Justification #4 – Condemning others – "It's really their fault." This is about blaming anyone but the guilty party...the victim, an accomplice or anyone else to share in some measure of responsibility. In law enforcement interrogations, this is most often used in sex cases. The interrogator blames the victim so the suspect will feel a reduced level of emotional guilt and confess to the action. It can still be useful in less dramatic situations.

"If the insurance company had taken care of their obligations the first time around, you wouldn't have had to fudge this latest 'accident.' Companies that treat people ethically are given the same consideration, but companies that act without conscience deserve what they get. They brought this on themselves."

We are all familiar with these justifications because at one time or another we've either used or wished we could use theses excuses for our own regrettable behavior. Choose the justification best suited for the situation and develop it appropriately thereby bringing the confrontation toward a conclusion.

TIMEOUT: What justification(s) would be most appropriate for situations I have encountered?

Closing question

During the confrontation you will sense, at some point, the subject is ready to provide an admission. That is the time to move to the closing question. If this happens after the initial accusation, skip theme development entirely and move right to the closing question.

The closing question, or "alternative question", as it is known in law enforcement circles, is a two-sided question that avoids a direct admission of guilt without the possibility of any qualifiers. It allows the suspect to tell the truth by making a single admission which also eases their conscience.

Both sides of the question must presume guilt. *"Did you take the money to help your family or was it for the excitement to see if you could get away with it?"* Never ask a general guilt question like, "did you do it?" And never allow one side of the question to be a denial of admission. For example, *"did you throw the eggs at the Johnson's house or just know who did?"* This is an improper closing question because one side presumes innocence. A properly phrased closing question would be, *"was it your idea to throw the eggs at the Johnson's house or were you pressured into it?"* Either answer is a tacit admission he threw the eggs.

The nature of the closing question should be based around your selected theme. Alternatively, you can base the question on the where, when, and how of the offense. *"Had you been planning to slash his tires or was it just something that popped into your head?"*, or, *"did you cheat on me before I left on my business trip or did it happen while I was away?"*

The contrast between the two choices should have a clearly preferred choice. One side should focus on the justified action as developed by the theme, the other should focus on the "negative" side of the question, *"Did you spread those rumors about Bill doing drugs just to even the score or are you just a sadist that truly enjoys watching others endure pain?"* People often accept the positive side to prevent others believing in the negative alternative.

One-sided questions can still be used. Even then, never ask directly as the preference would be a flat denial. Focus on the thoughts and emotions of the suspect, *"You wish you could take it back, don't you?"*, or, *"I can tell you feel sorry about this, don't you?"*

Although tempting, don't just ask the closing question and wait for an answer. You need to use supporting statements that strengthen the pillar of whichever theme you focused on. Continue to speak about how the choice they made is morally excusable, or that it isn't a big deal, whatever supports your initial theme. Think of it as continuation of the major theme. *"[Closing question] Did you take the money to help your family or was it just for the excitement to see if you could get away with it? [Pause briefly for an answer. If you don't get one, continue theme] I'm sure the money was for your family. You're not the type of person to just take it for himself. Or are you?"*

Repeated denials show the closing question you selected was the wrong one. Try a different closing question, and if that fails, go back and pick a different theme. Work on it until you feel the time is right to revisit the closing question again.

TIMEOUT: What closing questions would fit the situations and themes I previously identified?

Dealing with denials

How you handle denials shapes the level of difficulty in getting the admission. *The more someone denies involvement in a situation the less likely they are to tell the truth later.* Throughout the confrontation phase, your primary goal is to discourage the person from becoming entrenched in repeated denials.

Weak, half-hearted denials should be ignored as you move from the initial accusation into the justification. As you talk over them, their denial will stop. If they continue to cut in with a denial, a "stop hand" with a shake of the head as you continue speaking is normally enough to dissuade any further interruptions.

For more forceful interruptions you may try interjecting quick comments that grab their attention and stop the denial. *"Brian, before you say anything else, let me explain how important this is…"* or *"Brian, I'm not done! Let me explain the whole story…"* Another option is to reword the initial accusation. After the confrontation statement if they say, "I didn't do it!" you reply, *"As I said, after talking to you (and others) it's clear you did it. That's not in question. The reason I'm here now is to get your side of the story and find out why you did it. (Move on to the justification)"*

Common behaviors emerge that differentiate innocent denials from guilty ones. As always, these are not determinative, but suggestive.

Innocent denials:

- Are spontaneous, direct and forceful
- Build in intensity until the suspect wins the verbal battle and turns the interrogator into the listener
- Don't include questions
- Stay on point and don't change the subject until the matter is resolved

Guilty denials:
- Move from weak to apologetic
- Can be consistent but lack emphasis, emotion and conviction
- Include questions like, "Why do you think I did this?" and "How can you be sure?"
- Contain oath qualifiers and defensive responses like, "You're just out to get me."
- Seek to change the subject

WHISPER ALERT: Admission or denial, no one wins. Pick yourself up and dust yourself off.

The most important thing to remember is each time a denial is fully voiced, your chance to secure an admission drops. Do everything in your power to stay on point and don't let them finish a statement of denial. The admission phase is about your ability to persuade them that coming clean is the best and only option.

Unlike the impressive performances of our favorite detectives, our statistical success rate will be less than perfect. You will live through to the end and your skills will improve, but even with your "A" game success is not guaranteed. There are many uncertainties in life and this is but one.

* * *

FORGET-ME-NOTS

- Eliciting deception cues starts with a <u>conversation</u> that begins with an open question and moves to a series of closed questions.
- Two of the most powerful techniques to use during the conversation are bait and presumptive questions, both of which cause the subject to believe you have incriminating evidence. These are the best times to look for deception cues.
- When deception is apparent, move from conversation to <u>confrontation</u>:
- Make clear you are certain they are guilty
  - Offer a justification that they can latch onto to ease their guilt
  - Phrase the closing question in a way that eases their conscience **and** presumes guilt no matter how they answer, "Did you steal the money for fun or because you were truly desperate?"

* * *

WE STILL FAIL

Even after spending time, energy, patience, and practice learning the information in the last two chapters, we may still fail at detecting deception and learning the truth. Both indicting the innocent or believing the liar may damage personal and professional relationships. Approach the process with humility and realistic expectations to be better armed to deal with deception and learn how to separate the truth from the lie.

Another reason for failure has nothing to do with improving the skills you've cultivated. Some people are just good at lying and getting away with it. They emit no deception cues and their answers seem truthful. Significant time in their presence, however, betrays a darker side difficult to articulate. We all deal with them, if not on a daily basis, regularly enough to take a closer look. And conveniently they have a common name:

psychopaths.

8

Psychopaths among us

"I don't feel guilty for anything. I feel sorry for people who feel guilt."

-- TED BUNDY

Murdering psychopath. Psychopathic serial killer. Deranged psychopath. The term psychopath conjures up slightly different images for all of us because of the words commonly used alongside it. Do a google search for "famous psychopaths" and all the results show a string of serial killers and mass murderers. The depiction of psychopaths in literature and film often bear little resemblance to the real thing, in part because deciding on the distinct characteristics of a psychopath has been a century long process.

Psychopath? yes...   ...but so is he

WHAT'S IN A NAME?

No psychiatric organization approves a diagnosis of psychopathy (pronounced si-COP-a-thee but often wrongly pronounced SI-co-PATH-ee). The equivalent diagnoses used in psychology are "antisocial personality disorder" and "dissocial personality disorder," but never psychopathy.

The condition was recognized even before it had a proper name. As early as 1801, French psychiatrist Philippe Pinel described a condition he called "mania without delirium." In 1835, English physician James Prichard described the same condition as "moral insanity" (Berrios). Over time, these concepts became linked with the term psychopathy.

The word itself was first used in Germany in 1847 and had a general meaning that applied to nearly all mental illness. The word *psychosis* was also used and was just another way of specifying "an abnormal mental condition." By the 1930s, the slang term "*psycho*" became a shortened form of both *psycho*pathic and *psycho*tic. The common root of both words, and the slang usage, has led many to confuse the meanings of these words, but as we'll see they are quite different.

BUT WHAT IS IT?

Psychopathy is a personality disorder where a person shows a profound lack of empathy for the feelings of others. When made aware of other's feelings, they still show no regard for either the person or their well-being. They, themselves, have a reduced capacity for experiencing emotions, particularly love and friendship.

<u>*Physiologically*</u>, psychopaths have an impairment of the amygdala which as we remember, is part of the brain's limbic system. It is this impairment that accounts for the complete lack of empathy (Blair). The amygdala also handles the "freeze, flight, or fight" response, which is how we respond to fear.

Therefore, a psychopath can lie convincingly because they do not experience fear and anxiety in the same way the rest of us do and will not emit any nonverbal signals of discomfort or deception, unless done intentionally. Most of their verbal responses, likewise, will not betray any deception cues. However, they can be identified through a number of their characteristics.

They ignore social, legal and moral standards of conduct to achieve immediate gratification. They express greater willingness to take part in immoral and antisocial behavior that is both deceitful and predatory. They have no need to internally rationalize their behavior, but will do so outwardly if questioned about their activities. They know the difference between right and wrong, they just don't care.

A primary characteristic of psychopathy is extreme egocentricity. They are the central figure upon which the sun rises and sets. A psychopath views himself as the star of the film—and everyone else is playing the part of an extra, and this worldview colors, and gives context to, all of their behaviors.

The psychopath's antisocial behavior creates heartache for the people connected to them because of their profound lack of empathy, especially for those closest to them.

<u>*Behaviorally*</u>, true psychopaths are more likely to commit acts of aggression—both reactive and premeditated. Reactive aggression is a response to anger, frustration or anxiety aimed at hurting someone. Ploughing into someone else's car in a fit of road rage is a clear example of reactive aggression. Premeditated aggression is a calm, calculated decision to engage in aggressive and/or violent behavior. It is

aimed at achieving a particular objective, such as robbing a bank at gunpoint, as an extreme example.

While they can be violent and callous, their disposition is often the opposite, in that they can possess superficial charm and an affable nature enabling them to more easily deceive and manipulate others. They are just as likely to use a convenient compliment, clever lie or melodramatic apology instead of a kick to the head. But these are all just tools to be used in the right setting if it gets the psychopath what he wants.

Failing to accept responsibility for their actions is another trait psychopaths share. Anything that happens is the fault of someone or something, but never himself. Apologies are never genuine because the psychopath feels he has nothing to apologize for. Apologies are solely to avoid consequences and enable the psychopath to continue his systematic manipulation of others.

Psychopaths seek constant stimulation and easily become bored with people and situations. Since they don't feel fear the way a normal person does, they resort to extreme behaviors such as inflicting pain to generate some level of emotional response that most of us would classify as over-the-top.

*　　*　　*

Most psychopaths lead relatively normal lives. Most don't do drugs, commit crimes or enjoy hurting people. Many follow a utilitarian lifestyle interspersed with Judeo-Christian ethics. They know the difference between right and wrong and want to be good. Why? Because a peaceful and orderly world is more comfortable to live in. They are lawful because it's the best calculated decision for their life and lifestyle, not because it's "right", in any moral or ethical sense of the word.

Psychopathy and Psychosis. Potato-Potäto?

In the early 19th C., "psychopathy" and "psychosis" were both general terms for mental illness, and although commonly confused, have evolved to represent very different conditions. As we've seen, psychopathy is where a person feels no empathy or emotional connection to others. Psychosis, however, is a family of disorders characterized by the inability to determine what is real from what isn't.

Hallucinations and delusions are common symptoms in psychotics. People with delusional disorder, schizophrenia and bipolar disorder may all suffer psychotic symptoms. In general terms, they may see and hear things that do not exist, and come to believe in things that are not true. Unlike psychopaths, psychotics do not necessarily lack compassion and empathy for others. Any immoral or antisocial behaviors are due to their difficulty in assessing reality rather than a callous disregard for others.

Psychopaths, by contrast, have no trouble distinguishing what is real and what isn't. They know exactly what they are doing and have the mental capacity to know right from wrong. Any immoral or antisocial behaviors are done intentionally, but without guilt.

Psychopathy and Sociopathy. Tomato-Tomäto?

The term sociopath is confusing, even among legal and psychiatric professionals. With the understanding of the concept of psychopathy, there exist various meanings of "sociopath."

The differentiation between these terms is difficult. For some (myself included), the word sociopath is used interchangeably with psychopath. The only difference is the word "psychopath" carries a stigma that "sociopath" does not. Being more socially acceptable, the word is in more common usage today. There are people with the self-awareness and intelligence to know they are emotionally different from others and actually call themselves sociopaths but would never self-identify as a psychopath.

Usually, though, psychopath refers to criminal and violent types, whereas sociopath refers to the law abiding psychopaths that rarely exhibit violent tendencies. This same differentiation is known by other terms like, "successful psychopath", "compensated psychopath", and "Machiavellian". These are all terms that describe a ruthless professional that will do "whatever it takes" to get the job done. While they do not always act ethically and may even appear morally bankrupt, they keep to the letter of the law, particularly if there is any risk of getting caught. The only thing separating a psychopath from a sociopath in this definition is that the *sociopath possesses greater impulse control, intelligence and long-term planning.* *This makes a sociopath far more dangerous and difficult to handle.* This is the meaning the public most often associates with the word sociopath.

Psychopathy...not just a boy's club.

When "sociopath" is used, you should now be able to gather the meaning from the context, although I will avoid its use altogether.

Psychopathy and gender

When we think of psychopaths, we think of men. This is because most research on psychopaths is done on prison inmates that have shown clear antisocial behavior. There is a growing body of evidence that psychopathy is also a serious condition among women. It may not be diagnosed as often in women because it may manifest itself differently than it does in men.

The manipulation by psychopathic women may take the form of extreme flirtation and toying with men in a way that gives them control and may be misdiagnosed as *histrionic personality disorder.*

Also, the extreme impulsiveness of psychopathic women may manifest itself as self-harm, whereas in men it shows up as violence toward others. In women, such behavior is often diagnosed as *borderline personality disorder* (Forouzan).

It is possible that these diagnoses have identical, or similar, pathologies, but express themselves differently along gender lines. At present, this is unproven, but is an intriguing idea to consider.

Psychopaths and violence

Not all psychopaths are violent, nor do they all engage in criminal activity. Their antisocial behavior hasn't risen to a felonious level (or perhaps they haven't gotten caught yet). In most cases, however, the nonviolent psychopath has opted to forgo violence as it is not in their best interest. They still use manipulation, coercion, lies, guilt, intimidation, and every other nonviolent tool that helps them achieve their goals. Psychopaths have no moral qualms with violence, but the smartest among them realize that its use is counterproductive in the long-term.

Although many psychopaths are non-violent, they make up a disproportionate percentage of the prison population. While impossible to calculate precisely, about 1% of the general population would meet the clinical definition of psychopathy, yet they comprise 25-35% of the prison population (Nicholls). Psychopathic inmates have committed more crimes, a wider variety of crimes, and are more violent, on average, than the other inmates (Serin, 1991). These same inmates were more violent during the commission of their crimes and are four times as likely to commit another violent crime after release than their non-psychopathic counterparts (Porter, Hemphill).

Right about now some of you are thinking, "Only 1% of the general population are psychopathic?!? You got us all worked up making us think there were psychopaths around every corner!" *Actually, there are!*

Psychopaths around "almost" every corner

As our collective understanding of neurological conditions improves, we know they are not binary—on or off, true or false, yes or no. Many disorders happen on a continuum where some cases are not severe enough to warrant a clinical diagnosis.

In 2013, the American Psychiatric Association created a new diagnosis called Autism Spectrum Disorder (ASD) to place different subtypes of autism under a single umbrella. This diagnosis recognizes the condition may have different symptoms of varying intensity, but the same pathology is at work. Likewise a nonalcoholic with a drinking problem would be on the "alcoholic spectrum." The descriptive term is "almost alcoholics." The generic term is the "almost effect" –where a person may shows signs and symptoms of a particular condition without meeting the stricter criteria of a formal diagnosis.

*   *   *

In 2012, Ronald Schouten and James Silver applied the almost effect to psychopathy in <u>Almost a Psychopath</u>. They contend that many people exhibit behavior that falls outside the bounds of "normal", but falls short of meeting the strict criteria for psychopathy, which clinical psychiatrists call "subclinical psychopathy." The symptoms exhibited by "almost psychopaths" cause problems in their life and the lives of those around them. As with other "almost conditions", those exhibiting subclinical psychopathy do so on a spectrum ranging in the frequency and intensity of their antisocial behaviors. Their outward behavior is less harsh and appears less often. They may not completely lack an emotional response to the joy and pain of others, but the response is more muted.

Executives and successful professionals that are "almost psychopaths" show a high level of competence, order, and self-discipline. These are not the people that become serial killers. They are more likely to be described as backstabbers, opportunists and bullies. True psychopaths rate higher in irresponsibility, impulsivity and negligence (Board & Fritzon). A true psychopath is less likely to be successful and would be unable to hold an executive position for a significant length of time.

Almost psychopaths have an easier time living among people and having lasting relationships. Although they blend in better than true psychopaths, they are still not likely to be model employees, neighbors, spouses, or parents. They get along well enough at work and at home to keep a job and maintain family relationships, however dysfunctional. They use others for their own selfish motivations but are skillful at walking the fine line to avoid permanently alienating those closest to them.

When they go too far, they appear earnest when providing an endless parade of apologies and excuses for why their behavior isn't their fault. They make promises and grandiose plans to salvage relationships and are often successful because of their charm and apparent sincerity.

While the percentage of true psychopaths is ~1% of the population, the number of almost psychopaths is many times higher. So in any modest size group, you are likely to be in contact with at least one almost psychopath.

Before you start looking at your companions suspiciously and questioning yourself, take a breath. We all do things we're not proud of sometimes, but that doesn't make us psychopaths. It is only when a long-trending pattern of disregard for others emerges that one might be considered on the psychopathic spectrum. While there is no magic point when this happens, if one's life is defined by completely self-interested decisions and demonstrating no regard for others (teenage children exempted), they may have psychopathic tendencies.

We can all be small-minded, bigoted and hateful *at times*, but that doesn't put us on the spectrum. So if not you, and not me, then who are these people?!

(Throughout the rest of this chapter, I will use the terms psychopath and almost psychopath interchangeably.)

SO WHO IS WHO? (OR IS IT WHOM?)

The only acceptable clinical and legal diagnosis of psychopathy was created by Dr. Robert Hare in the 1970s and is uncreatively titled Hare's Psychopathy Checklist (PCL). Subsequent revisions to the checklist are known as the... wait for it... the Hare's Psychopathy Checklist-Revised (PCL-R).

It is a psychological assessment tool for trained personnel to use on subjects in a controlled environment. True psychopaths score in the top 25% on the PCL-R. Almost psychopaths score in the middle range, between 25-75%. As noted, studies in the U.S. show that anywhere from 5-15% of the general population would rate as an almost psychopath on the PCL-R. *This means that in any group of 20 people, up to three of the group members may be almost psychopaths.*

Most of us don't have a copy of Hare's PCL nor are qualified to administer it. So given the prevalence of this condition, we need a simpler way of identifying the likelihood that someone falls into this category. The primary characteristics of all psychopaths are that they:

- Are superficially charming and personable
- Lack empathy so they neither understand nor appreciate others' emotions
- Show no true remorse when they hurt others, but may demonstrate remorseful behaviors to evade the consequences of their actions
- Easily transfer blame to others when they are criticized and have an answer for everything
- Have a difficult time expressing their feelings and maintaining lasting relationships
- Avoid responsibility when it suits them to do so
- Lie often, even for trivial and inconsequential reasons
- Expertly manipulate others for their own benefit
- Possess a grandiose sense of self-importance

You were thinking of one or more people in your life before you even finished going through this list, right?

TIMEOUT: Don't just skim the list. Think of specific instances where you recognize these traits in individuals.

When making an objective and dispassionate assessment, if someone meets all or most of the criteria on this list, there is a greater chance they may fall on the spectrum. As with detecting deception, we need to maintain objectivity when trying to make these types of assessments. We aren't looking for a clinical determination; rather, we just want to know whether it is likely that the person we are dealing with falls on this spectrum, and if so, we must change our behavior accordingly.

* * *

Even if we find someone that possesses some or all of these traits, it still does not mean they are clinically psychopathic, as this can be easily mistaken for several other conditions.

Psychopathy is most often confused with Narcissistic Personality Disorder because both share a lack of empathy and entitled sense of self-importance. However, narcissists rarely have a history of antisocial behavior and are less likely to act out maliciously. Additionally, psychopaths generally know they differ from other people and are better able to alter their behavior to conform to the social groups they inhabit. Narcissists believe they think and feel the way others do so they are less willing and able to alter their behavior, even when it is in their best interest.

As mentioned earlier, Histrionic Personality Disorder and Borderline Personality Disorder also share traits with psychopathy (such as manipulative behavior), and may be a more typical manifestation of psychopathy in women. Even if some women meet the criteria for psychopathy, cultural bias might cause psychiatrists to misdiagnose the condition.

Other possibilities include physical trauma, such as brain injury; emotional trauma, like post-traumatic stress disorder (PTSD); other mental illnesses like bipolar disorder; or substance abuse disorders.

* * *

Because our approach is functional, not clinical, it doesn't really matter which condition someone has–NPD, HPD, BPD, psychopathy, etc. If they meet most or all of the criteria above, we need to alter our approach when in their company.

HOW TO DEAL WITH ALMOST PSYCHOPATHS

Because almost psychopaths make up a statistically significant percentage of the population, it is critical to understand how to handle interactions with them. We are not talking about hardened criminals or wildly violent psychopaths, but the more restrained variety whose impulse control allows them to move more skillfully through society. These people may be our neighbors, co-workers, bosses, relatives, friends, family, and lovers.

Awareness is the first key to success. Whenever you feel manipulated or coerced, take a step back and ask yourself if this person normally behaves in this fashion or is it an aberration? What are your instincts telling you? It's difficult when dealing with a psychopath because their manipulation can override your instincts. What, for example, was your initial feeling on your first meeting? Listen to that little voice inside your head regardless of what others think or say. *When you have made a determination that an individual fits the profile outlined above, you must take steps to minimize the control this person has over you.*

What to do

Avoidance. These are difficult people to deal with so if you can cut the cord on the relationship you will be better off. Change your coffee break time, cultivate different social activities. Maintain as much physical and emotional distance as possible. Keep in mind that the quality of the relationship will not improve over time. They will not change and become something they are not. Nor should you.

This is especially true if you are particularly sensitive and empathetic. Psychopaths are drawn to these personality types as they are easiest to manipulate and manage. To the psychopath, relationships are competitions to gain the upper hand while keeping the other person off balance. The more you can avoid this person the less chance they have of wielding control over you.

Sometimes avoidance isn't a realistic option. Maybe they are your boss, or someone even closer to you. If that's the case, you will need to apply different strategies.

Adopt the correct frame of mind. Focus on being in the right mindset instead of obsessing about their behaviors. Remember what drives an almost psychopath. They aren't motivated to help others; instead, they are motivated by having power over people to get what they want—control, money, sex, etc. Even if they do something that appears to be generous or kind hearted, there's a hidden motivation.

Remember, too, that psychopaths are expert manipulators. They can be charming and can quickly get everyone "on their side." They often pit people against one another to achieve some objective, or just for the challenge of doing it. (My mother was the first person I knew that used this as a criteria in evaluating potential long-term employees after a probationary period. If they were divisive and seemed to enjoy disharmony, they were considered ill-suited for the job, even if their work product was satisfactory.)

In romantic contexts, they are often involved in affairs. In the workplace, they make themselves look good in front of the boss, even if it requires sabotaging the efforts of others or throwing other coworkers under the bus. In social circles, they start drama that forces people to take sides, as they attempt to move people like pawns on a chessboard.

When dealing with psychopaths, just know these events will happen, and will happen repeatedly. *You can't control these situations, but you can control how you respond.* Never allow someone to take you out of your game. Don't allow yourself to be thrown off balance by someone who is seeking to exert control by manipulating people and situations. They will try to push your buttons and evoke an emotional response from you. By maintaining your self-control, their game fails and they will quickly become frustrated and move on to an easier target.

Conversational Awareness. It is important to always be on your guard when interacting with a psychopath. Even though you're not in a courtroom, anything you say can, and will, be used against you. Therefore, you must remain hyper-vigilant when conversing. Even casual, social chats are places where a psychopath looks to gain information to use to his advantage. *Especially* casual, social chats.

Instead of letting them steer the conversation, speak up and move the discussion in directions you choose. If you can keep the exchange in comfortable territory, they will have little chance to catch you off guard and unawares. Move the flow of conversation to emotionally neutral topics. If they still try to harass you with insults or disparaging remarks, change the subject, and be prepared to do so as often as necessary to prevent them from gaining the upper hand. Through this process, remember to stay positive and upbeat. If they think they are getting to you, they will be emboldened to continue.

Never share personal information. Don't talk about your likes and dislikes, hobbies, pet peeves, or even your loved ones. Psychopaths will use this information to gain an advantage, even a social advantage. Be wary of even sharing your opinions around them. If you let them know when your feelings are hurt they will be more likely to repeat the behavior or engineer situations so it happens again and again. This advice may be particularly difficult for emotive people that love to share the details of their lives. If someone close to you is on this spectrum, force yourself to hold back from sharing as much as you normally would.

This caution also extends to your ambitions and plans. If a psychopath knows your goals ahead of time, they might use that knowledge to discourage or hinder you. Wait until you have completed your task before sharing the information. If you've decided to quit your current job as soon as you find a suitable replacement, don't mention a word of it until you are actually on your way out the door. Otherwise, they are likely to make things difficult by holding this information over your head, or spilling the beans outright.

Guard not only what you say, but be skeptical about anything they tell you. They aren't only working against you, but against others. Anything said about a person or situation needs to be taken with a very large grain of salt. Remember, too, that psychopaths are highly skilled at pushing people's buttons. Anticipate this and you'll be less likely to be surprised. Stay calm and composed no matter what is said. If they tell you you weren't invited for drinks after work because nobody else wanted you there, get the facts from others first.

Let them know you have nothing they want. Provide no details about your finances, and keep your records secure. Create the impression you have little money and you won't be viewed as a target. Create the impression you are not well connected. If they're after the joy of making people feel uncomfortable, then never let them see you're uncomfortable. They will soon move on.

Direct Approach. If the above strategies do not work, then you may consider a more direct option. This will not work for everyone so consider your options carefully before diving in. It requires a quiet yet confident demeanor to pull off but if you can do it, getting a psychopath to disengage from you is well worth the effort. Do NOT attempt this with a person prone to violence or one that angers easily. This is for the individual of more typical disposition whose lack of empathy allow them to manipulate people and situations without threats of violence.

The idea is to let him know you know what he is doing *and* that it will not work. If he lies, either to you or in a group setting, *call him out on it.* Don't be accusatory and shout out, "you're lying!" Remain dispassionate and just say, "that isn't true because…" and explain yourself as plainly as possible.

If he attempts to antagonize or criticize you, calling him out as with a falsehood would not be appropriate. But there are two strong options. First, just smile wryly right at him with a twinkle in your eye as if to say, "How cute. I know exactly what you're doing and it is never going to work." Don't let any contempt or malice show through on your face, however difficult it might be. This not only lets him know it didn't bother you and was unsuccessful, but everyone else in the group will be made consciously aware of his behavior through your expression. Avoid accusations and keep all conversations light and pleasant. It is not what you say but how you say it that frames whether you will be perceived as hostile by the psychopath. *Being direct does not mean being adversarial.*

Another direct tactic is to use narrative voice. When he says something that begs a response, either alone or in a group, comment on his comment and why he said it. "We shouldn't let Jane handle this one. She'll screw it up, like usual." Here, a direct, narrative response from Jane might be, "Nice… you think by tearing me down in front of others you'll come off looking better?!? I hope it works out for you." The greatest effect is achieved if Janet remains calm, pleasant, and appears almost amused. Or perhaps, "Joe just isn't putting in the effort we need. We're in danger of missing our deadline but I'll make sure things get straightened out," should be met with the response, "Well done! You're trying to get everyone to believe the project is in trouble so that when we deliver on time you can take full credit for 'turning things around.' But, actually, the project is in great shape and as of now, we're right on schedule. But nicely played."

Both simple examples are situations I was caught in and the responses are exactly what I said. Early in my career I was working on a project for the Department of Defense. My direct supervisor at the time exhibited many of the behaviors described in this chapter. In one-on-one conversations he would tell me how well I was doing and how he appreciated all the work I was putting in on the project. In small groups, and even team meetings, he would make derogatory comments about both my work ethic and the quality of work I was producing. Later, I found out he was saying the same things behind my back to anyone that would listen. He never accepted responsibility for anything and enjoyed making others feel bad about their work and themselves.

The responses quoted above were said in a very good-natured way and while they may seem somewhat extreme, came across as less harsh due to the manner in which they were said. You will need to find your own voice and your own comfort level with responses in these types of situations, but highlighting their behavior is a powerful technique if the more passive approach fails to work.

After a few weeks of making sure his these comments were called out via the narrative voice strategy, the problem slowly died down and eventually stopped altogether. He didn't change, but rather decided it was more troublesome to continue attacking me in front of others and moved on to easier prey.

Get Help. For more serious situations, whether violent or just extreme behavior, getting help is your first priority. If you are emotionally susceptible to a psychopath and he is having a negative impact on your life, talk about it with someone who isn't involved. Get professional help from a therapist or psychologist who can help you work through the situation and give you the tools to handle it.

Someone specializing in these disorders can help you understand how the psychopath manipulates you. This allows you to see the relationship for what it is, which breaks his power over you and his control is minimized. Everything becomes easier when you understand the motivations and tactics of the psychopath.

Predatory psychopaths convince their victims the situation is their fault and they need to try harder to work things out alone. This tactic is particularly effective when the victim is isolated from family and friends. If you, or someone you know, is trapped in this situation, getting professional help is vital to move forward.

Help means more than just speaking with mental health professionals. Friends, family and colleagues are a terrific source of help. In the workplace, if you feel the person is trying to undermine you, it's important to collect evidence. As psychopaths are often popular, it may be difficult to get others to believe you unless you have proof. Save emails and texts that corroborate your side of the story. When you have sufficient evidence, take it to your boss, or to human resources, or any other party tasked with handling these types of grievances.

WHAT NOT TO DO

Do not try to "fix" them. Studies show that therapy, medication, incarceration, threats, pleas or trying to "teach empathy" are all failing strategies. These attempts only frustrate both parties and waste time. You cannot cure a psychopath and you cannot make them a better person. Even a commonsense notion like explaining how and why their actions cause others pain is a strategy doomed to fail.

Do not become indebted. Psychopaths gain power through situations that puts you in their debt. Do nothing that could be used to control your behavior. Borrowing money, accepting gifts or favors, or even an offer to help you out of some situation all create a social imbalance that a psychopath will exploit to get what they want.

Do not confront them. Don't accuse them of being a psychopath. Any accusations of wrongdoing at all will become mired in negative feelings and could end in a heated exchange. You stand to lose more than they do, so don't do it.

Do not issue demands. Ultimatums and threats are other types of confrontations to avoid. The psychopath sees these power plays as games. They will work to gain the upper hand which will sharpen their skills to more easily prey on others. Resist the urge to engage in any kind of mind games with a psychopath. Don't try to out think them. Focus on yourself.

*   *   *

As your awareness of these personality types grows, you'll have an easier time spotting who they are and how they are trying to manipulate people. Armed with this knowledge, you'll be ready to both avoid them and counter their attempts at taking control. As a result, you will feel less anxiety and uncertainty when you find yourself around them.

WHISPER ALERT: Identify the 1%: Red light! -- Suspect the 5%-15%: Yellow light! -- Interacting with the rest: Green light!

This chapter only appears to be a detour, but it is imperative you have some understanding of these clinical personalities in order to recognize and deal with them. Without this knowledge, you risk being ensnared in their trap. Your goal is to become a Human Whisperer, not a victim!

*   *   *

FORGET-ME-NOTS

- <u>All</u> psychopaths have profound lack of regard for others and will ignore social, legal and moral standards if they deem it in their best interest. <u>Successful</u> psychopaths (sociopaths) possess greater impulse control, are better able to plan long term, and rarely operate outside the law.
- "Almost psychopaths" (5-15% of the population) are often high achievers and they are always master manipulators. They exhibit the same behaviors as true psychopaths, although less extreme and/or less frequent.
- Options when dealing with psychopaths: politely avoid, adopt an unruffled frame of mind, never over-divulge, occasionally employ the direct approach, and above all else, **seek help**.

*   *   *

So far, we've taken a long look at how to both read and connect with people. That's all well and good, but the mark of every great Whisperer is how well you can utilize the tools of persuasion. The remainder of the book is dedicated to exactly that.

9

Dipping a toe into the pool of persuasion

There are myriad books on the subject of persuasion and influence written to turn us into master persuaders. Alas, the techniques go unused and the books are relegated to a prominent place on our bookshelf, so we can proudly *suggest* to visitors, without directly boasting, that we have skills to be envied! We succeeded in reading all 300 pages, but beyond that, our ability to persuade remains unchanged. Some of the strategies may have even been tested and found not to work consistently or even at all.

Failure is common because these books treat the topic of persuasion as a single concept. Generic strategies are plugged in without regard to context. One well-worn strategy is to become "more likeable." While good advice, this doesn't help us with our friends, most of whom should already like us well enough! Other advice to create deeper bonds and emotional connections doesn't help us with the person behind the customer service counter refusing us a return without the receipt.

Different situations require different strategies. It's best to think about the end goal before figuring out which specific strategies to use in pursuit of that goal. Persuasion typically has one of the following end goals:

- Get someone to grant you a favor (self-interested persuasion)
- Influence a longer lasting decision that does ***not*** benefit you directly
- Change someone's mindset

Each of these will be discussed in turn.

The starting point is to have a clear idea about what you're trying to accomplish. Too often, we shoehorn one persuasive technique for the wrong task. We need different tools to cover a wide variety of situations. If we rely on just a single technique without understanding why and when it should be applied, we exemplify Abraham Maslow's wisdom: "When all you have is a hammer, everything looks like a nail."

We need to tackle some basic questions before moving into specifics. First, we need to think about whether or not this is even ethical. Is it right to exert influence over someone else's thoughts and actions? Second, we need to understand the two fundamental means by which people make decisions.

THE ETHICS OF PERSUASION

"You are here to make a difference, to either improve the world or worsen it. And whether or not you consciously choose to, you will accomplish one or the other."

--RICHELLE E. GOODRICH

Influence. Persuasion. Manipulation. Deception. No two people understand these concepts in exactly the same way. Some feel they are synonymous as all create involvement in the lives of others. Some focus on how each word carries subtle shades of different meaning. Some feel that while one concept is acceptable, others are terrible actions to be avoided at all costs. Just because you *can* learn to exert influence, persuade, manipulate and/or deceive doesn't necessarily mean you *should*. Which prompts the question, "Is engaging in this type of behavior ethically defensible?" Well... yes!

We influence each other every second of every day. Every conversation persuades someone of something. Opinions are being altered about either the subject matter or the speaker. Even if the revelation is something as simple as, "I really don't enjoy this conversation!"

The nature of this influence is often hidden because we aren't consciously aware of the psychology and motivation behind why people do what they do. You exercise persuasive behaviors even if you are unaware of it. Most of you already use some of the techniques in this very book. By stepping back and taking a closer look at what works and why, you're refining strategies you already use. The act of *consciously* using these techniques doesn't magically render them unethical. It just makes them far more effective.

Some techniques, however, clearly cross the ethical boundary. There is a difference between persuasion and manipulation, between influence and deception. While the location of that boundary may vary from person to person, there are some techniques that would (almost) universally be considered over the line:

- Lying: misrepresenting the truth to achieve your objective
- Lie of omission: leaving out some, or most, of the truth
- Intimidation: using subtle or overt threats that may be psychological or even physical

- "Guilt trip": telling the victim they are selfish, have it too easy, or don't care enough about others to exact the desired behavior
- Shaming: using sarcasm and insults to damage self-esteem creating feelings of inadequacy
- Hostility: falsely accusing someone who stands up for themselves as being an instigator of problems

These are just a few tools of manipulators. These aren't the kinds of techniques you will find here. Our focus is on the use of non-manipulative ideas proven to be successful. Of course, you may feel that a certain strategy crosses the line of what you feel is ethical. In that case, listen to your conscience and don't use anything you feel is inappropriate.

* * *

Throughout the next few chapters you will hear the terms "subject" and "target" used to describe the people on whom we are using persuasive techniques. For some, this may connote the idea they are "marks" to swindle or hustle. This is *not* what is meant. It is simply a shorthand way to differentiate between the *persuader* and the *persuadee*.

HOW PEOPLE DECIDE

> "Today, if you are not confused, you are not thinking clearly."
>
> --IRENE PETER

Before discussing specific techniques, it's important to understand *how* people make decisions. In simplest terms, we either use our higher order brain processes (remember our executive functions?) to analyze competing data and reach a conclusion, **OR,** similarly to how our limbic system processes our response to danger, we put ourselves on autopilot and make a snap judgment.

HEURISTIC VS. SYSTEMATIC PROCESSING

In the study of animal behavior, the phrase *fixed action patterns* describes an instinctive response to a given stimulus and is normally used in connection with lower order species (mammalian brain). Once an animal experiences the triggering stimulus it will engage in the automatic response.

The behavior of turkeys provide a clear example of this. When a turkey mother hears the chirping of her chicks she gathers them under her for warmth and protection.

In one experiment, a stuffed polecat, which is a natural enemy of the turkey, was fitted with a tape recorder to play the chirping sound of a turkey chick. When the mother heard this sound, her fixed action pattern was fired and she gathered the polecat under her, disregarding the sight, touch and smell of the imposter, and treated it as one of her own offspring. As soon as the sound was turned off, she attacked the polecat realizing it was an intruder (Fox).

At first blush, it seems like ridiculous behavior but remember that in nature this instinctive behavior would always achieve the desired result–protecting the offspring from would-be predators. Immediacy is crucial. Instead of taking the time to smell, feel, see and hear a chick every time it makes a sound, the fixed action pattern allows the turkey to immediately react to the sound of the stimulus trigger.

Human beings, with our superior intellect and higher functioning brains, are not immune to our own version of fixed action patterns. The only notable difference is that most of our behaviors are learned rather than inborn.

*   *   *

In the modern era, we are assaulted by a never-ending stream of stimuli. Technology plays the largest part with televisions, phones, and computers all competing for our time and attention. All of these devices let us access email, text, social media, online shopping, online banking, well... online *everything*.

Technology is not the only demand on our time. The requirements of our families and jobs are broader than they've ever been. Not that this generation works *harder*, but we're asked to perform a *wider variety* of tasks than ever before. All these demands put us in a state of *continuous partial attention* where no one thing has 100% of our focus.

No one has the time or energy to thoughtfully and critically examine every decision made in the course of a day. Instead, we rely on mental shortcuts (think of them as "rules of thumb") to help us navigate our rapidly moving and complex surroundings.

These shortcuts are our fixed action patterns. Just like the turkey mother, we respond automatically to specific stimuli. Understanding and exploiting these stimuli allow us to fashion more effective ways to influence others.

In a now famous experiment, people in line to make copies were approached by a potential line cutter and asked, "Excuse me, may I use the Xerox machine?" Only 60% complied with the request. The request was then changed to include a legitimate reason for cutting the line. This time people were asked, "Excuse me, may I use the Xerox machine <u>because I'm in a rush</u>?" Now the rate of compliance shot up to 94%. This makes sense as people with a genuine need to cut the line would be allowed to do so. (The other 6% were no doubt in a rush as well!) So far, so good.

The amazing part is that when changing to a nonsense reason like, "Excuse me, may I use the Xerox machine *because I have to make copies?*" the compliance rate remained virtually unchanged at 93%. There is no legitimate reasoning here. Of course you have to make copies; everyone in line has to make copies! It was the use of the magical word *because* that created an automated response to assume the reason given would be a valid one. *Once we hear the word "because" we stop listening to the rest of the sentence and grant the request without thinking* (Langer).

These mental shortcuts to reach quick, automatic decisions are called *heuristics*.

This is how we make *most* of our decisions. As in the animal world, we do this because it works *in a vast majority of cases*. If we can expend little or no brain power on dozens or hundreds of small decisions a day and only get a couple of them wrong, these are odds we can live with. (So next time you're late to work instead of saying, "Sorry I'm late!" try this, "Sorry I'm late, but there was a situation and I'm late *because* of it!")

The most important book on this subject is <u>Influence: The Psychology of Persuasion</u> written by Robert Cialdini in 1984. He discusses this from the perspective of advertisers, salesmen and anyone whose job it is to persuade you to give up your time and money. He labels these people "compliance professionals" and exposes their tactics by explaining the ways in which they take advantage of heuristic thinking. Most of the book focuses on how retailers and mass marketing can affect us in surprising and unrecognizable ways. His hope is that by acquiring this knowledge we will be better prepared to ward off attempts by the less-than-reputable to be unduly influenced. (And of course, he popularized the "turkey experiment" making it a classic example of the fixed action pattern phenomenon.)

*   *   *

Systematic processing, by contrast, is the critical analysis of information that requires focus and concentration, and for that reason is used less often and is reserved for bigger decisions. The more decisions we can make heuristically, the more mental cycles we can devote to analyzing life goals, how to reach them, big purchases, and vacation plans, all of which require more detailed thought.

Since Whispering is practiced primarily one-on-one, we are going to adapt

Heuristics represent the shortest point from A to B. Systematic processing is a LOT more work.

these, and other, concepts to work in casual conversations instead of focusing on mass media and sales tactics. By leveraging this information, it is possible to persuade others both systematically and heuristically in subtle ways that do not appear heavy handed.

TIMEOUT: How many heuristic decisions can I identify in my personal, social and professional life?

ACTIVATING HEURISTIC THINKING IN OTHERS

Many of these strategies to influence others require the use of heuristic responses. Fortunately, most people's default response is to rely on heuristics, but there are ways of reliably placing people in this mode of thought.

Mood. Not only are people in a good mood more likely to comply with a request in general, but are also less likely to critically evaluate a message (Bless). People in a bad mood tend to remain skeptical of any message and tend only to be swayed by the strongest and most convincing arguments (Kuykendall). Make sure you wait until your subject is in a good mood before making any request. Otherwise, you run a greater chance of refusal.

Arousal. People in a state of arousal are also more likely to rely on heuristic processing. A scary movie may arouse fear, for example. In one study, people induced to arousal via exercise were more influenced by celebrity endorsements, which is a heuristic we use to identify quality (Sanbonmatsu). If you need to ask someone a favor, wait until they've just had a great workout, returned from the gun range, a scenic hike, or any passion they have that will induce a state of arousal *and* put them in a good mood. Chances are high that by linking the two criteria (arousal and mood) they will *not* systematically examine the request.

Complexity. Conventional sales wisdom says keep your message simple. But there is a time where you want to create a message that is a little harder to analyze. By making the message a little more difficult to follow, you decrease the motivation and ability of someone to critically evaluate the message. Therefore, they stop trying to analyze and shift into heuristic thinking to make a decision.

This was demonstrated in an experiment where gourmet cheese was sold using a difficult-to-read font. This made it harder to analyze the product, but since a pleasing aesthetic was predominate it became a better seller. People relied on the visuals and packaging to determine whether the product was worth buying (Pocheptsova). If the message is too complex, however, you run the risk of someone shutting down entirely (or heightening their suspicious nature) and heuristically denying the request without any thought at all.

That's fine for sales in the grocery aisle, but how can we leverage the complexity principle in real life when speaking to someone? A great way to change the thought process of a person is to use a technique behavioral psychologists call a *pattern interrupt*. This is something designed to break someone out of their current mode of thinking. In the case of phrases, you get the person to expend mental cycles on the question and temporarily interrupt their thoughts. It needs to sound as though it belongs in the conversation and not an attempt to radically change the subject. If someone is complaining about their day, you can't just pop out with, "I like Mickey Mouse… do you?"

You need to ask a question complex enough to force them to think about the answer, which not only gives you time to compose your thoughts, but also gives you a chance to respond with comments designed to further get them thinking heuristically. A few quick examples are:

- "Why aren't you telling me what you thought you knew?"
- "Are you unaware of what you haven't forgotten?"
- "How can you agree with ideas you haven't heard?"
- "Can you visualize these misremembered ideas?"

In each case, it will cause a brief dead zone in the conversation while they're processing the question, giving you time to redirect the speaker. <u>Make sure you continue speaking before they're able to completely analyze the question</u>. They need to be nudged onward in the conversation and if they're unable to fully process your pattern interrupt statement they are far more likely to move back into heuristic thinking.

The most difficult part of using pattern interrupt statements is finding phrases that correspond to how you naturally speak. For some, one of the above examples may fit your natural speech patterns. Others may have to come up with a different phrase that doesn't sound out of place but still achieves the intended effect. Work at inventing a phrase (or rewording one of the above examples) to more naturally reflect how *you* speak.

Whisper Alert: Pattern interrupts help maintain the target's heuristic thinking.

Pattern interrupts can be other than phrases. Snapping one's fingers, making an odd sound, slapping your leg, all of these things immediately grab your target's attention. Those precious moments have interrupted their existing pattern of thought, which you can use to redirect them to *your* thought process.

TIMEOUT: Where and when would I need to create heuristic thinking in others?

ACTIVATING SYSTEMATIC THINKING IN OTHERS

At other times, you may want someone to critically analyze information to arrive at a meaningful decision. If they are on autopilot (thinking heuristically) you need to get their attention in ways that cause them to focus on the information. Let's say you work for a company trying to sell goods and services to another company. That person might be heuristically denying your request, just reflexively saying "no." How can you move them to into another mode of thinking?

Caffeine. Research shows that caffeine enhances systematic processing. In one study, a group of students, all opposed to voluntary euthanasia, were exposed to compelling arguments supporting it. Those consuming caffeinated drinks were more persuaded by the arguments because they were more thoroughly examining the issues via systematic processing (Martin). The lesson here is if you want to convince someone through the power of argument take them to Starbucks first, or buy them a soda. It won't guarantee success, but they will be more likely to seriously think about and consider your line of reasoning.

Pique technique. Making an unusual request, or making a request in an unusual way forces people into a systematic evaluation by piquing their interest and curiosity. In a study where panhandlers asked passersby for 25¢, 37¢, 42¢, or "any spare change" found that the unusual requests (37¢ and 42¢) yielded a higher rate of compliance. People expected requests for a quarter or for any spare change, but the odd request forced people out of heuristically denying the request and into a true evaluation of the request itself (Santos).

Other experiments have validated this finding that when people experience an unusual request it short-circuits their heuristics and forces them to think about the request more closely. Therefore, if you want someone to really evaluate a request, find a means of presenting it in an unusual way.

Rhetorical questions. Asking rhetorical questions throughout a conversation impacts your persuasiveness by subtly encouraging them to think about the answers to the question. Transform a statement into a rhetorical question by prefacing it with a statement like, "Doesn't it seem to you like…" or "Wouldn't you agree that…" This technique will have them asking themselves, "*why* does it seem to me" or "*why* would I agree" and add a level of gravity to make a correct analysis. To ensure it is received as a rhetorical question and not an invitation for debate, don't ask it as a question. The emphasis should be on the subsequent point:

"Wouldn't you agree that the new contract proposal is essentially identical to the old one. (no pause) For one thing, the project scope remains unchanged. For another thing…"

A quick note of caution here. Arguments on topics of **high personal relevance** to the listener are *less* effective when using rhetorical questions, as they are already motivated to process the information systematically. Therefore, only use this technique when the subject matter is of low personal relevance to the listener and you want them to think systemically (Petty).

* * *

Depending on your goals, decide how you want your request to be processed so you can use the correct techniques to enhance your influence. Too often, expert advice on persuasion doesn't factor the listener's method of evaluation into the equation. Using a heuristic technique with someone who should be thinking systematically is likely to fail, and vice-versa. This may cause you to wrongfully conclude that the technique in question doesn't work.

Motivational direction

Besides the need for a subject to be guided into either heuristic or systematic thinking, another overlooked factor is *how* people are motivated to act and make decisions. Aside from deciding in their best interest, an individual's motivation is also either *toward* what they want or *away* from what they don't want. "Toward motivation" is goal-oriented while "away from motivation" is focused on identifying problems and finding solutions. Stated another way, *toward motivated people* are seeking what they want, while *away from motivated people* are avoiding what they don't want.

While everyone is influenced by both factors (think of "the carrot and the stick"), and while a specific issue may create only a temporary shift in motivational direction, we all tend to be pulled more strongly in one direction or the other.

Managers are taught to figure out each employee's motivational direction and incentivize them accordingly. Toward motivators want to get somewhere–to a better pay rate, a better job title, greater benefits, or just more recognition. Away from motivators seek escape from overbearing oversight, fewer demands on their time so they can focus on the problem(s) at hand with less stress and anxiety. Misapplied incentives due to ignorance of an employee's motivational direction result in frustration for the employee and management. So it's important to understand the concept *and* how to apply it.

Advertisers use specific words to engage both types of people. Words like: *fun, enjoyable, pleasant, entertaining* entice toward motivators. Words like: *security, peace of mind,* and *stress-free* trigger the away from motivators.

If you were selling a car and needed to appeal to an away from motivator, you might say, "Buying this car will allow you to *avoid* expensive maintenance and the headaches of all-too-common repairs." The emphasis is moving away from the undesired effects of repair. By contrast, the toward motivator might be enticed by saying, "Buying this car brings you not only the admiration of people who can appreciate a high performance vehicle like this, but also gives you the most luxurious car you will ever own." Here the emphasis is on moving toward admiration, respect and luxury.

In business settings, if you're trying to sell goods or services, you can focus on *avoiding* cost overruns and lost productivity –OR– you can explain how your offerings can help them *achieve* both their short-term and long-term goals.

A quick test to determine in which direction a person's motivation lies is to use the magic word "freedom." It's a neutral word that allows for either type of answer. Ask someone the question, "If you had complete *freedom*, what would you do?" Then listen to the *first* thing they say. Most people will give several answers that include both toward and away from motivators, but it's the *first answer* that is the most telling. If the first thing they say is, "I'd quit my lousy job" or "I'd move out of my apartment" their motivation direction is away. If, however, their instinctive response is something like, "I'd move to a tropical paradise," that indicates a toward direction.

Whisper Alert: Ask the "freedom" question to confirm motivational direction.

Keeping the concepts of heuristics and motivation in mind, let's finally open up the toolbox and take a look at some persuasive techniques in action. But remember, the persuasive tool you use depends on your objectives:

Favors are the easiest to understand and are a perfect place to begin filling our toolbox. Sometimes favors are requested of people we know and sometimes not. How we approach a friend to ask for a ride to the airport, or God forbid, to help us move, requires different strategies than dealing with an office supply store cashier that won't accept our coupons. What these requests have in common is that they are things we need someone to do *for us*. It normally involves just a single action on their part and the favor is paid.

Decision making differs from favors (and is more difficult to achieve) as it requires a more lasting change and is presumptively for the decision maker's benefit. Sales and marketing professionals spend most of their energy on this sphere of influence, trying to get people to buy the goods and services they are hawking. When we work to get a family member to exercise more or get a colleague to take a more active involvement in a project, we are trying to affect the decision making process.

Changing a mindset is the most difficult form of persuasion as it requires a person to see the world at least a little differently than they did before. The upside is that, if successful, it will naturally affect their behaviors in positive ways consistent with this new mindset. These new thoughts don't need to be antithetical to what they currently believe, nor do they require a radical new outlook. Even the most subtle of changes in outlook can yield dramatic changes in behavior.

*   *   *

FORGET-ME-NOTS

- True persuasion does not mean acting unethically or manipulatively.
- Heuristics are shortcuts to simplify the decision-making process. Most influential techniques operate at this level.
- The persuasive tools you will use depend on your *objective:* getting favors, altering decisions, or changing mindsets.

*   *   *

10

Can you do me a favor?

"Most people return small favors, acknowledge medium ones and repay greater ones with ingratitude."

--BENJAMIN FRANKLIN

The simplest form of persuasion involves getting someone to do something for you. A simple task, performed once and the favor is paid–whether asking someone to pass the butter, asking a coworker to help us out on a project, or appealing to our spouse to remain pleasant when the mother-in-law pops in for a visit. The situation, the current emotional state of the target, how well the parties know one another, and the size of the favor, are all elements contributing to the likelihood of the request being granted.

We noted in chapter 4 that children ask far more questions than adults (75-20%, on average). The majority of their questions focus on learning about the world around them and uncovering some mystery of life, such as, "What does Santa smell like?" or "Why were curse words invented if we aren't allowed to use them?"

Adults' questions, by contrast, are disproportionately focused on asking others to do things for them. We do it so often we don't realize how much of our conversation consists of asking for something. To increase our chances of success when asking for a favor, let's start with some general ideas before ramping up to the bigger strategies.

SIMPLE STRATEGIES

A few guiding principles at the outset will help you achieve your goal:

Mood. Just as we learned a good mood increases the likelihood of heuristic thinking, someone in a good mood is more likely to do something for you than someone in a bad mood. (By now you're probably thinking, "No way! Really?!? What a fantastic bit of insight!") Where possible, wait until someone is in a good mood before asking a favor–after a good meal or when they're coming back from a fun activity is a great time to hit someone up.

Unfortunately we aren't always in a situation where we can wait for someone's mood to adjust. All hope is not lost. Insist they will *feel good* about your request and that it *won't take too much effort* on their part. If possible, remind them of a time when it made them happy to be able to help someone else out. This has a twofold effect: first, it offers the promise of improving their mood if they help someone out again. Second, it supports the notion that they are the type of person that helps others out, so they are more likely to try to live up to that self-reinforcing belief.

Suppose you need to ask a co-worker to switch shifts. They are not in a good mood but you know you won't see them again until it's too late to ask for the switch. Here is one way to make the request:

"Nancy, do you remember when you swapped shifts with Simon last month so he could attend his friend's wedding? He was so grateful for your help. When you covered his shift we were all smiling and laughing about how ridiculous he would look in a suit. We probably had a better time than he did! I am hoping you will be able to extend your generosity and kindness again. I'm going out of town next week and need to swap shifts. If you can make it work with your schedule I'd be grateful. To make it easier on you, I will offer any of my days off to cover your shift. Can you do it?"

This request lets them know they will enjoy the good opinion of others by helping out, it won't be too big a deal, and you really appreciate their assistance, all of which make compliance more likely.

"The Last Option." If someone thinks you have several options in getting assistance, their own sense of responsibility is reduced. Make sure they know you have no one else who can help. By making that clear, they will feel an increased pressure to comply with your request.

(This principle is further discussed through *diffusion of responsibility* in the next chapter, where the greater number of bystanders means a person with a medical emergency is *less* likely to get help. Everyone assumes that someone else will be responsible for getting help so they don't have to worry about it and no one calls 911. You are more likely to be rescued if there are only one or two other people present! The same principle is at work when they know they are the last option.)

Responsibility. We learned in chapter 4 that the homeless engender the least amount of empathy of any group because of a pervasive assumption that many homeless people are victims of their own poor decisions. It is therefore easy to imagine a situation where someone steps over a homeless person to get to an injured dog or cat. "Awww, the poor dog never hurt anyone, but the homeless guy drank himself into the gutter." Empathy takes a nosedive when there is a belief that the person needlessly created a difficult situation.

If the subject feels the situation was not of your doing, the chances of compliance with your request rise dramatically. Don't let them think that you "got yourself into this mess" because their desire to help you will diminish. This isn't to suggest you should lie, but where possible, stress how this situation came about due to factors beyond your control.

Us vs. Me. Instead of framing a request as a matter of *you* helping *me*, make it about *us*. If you are asking someone to man the phones for a benefit concert, don't say, "Can **you** help **me** fill my quota to man the phones?" Instead, make it about *us*, "Can you join **us** in the fight against pediatric cancer by manning a station during the benefit show?" It's not about them doing you a favor anymore, it's about becoming part of something bigger. Not every favor can be framed in such a manner, but wherever possible, use it because this idea is strongly correlated with a successful request. (This request could improve their self-esteem by doing charitable work and possibly be reinforced with the "last option" principle to increase a favorable answer.)

Timing. When the event is farther in the future, the more likely the subject will comply with your request. Waiting until the 11th hour to ask someone to do something *you knew about in advance* makes it even less likely you will gain their compliance. A last minute request makes people feel that you're "putting them on the spot," which creates a negative impression. For many people in this situation, they will just say "no" as their automatic response when feeling pressured by time or circumstance. The bigger the favor, the farther in the future it should be requested.

*   *   *

Use more than one of these strategies in a single request to increase your chances even more. Construct a request that naturally accounts for more than one of these ideas. For example, right before someone goes on a week-long vacation, ask them to work extra hours when they get back. In this made-up scenario, let's pretend the extra work is to account for recent layoffs. This accounts for mood (since you asked right before they leave on vacation they will be in a pleasant frame of mind) and timing (since they are going on a long vacation, the request is far enough in the future so as not to generate any unnecessary pressure). And as I'm the one making up this story, let's just say they agreed to do the work! See how easy it is?

TIMEOUT: List some scenarios applicable to requests you might make.

Please like me!

> *"And I can't deny the fact that you like me right now. You like me!"*

--SALLY FIELD

People are most likely to agree to a request if they know and like the person. This is why you have little difficulty in getting your friends to do you a favor (assuming your friends both know *and* like you). It is more difficult dealing with people you do *not* know, or do not know well. They don't know how wonderful you are or what obstacles you have overcome, and at this point, they don't care. In these cases, all you have going for you is "likeability potential".

Didn't we already discuss how to be likeable in chapter 2 with power, warmth and presence? No, because charisma is not the same as likeability. A *charismatic person* has "magnetic" charm that inspires devotion and attracts others to their beliefs, and is one of the most powerful tools of the Human Whisperer. A *likeable* person is easy to talk to and enjoyable to spend time with, but they don't necessarily inspire awe or confidence. The most successful

Being well-liked means more than getting online feedback!

whisperers are both charismatic *and* likeable but it is certainly possible to have one without the other. While Donald Trump certainly exudes an authoritative charisma that many find compelling, few would accuse him of being overly likeable. Michelle Obama, by contrast, is engaging, well liked and passionate, but she doesn't inspire that same level of charismatic devotion. So in addition to being charismatic, you also must work on being likeable.

As with charisma, it is important to remember these strategies aren't to be "turned on" only when you need something. You need to *be* likeable as your default so eventually you can exhibit likeable traits without conscious thought. Being a genuinely likeable person has far ranging benefits above getting preferential treatment or getting someone to do you a favor. Likeability creates goodwill where perhaps none existed, allows people to feel good about you and themselves, and sets up an environment where people will always welcome and enjoy your contribution to the conversation.

Our toolbox must contain both long-term and short-term likeability strategies. Long-term strategies are best used for people in our lives that we are going to see often, or at least on a semi-routine basis. Short-term strategies are reserved for people that we will only see once (or very infrequently), like a hotel desk clerk, someone in the returns department, or a distant friend-of-a-friend.

Long-term likeability strategies

It is important to be likeable not only for new people we meet, but for our old friends that deserve the best "you" you can give them. Make a concerted effort to be more agreeable and pleasant. Even old friends can tire of self-absorbed behavior and may eventually prefer to spend less time in your company. Some of you may be thinking, "Well, that's just not me. My friends love (or accept) the fact that I'm a disagreeable SOB. I apologize for nothing and that's just the way it is." If that's you, save yourself a little time and skip to the next section. The rest of you, read on.

Warmth. Friendlier, warmer people are seen as more likeable. Think of the strategies in chapter 2 directly related to increasing your warmth: smiling, eye contact, and speaking strategies. By adding these behaviors to your baseline, you can become more likeable right away. Turn up those warmth-related attributes; and if necessary, turn down the traits related to power.

Frequent, positive exposure. The old adage "familiarity breeds contempt" isn't true (unless you're the guy described above). The *more* time you spend with someone, the more they will like you. Some people think that to be liked, you shouldn't "wear out your welcome," but studies have shown that we are most attracted to the familiar (which doesn't mean suffocating others). Set up opportunities and situations to spend time with the people you would like to befriend. It doesn't need to be an all-day affair, even a few shared minutes can have an impact.

Exposure to others shouldn't only be *frequent*, but *positive*. As much as possible, ensure you are associated with positive feelings. A simple rule of thumb is not to be the bearer of bad news. (We all know someone who will call immediately with bad news but the good news is never urgent.) People feel they can separate the message from the messenger, but frequent association between you and negative emotions creates an uncontrollable, subconscious link. Better to talk to people when they are in a good mood; or better yet, when you are in a situation to put them in a good mood with a well-timed joke, funny anecdote or just good news. The good feelings they have when you are around become associated with you. If every time you are around they are happy and in a good mood, they will seek out your company.

Follow this simple rule: leave everyone in a better mood than you found them. Choose your greeting: "Your smile brightens my day!" vs. "Looks like a bad hair day for us!" While conversing, you don't need to be a master story teller (or even very funny). Most people's mood improves if they feel heard, so just through the act of listening you can engender positive feelings. Let them know you understand what they're saying without offering advice reflexively. Even if it goes consciously unnoticed, over time people will come to associate your presence as positive and enjoyable.

Reciprocal affection. *How someone feels about you rests on how you make them feel about themselves.* This seems to be common sense but it's amazing how many people behave as if this is a foreign concept. Many attempts at achieving this rest on compliments that can come across as insincere; or worse yet, only given due to an ulterior motive. <u>*Reverse*</u>

You won't believe this but she is the nicest person you'll ever meet!

<u>*Gossip*</u> is a way of expressing those thoughts without coming across as fake, creepy, or disingenuous. This is where you talk behind someone's back, but only say positive, uplifting things. It will feel unusual at first since this is not the norm when talking behind someone's back.

The nice thing about reverse gossip is that, just as with regular gossip, your comments *will* make their way back to the subject. It may not happen immediately, but it will happen. When they hear what you were saying *to other people* about their hard

work, sincerity, sense of humor, or other *genuine* compliment, it has far greater impact than if it were said directly.

Once you see how strongly this concept works, you will want use it as often as you can! Make reverse gossip your default way of talking about others, and you'll **never** have to worry if something you said will get back to the person. In fact, you'll be hoping it does! Additionally, people to whom you are gossiping will see you in a more positive light as well. If you develop a reputation as the person that says good things about others, it makes you more likeable even with people you haven't gossiped to or about.

The downside to reverse gossip is that there is a delay between the time the compliment is given and the time it is received by the target. A more direct, yet still subtle, strategy is to use a <u>*third-party compliment*</u>. This is when you make a complimentary statement to a third party about the subject, but do it while in their presence. It may be as simple as, "Jennifer, don't you love Angie's earrings? They're gorgeous!" You're aren't addressing Angie directly, you are telling Jennifer how much you like them. It seems a small thing, but it comes across as more genuine and spontaneous. Another example might be, "Bill, you didn't tell me Eddie was so funny!" This is a more natural way to give Eddie a compliment without turning to him and saying, "Hey Eddie... you're funny, man."

No matter what techniques you use to get the word out, once a person is aware that you like and admire them, those feelings will naturally be reciprocated by the other party. <u>*People like people who like them.*</u> It's an unavoidable heuristic response. Once someone has decided you are worthy of their friendship and goodwill, getting a favor is only a matter of asking.

TIMEOUT: Which long term strategies do I presently use? Which long term strategies should I employ and how might I implement them?

Short-term likeability strategies

Often we are in situations with people we've just met and won't be seeing again. The previous strategies won't work because they require time to take root. For these situations, use these short-term strategies which produce more immediate results, increasing the chance a request will be granted.

Similarity. We find people more likeable if they resemble us in appearance, thoughts, or interests. Similarities in physical features, like a similar height or body type, require no comment as they are self-evident. Whether your target is wearing a suit or jeans, where possible, you should mirror their relative level of dress. It creates the unconscious feeling that "this person is like me." Any similarity, no matter how inconsequential, can boost your connection with the target and increase your likeability.

The nature of the similarity doesn't need to relate in any way to the favor requested, you just need to have *some* connection with the other person. For it to be most effective, however, the similarity should be *rare* rather than *common*. "Do you like pizza?... Me too!" While that demonstrates a similarity, the ubiquity of that preference doesn't move the needle in terms of likeability. So look for similarities that are distinct, unique and unusual. "Wait a second, you collect antique fingernail clippers?...Me too!" Whether they be common interests or viewpoints, it is these things that create a bond between people that generate rapport and feelings of kinship.

Two groups of test subjects were told they had fingerprint features in common with someone else in the group (a plant by the experiment team.) After the experiment, the plant asked the subjects if they would read an eight-page essay and write up a one-page critique. The first group was told that the fingerprint features they shared were *common*, and those subjects complied with the request 55% of the time. The second group was told the fingerprint features they shared were *rare*, and those test subjects complied at a rate of 82%! The rarity of the fingerprints (which is an inconsequential similarity) resulted in a compliance increase of nearly 30% (Epley & Whitchurch). So find a hobby, point of view, or topic of interest you both share, and <u>the more unusual the better</u>.

Helping. Many people believe the best way to become liked is to do something nice or helpful for your subject. This may work to some degree, but the reverse is even more effective - get *them* to help *you*!.

To understand why, think about what happens when we hurt someone, physically or emotionally. It turns out we are driven to *dislike* that person! Our brains are in a constant battle to maintain cognitive harmony between our thoughts and actions as we learned in chapters 2 and 3. Remember how your conscious body language can alter your thoughts? Likewise, the act of hurting someone causes your brain to go through a similar thought process, "This person was hurt by me. If I hurt a good person, even by accident, that makes me a bad person. Since I know I'm not a bad person, this person must not be as good as I thought." With this logic, your brain is able to make sense of your actions.

The process works in reverse for the same reason. We like a person *more* after doing something for them. Your brain concludes that you would only be helpful to a person that was deserving, therefore if you help a person, in whatever capacity, you unconsciously conclude that this is a good person worthy of your energy and assistance. Let's apply this from the perspective of the subject.

To get someone to like you more, get *them* to do something for *you*. It can start out small, "Can you hand me that pen?", "What time is it?", "Do you know a good place to eat around here?" *Anything* that puts them in the frame of mind of helping you creates a sense of goodwill toward you which can be used to ask for a larger favor.

It is widely assumed this "foot-in-the-door" technique works because you are conditioning the person to comply with your requests, but this is only partly correct. More significantly, with each thing they do for you, *you* become a person of greater esteem to them. This process happens outside conscious realization of the subject, making it both subtle and highly effective.

Self-deprecation. The most likeable people are ones that can do something embarrassing and laugh at themselves about it. By ignoring the faux pas you create a tension that is easily diffused by acknowledging the situation and smiling (or laughing) your way through it. Only a person that is confident in themselves can laugh at their mistakes without fear of appearing vulnerable. It not only keeps things breezy, but it humanizes you, making you more likeable.

You don't need to wait for a mistake to show your humanity. Feel free to drop an occasional, light comment about something you aren't good at. In the course of a conversation, you might say, "my organizational skills are horrible!" or "I've got the worst fashion sense when it comes to hats!" But don't overshoot the mark by divulging too much, "I'm a sexual compulsive with intimacy issues fearing that I'll never find love." Some things are better kept to yourself! If you can find the right balance, these types of comments serve to humanize you in a way that let's people know you don't take yourself too seriously, and you make no pretense about being perfect.

TIMEOUT: Which short-term strategies do I currently use and how might I incorporate others?

If you maintain a happy and positive outlook on life you'll find that most of these strategies occur naturally or very quickly become your standard way of dealing with people. If you are a likeable person, people you know and people you don't will accommodate you in ways that will mystify your less agreeable friends and acquaintances.

The power of liking

In the summer of 1987, between my senior year of high school and freshman year of college, I took a sales job with Vector Marketing, which at that time was the only distributor for Cutco knives. Having spent a weekend in upstate New York at a crash course seminar to learn all about knives and how to differentiate good ones from bad ones, I was ready to start selling.

Vector mandated that you first sell to friends and family, which isn't an unfair request because the product was (and still is) stellar. The thinking is if you don't believe enough in the product to sell to people you know, then you shouldn't be selling it to anyone. At the conclusion of each house call, you ask the person for a list of ten names of other like-minded friends that wouldn't mind hearing the same pitch. Since my sales rate was about 95%, those customers were happy to provide a short list of names, because they had seen that the product was legit. (As for the other 5%, we'll get to those later!)

At the start of each week, I would go through the list of referrals and set up my appointments for the week. With each phone call I would mention who gave me their name and ask for an appointment. Unlike regular cold calling, my referral success rate was also sky high, about 90%. The power of liking is so strong that the mere mention of a well-liked person's name was enough to accept a teenager's invitation for an hour long sales pitch! There was no social pressure to accept the invite as the referrer wasn't part of the conversation and I made clear that whatever they decided wouldn't get back to whomever gave me their name. People accepted this invitation based solely on my dropping the name of a person they liked. Turning me away in this instance would be like rejecting their friend. By collecting ten names per appointment, by summer's end I had over 1,000 referrals that I didn't even have time to contact. There is power in being well-liked, even if you aren't in the room!

This simply illustrates the importance of learning and practicing long-term and short term likeability strategies! Speaking of names...

What's in a name?

The final, and perhaps most important, strategy in being well liked, is to *remember* everyone's name you meet and *use it* at least twice in every conversation. This should be used for all situations, both short and long-term. The greatest sound to everyone's ears is the sound of their own name. When people remember our name in conversation, we take notice of it. When they remember our name days or weeks later, we never forget it. Dale Carnegie told us this 80 years ago in *How to Win Friends and Influence People*, but we still aren't listening (a **great** book, still worthy of your time and attention).

It's happened to all of us. You get introduced to someone and not 5 seconds into the conversation you realize you don't remember their name. You end up hoping they don't use *your* name because you have no way to reciprocate the greeting. "Nice meeting you, William" is met with, "And nice meeting you...buddy." It is an inauspicious way to begin.

Many of us believe that we are "horrible with names" and are seemingly quite proud of this fact by telling other people about it, "Nice to meet you, John. By the way, I'm horrible with names, so I probably won't remember that!" What a bad start. But by making this admission, we make it easy to forget people's names without even trying, because we are "horrible with names." It becomes a sort of self-fulfilling prophecy. So, STOP telling people that you are "horrible with names". You aren't.

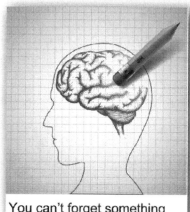

You can't forget something you never bothered to remember in the first place!

You just haven't come across a workable process to remember names–until now.

A workable process–COAR–concentrate, observe, associate, repeat.

Concentrate. You didn't forget a name within 5 seconds; rather, you never heard it in the first place because you weren't really listening. The first step in remembering names is to concentrate only on their name when you hear it. Don't think about what you're going to say or how you're going to say it. <u>Focus exclusively on the sound of their name</u>. Although it sounds obvious, I would bet my last dollar that less than 10% of people actually do this. Don't get so preoccupied with giving your name and story that you only hear the sound of your own voice. Make it a habit to focus on the name of everyone you meet rather than tuning out for fear "you won't remember it anyway." You can remember it, and you will. If you generate the mental effort to focus on their name you will *feel* right away that your brain is using muscles it hasn't exercised in a long time, if ever.

Observe. As you hear their name for the first time, look at the person you're speaking with. Notice the sound of their voice. Do they have an accent? Gruff or smooth voice? Notice their facial features, their hair, their clothing, their shoes. What one thing stands out to you the most? Do they have a noticeable freckle? Perhaps they have a John Waters-type pencil thin moustache. Whatever the case, it shouldn't take more than a second or two (with a little practice) of zeroing in on *one* feature of the person. Physical features are better than clothing or accessories because the next time you see them they will be wearing something different and your association may not work as you expect.

Associate. Take that one thing that stands out to you the most and create an image that associates the name. This idea is a variation on a "peg" memory system, so the more absurd the image, the more likely to you are to remember it. Everyone's brain processes impulses via different routes, so some types of association will work better for some than others. Here are a few examples of people I've met recently and how I associated their name:

- Pam: She had a relatively flat face which is the first thing I noticed. So my mind went from "Pam" to "Pan" and I thought that's what she'd look like after getting hit in the face with a pan.
- Dave: Had bleach blond hair which took me to the word "Day" as in "Day.....ve" and I imagined the brightest sunrise behind his head that lit up his head and made his hair look so blond.
- Rose: Was dressed all in black and I thought, "She is dressed too darkly. She could use a rose pinned to her lapel to give her some color.
- Billy: He had a well-trimmed goatee. This one was easy. Billy-goat.

It may seem silly, and it is. More importantly, it works! I never forgot their names or the hundreds of other people on whom I've used this system.

Some people have an easier time linking to images. Other people prefer to rhyme a name. Let's say you meet Jessica, and if it fits, someone might think, "Jess looks like a mess." Another strategy is to link them to another person you know with the same name, even if they don't have similar features. I once met someone named Dan with long hair. My brother's name is Dan but his head is clean-shaven. So I thought, "if Dan had never shaved his head, he'd look like this guy." Again, once you make some odd association, it won't be easily forgotten.

All of these strategies can be mixed and matched. The more you put this into practice, the better you'll get at it. If you fail the first few times, don't get discouraged, stick with it. It's only through repetition that you'll get good. Eventually, you'll be able to join a group of 6 or more people that you've never met, hear all their names *once* and use those names throughout the conversation. People will not only remember it, they'll openly talk about it, "How do you remember everyone's name?!?" It's difficult to articulate in writing, but when you create an association, <u>you just remember it</u>.

Repeat. Finally, once you've created that association, say their name in your head 5 or 6 times and then say their name *out loud*. If you meet Jerry, whose rosy cheeks look like two berries... Jerry -> Berry, once you create the association say his name out loud, "So, Jerry, what do you do for a living?" Don't wait until the end of the conversation. When you repeat the name in your head, think of the association at the same time. It may sound like too much for your brain to handle at once but it isn't. Once you try this a few times you'll realize that you *can* do this and it isn't as hard as you thought it would be. Then when you're trying to recall a name (even if it takes you a second or two to reconstruct the association) you will be able to do it.

It should go without mentioning, but I'll mention it anyway: don't discuss the associations you're creating in your head. Sometimes they may not be flattering (see Pam above) and of course it isn't done to hurt anyone's feelings or make anyone feel bad about themselves, it's simply a mnemonic tool to remember names. Also, sometimes my associations get a little "blue," which can make remembering the names even more fun!

WHO'S IN CHARGE, HERE?

"You will respect my authoritah!"

-- ERIC THEODORE CARTMAN, SOUTHPARK

From youth, we are taught to obey those in authority over us. It is such an ingrained mindset that when confronted with doing the unthinkable, if in the presence of an authority figure, we will do it anyway. Back in Chapter 4 we discussed the "Milgram experiments" and how people would (apparently) give near-lethal electric shocks to test subjects at the urging of an authority figure in a white lab coat.

This experiment, and the dozens that followed, forcefully demonstrates the power of authority. Our heuristics are activated when someone in charge instructs us to do something. We just comply without thought, because we are conditioned to accept the legitimacy of the request if it comes from a person of authority.

It is important to recognize that the term "authority" doesn't only mean jurisdiction over others, or the power to enforce conduct or behavior. It also refers to anyone admired for wealth, stature, fame, intellect, or expertise. Those who fall into one of these categories will be viewed as an authority and people will show deference to them, even in areas unrelated to their status as an authority.

Celebrity endorsements give credence to the idea that we are just as susceptible to the *appearance* of power as we are to its *substance*. In the 1970's, Robert Young, who played Dr. Marcus Welby on television, became the spokesperson for Sanka coffee. The well-mannered actor generated an air of erudition and sophistication on his way to selling more Sanka than one would have thought possible.

Are these types of endorsements a thing of the past? Hardly. Jim Parsons, who plays theoretical physicist Sheldon Cooper on CBS' popular show "The Big Bang Theory," recently began a marketing campaign with computer chip manufacturer Intel. In each ad he rattles off a bunch of information about the power and performance virtues of Intel processors, and because he *plays* an intellectual giant on a TV show, we subconsciously translate that into some level of real-world genius that would qualify him as an expert in the subject.

We are becoming more consciously aware of these types of endorsements, which is why Cigna used humor with their celebrity spokespeople to poke fun at the entire celebrity endorsement concept. Their dream team of TV doctors included: Patrick Dempsey from "Grey's Anatomy," Alan Alda from "M.A.S.H.," Lisa Edelstein from "House," Donald Faison from "Scrubs," and Noah Wyle from "ER." Rather than trying to *blur* the line between their roles and their actual qualifications, they *highlighted* the line, best illustrated by Alan Alda who says, "I have no idea what I'm doing, I'm just a TV doctor." By making light of the celebrity "authority" endorsement, the ad campaign proved successful.

Overall, the longstanding success of celebrity endorsements illustrates that we are swayed, heuristically, as much by the *illusion* of authority as by authority itself.

What follows are the simplest, and most effective, ways for Whisperers to create this illusion even in the absence of genuine authority.

Titles

A title is the simplest way to acquire an immediate air of authority. Depending on the title and with whom you are speaking, it can have a dramatic impact on the tone of the conversation.

In the late 1990's, I taught as an adjunct professor with the University of Maryland. During this time, I would introduce myself with the title of "Professor." Initially it was just for fun, but I began to notice the effect the title had on others. Once people heard it, they seemed to hold my opinions in higher regard and were less likely to cut me off with their own interjections. If my title was brought into play *during* a conversation, it was striking how quickly they displayed deferential behavior. They would use words much too large and "bookish" for casual conversation and their grammar and syntax would morph into something more formal and precise.

Titles affect how you are viewed not only intellectually but *physically*. A visitor from Cambridge University was introduced to different groups of students as either a student, demonstrator, lecturer, senior lecturer, or professor. With each status level, the visitor's height was estimated to be a half-inch taller, so the difference between the student and the professor's projected height was a full two inches! So a prestigious title makes you judged to be more physically imposing *and* more worthy (Wilson).

The title creates the appearance of authority, and as a result, people will be more likely to comply with your requests, even if those requests don't relate to your area of expertise. In an extreme experiment, someone calling on the phone claiming to be a "doctor" ordered nurses to administer a lethal dose of an unapproved drug to a patient. 95% of test subjects complied. Without any real authority figure, a bare title over the phone was enough to gain compliance. This is in no way to disparage the job nurses do–unthinkable conditions, longer hours, and huge responsibilities. But *because* of the full scope of their job, they fall into the heuristic trap of complying with the "doctor's" orders. They don't have time to systematically examine every request they receive (Hofling).

If you don't have a job title or other honorific to generate authority, you have two choices.

First, you can get creative with your actual job title and hope it creates the desired effect. A bartender becomes a "Beverage Dissemination Officer," or a receptionist becomes the "Director of First Impressions." Get too creative and the title becomes more humorous and less authoritative, so find a title that achieves the desired effect.

Second, you can lie. This is only advisable for research purposes. In social situations, you can borrow from the "pick-up artist" and try using various, yet believable titles such as lawyer, doctor, professor, engineer or judge and watch how the conversation and the people change with that information. At the end of the conversation, you can even come clean and say, "I'm not really a judge...but I've always wanted to be!" It will get a laugh and you can watch them turn back into themselves now that they don't have to impress a member of the court! Of course, don't lie "for real" as this will only lead to the dark side. And if you do experiment with titles, make it believable. If you're wearing denim overalls and digging wax out of your ear with a screwdriver you can't believably claim to be a global hedge fund manager. Keep it in the realm of possibility.

Clothes

"Clothes make the man. Naked people have little or no influence on society."

--MARK TWAIN

People underestimate the veil of authority that clothing provides when getting someone to comply with a request. Even in 2017, when people are suspicious or even openly contemptuous of authority, the power exuded by what we wear has an impact on others' perception of us.

In one study designed to test how strongly we reflexively comply with authority, a man in the street tells another man, "That guy by the meter is over-parked but doesn't have any change. Give him a dime." When the speaker is dressed in street clothes the compliance rate was 42%, but when in uniform, the same man achieved a compliance rate of 92%!

This doesn't only apply to uniforms as people were more likely to return money "lost" in a phone booth if the requestor was well dressed. This operated on a sliding scale–the better dressed, the greater chance of success. Taken to an extreme, people trust their very lives to others based on how they're dressed. A man crossing the street against a traffic light was able to get 350% more people to follow him through the intersection when he was wearing a suit! (Bickman, Lefkowitz)

Clothing persuades at the heuristic level as well. When people see a well-dressed person, they instinctively assume this person has the status and the intellect to make the right decisions, which is why they will follow him through a crosswalk like he was the Pied Piper of Hamelin. It happens unconsciously, freeing our minds to focus on more important thoughts. Clothing heuristics tie into liking. We find people more attractive and likeable if they are well groomed and well dressed, and we already know that the more likeable you are, the greater your chance of success.

For the next month, try moving up a level (or two) from how you normally dress when going out. Stay observant and look for any differences in behavior from how you are normally received.

For me, I started wearing a nice looking sport jacket over whatever shirt I was wearing. People smiled more in my direction, nodded more to acknowledge my presence, and were generally more pleasant across every social situation. I was able to return expensive items without a receipt (from stores that require it) and get preferential treatment at restaurants and other retail establishments. Yes, other techniques were used as well, but the clothing is the first thing they notice, and if you're well dressed, it will put their brain on autopilot.

This concept is better, and more succinctly, explained by Thomas Fuller who said, "Good clothes open all doors."

Jargon

The term "jargon" carries such a negative connotation that a thesaurus likens it to: balderdash, drivel, gibberish, nonsense, twaddle, and mumbo-jumbo. It is negatively associated because it makes things harder to understand for people *outside* the associated field. For *insiders* (whether they be professionals or amateur enthusiasts) in that field, jargon improves communication because it is more concise and clearer. In the right situation, selectively peppering one's speech with a little jargon can further create an air of authority to which people respond.

Some jargon you can figure out through context and common sense. The point isn't to understand it when heard, but to **use it** in a conversation. What follows are varied examples to more clearly demonstrate what we mean by jargon. There are hundreds of words and phrases in each field but to use them effectively, you only need to learn one or two.

Business/corporate jargon:

- "Land and expand" - Using a "foot-in-the-door" principle to sell a small solution to a client, then expand upon that solution once inside the client's environment
- "Blue sky thinking" - This is modern jargon for "thinking outside the box," which itself is jargon for creative thinking that isn't constrained by preconceptions.
- "Drink our own champagne" - This means the business will internally use the same product they sell. Another phrase that means the same thing is "eating our own dog food," but champagne sounds better.
- "Pick the low hanging fruit" - Take care of all the easy tasks first before moving onto the more difficult ones.

Police jargon:

- "D&D" - Drunk and disorderly
- "Code three" - Emergency response required
- "DB" - Dead body

Computer jargon:

- "Box" - Is a computer, as in, "we need to replace all the boxes on the 3rd floor."
- "Ping" - To get someone's attention via text or email.
- "Middle school dance" - When two pieces of hardware are both waiting for the other to initiate communication, resulting in no communication occurring.

Some jargon gets used so much it moves into more global usage and is no longer considered jargon, but "slang." A good example of this is the aforementioned "thinking outside the box," which began as business jargon but is now more widely used. Whatever group you're dealing with, make sure you have a little bit of jargon you can sprinkle into the conversation.

As with clothing, jargon works on more than one level. If you're speaking with people that understand the jargon, they automatically like you because you've demonstrated that you belong. It's like knowing the "secret handshake." Their assumption of shared knowledge creates rapport and an immediate feeling of goodwill. This appeals to the "similarity heuristic" discussed earlier.

It works just as well when people *don't* understand the jargon as it appeals to the "authority heuristic." You appear to have a command of a subject area that they don't, or you at least have a deeper understanding than they do. This perceived expertise makes you an authority, but remember, the influence of authority works even beyond the limits of the subject matter in question. Just remember not to overdo it because you'll come across as overbearing which will *diminish* other's perception of you.

Whether it's medical workers, evangelical Christians, woodworkers, pilots, or vintage movie poster collectors, every group has its own jargon which you need to tap into in order to convey the proper authority.

GIVE TO GET (THE ART OF RECIPROCATION)

Throughout society, across all cultures, people try to repay others for what they've done. Repaying bad or evil actions is called revenge. Repaying constructive, helpful behavior is called reciprocity. You give back, or reciprocate, the treatment that you received. If you want someone to do something for you, do something for them first.

In a way, this is the reverse of the liking strategy where they do you some small favor, which subtly enhances your likeability. In this case, *you* are doing something first, and while it won't make you more likeable, it creates a feeling of indebtedness they need to resolve.

But isn't being well liked more important than reciprocity? Surprisingly, it isn't! The need to repay a social debt is so strong it even overpowers other forms persuasion, such as being well-liked.

Two tests were conducted where test subjects were waiting in a room. One of the subjects was an experimenter posing as a test subject. First, the experimenter left the room and came back with a soda for himself. Later, he asked the real subject whether they would buy some raffle tickets, and if so, how many. Everyone purchased a number of tickets based on how much they liked the experimenter–no surprise there. In half of the test cases, however, the experimenter also brought back a soda for the test subject. In these cases, people bought as many tickets as those people that liked him a lot but didn't get a soda, *even if they didn't like him.* In other words, when they felt a social debt, the compulsion to pay it off resulted in compliance with the request, *completely irrespective* of how much, or how little, they liked him (Regan).

This experiment showcased another powerful feature of reciprocity–*the favor given was unsolicited.* No one asked for the experimenter to bring back a soda, he just did it. Even though it wasn't requested, it still created a feeling of obligation in the test subjects.

Taken even further, if the gift is *unsolicited* and *unwanted*, it still works just as well! In the 1970s, the Hare Krishnas were a religious cult on the brink of financial collapse when they started soliciting for donations in airports and other public places with high volumes of foot traffic. They would give a small flower to the mark and ask for a small donation. The numbers of flowers that ended up in trash cans just outside airports across the country was a testament to the fact that these "gifts" were not wanted. But the power of reciprocity was so strong it resulted in an economic boon for the Krishna movement, as the majority of people that took a flower ended up giving a donation.

This method of getting donations became so popular in the 1970s (and even into the 1980s) other organizations started using it. Eventually, soliciting without a legal permit was banned from most public places. The power of reciprocity is evidenced by the fact that as a society, we fought it through statutory *avoidance* rather than directly saying, "No!" to solicitors. The rule of reciprocity is just too strong to violate.

PBS still uses this principle when fundraising on-air. During fundraising season you're likely to hear something like, "Thanks for watching. For a small $250 donation, we'll send you a gift. A DVD of the show you're watching right now..." Many people don't even have DVD players anymore, and most people record those shows directly onto some digital device, but people contribute anyway. Yes, in part to support the network, but a good percentage feel the pull of reciprocity for an item they don't even want and can't even use!

Another interesting conclusion drawn from the Regan study is that *the exchange does not need to be balanced.* The initial favor can be small, and as long as it creates a sense of obligation or indebtedness, the debtor will agree to a considerably larger return favor. The raffle tickets cost more than a single soda in the experiment above, yet people bought several tickets in an effort to cancel their perceived social debt.

The reason an unfair exchange works is that the initiator chooses *both* the debt-creating first favor and the subsequent debt-canceling favor. After the person receives the soda and then is asked to buy raffle tickets, there is no other available alternative to cancel the debt, so the most expedient way to correct the social imbalance is to agree to the larger favor. We jump at the first opportunity to regain equilibrium.

The principle of reciprocity:

- It is one of the most powerful forms of getting a favor, even stronger than liking
- The initial favor does not need to be asked for, or even wanted
- The return favor can be considerably larger than the initial favor

Practical uses for reciprocity

Rather than lurking around airports with flowers or having pockets full of trinkets and baubles to use as our initial favor, is there a more practical way to make use of the principle of reciprocity? Turns out, there is. If you ask for a big favor, get rejected, and then ask for a smaller favor, it heuristically activates our need to repay a favor. Robert Cialdini, Ph.D., was the first to articulate the concept of **reciprocal concessions** and offer an explanation as to *how* and *why* it works, "Suppose you want me to agree to a request. To increase your chances of success first make a larger request, one that I will most likely turn down. Then, after I have refused, you would make the smaller request that you were really interested in all along. Provided you structured your requests skillfully, I should view your second request as a *concession* to me and I should feel inclined to respond with a concession of my own, the only one I would have immediately open to me—compliance with your second request." (Cialdini, 2007, p.38). This technique has come to be known as the "rejection-then-retreat" strategy.

The crucial link is that moving from the bigger request to the smaller request is viewed as a favor. Saying, "no," to a big favor, then hearing a less demanding alternative means the other party has done you a favor by asking for something less than they wanted. Your agreement to the second request repays that favor. This should be clear enough but what follows is, to the best of my memory, a word-for-word exchange between a manager and an employee (who reported to a different manager, so tasking was optional).

Manager: "*I've got a report due for the directors but have other deadlines. Can you bang out a quick presentation for me to deliver to them? Not more than 4 or 5 pages I would think.*"

Employee: "*Umm... I don't have the time to do that right now. For the next couple of weeks I'm totally slammed.*"

Manager: "*No problem. I understand. But do you think you could do a quick intro for the presentation? Just hit the high points of the project... maybe a couple of paragraphs?*"

Employee: "*Sure, I can find the time for that! How soon do you need it?*"

Pretty clever of me, right? Not really. I was the employee. It wasn't until much later I realized what had happened. I could have said no to the second request too, and probably would have if not for the larger, initial request. But I automatically agreed to the smaller request, *without thinking*. This conversation always comes to mind when I think of reciprocal concessions and how heuristics work when agreeing to a favor.

*   *   *

Not only does reciprocal concessions work but it contains a few hidden benefits unearthed by additional studies.

Note that the *smaller* request doesn't need to be a *small* request. It just needs to look smaller in comparison to the original question. College students were asked to accompany a group of juvenile delinquents, as chaperones, for a trip to the zoo. Being alone with troubled kids of ambiguous ages for hours at a time in a public place is no small request, borne out by the fact that in the control group, 83% of the students declined to help. When test subject students were first asked to spend two hours a week for two years as a juvenile counsellor, *then* asked about the zoo trip, the success rate rose from 17% to 50% (Cialdini, 1975).

(The request cannot be *too big*, however. Research shows that if the initial request is too large or unreasonable, then the person will not agree to any subsequent request, however small or feasible. So when fashioning an initial request, you need to strike a reasonable balance with the larger first question, something that is not so over-the-top that they heuristically shut down any further request you make.)

Not only does this reject-then-retreat technique result in a higher compliance rate, but the number of people that *follow through* is likewise much higher. A Canadian study asked test subjects to volunteer two hours for two years, and after a rejection, they were then asked them to volunteer for two hours for one afternoon. The compliance rate was 76% vs. 29% for those who were only asked the second question. This is an expected outcome of the principle. What is more surprising, however, is that of those who volunteered, the rejection-then-retreat subjects followed through (meaning they actually showed up) at a rate of 85% vs. just 50% of those that were only asked the second question. It appears the added responsibility as the agent of change which produced the concession (by saying "no" to the first request) increased their participation in that concession (Miller).

For all those that follow through and are asked for future favors, the compliance rate is again higher for initial rejection-then-retreat subjects. In this study when subjects who came in to donate a pint of blood and then were asked to donate at some future date, 84% of the previous rejection-then-retreat subjects agreed while only 43% of the control group subjects agreed to come back (Cialdini, 1976). Why the disparity? If the reason was satisfaction with social participation, both groups would have volunteered again in roughly the same numbers. The difference is that the rejection-then-retreat subjects residually feel, in however small a measure, that they have been given a favor by letting them choose a much smaller way in which to contribute. When asked again, psychologically, it doesn't seem to be an undue burden in comparison to the initial request. The control group is clearly doing *us* a favor by agreeing in the first place so they don't feel compelled to continue giving their time and energy over what was initially promised.

*   *   *

Use reciprocal concession whenever you need a favor. You will be surprised how often people's automatic responses kick in and they just agree to that second request. Add to that they'll be more likely to actually do what they agreed to do *and* they'll be more likely to provide you subsequent favors. Given all this, reciprocal concession may just become the primary tool in your persuasion toolbox.

> **TIMEOUT:** Take a break and let the information sink in. While you're processing all of this, go ahead and post how much you've gotten out of this book to at least a dozen web and social media sites. No?!? Fine, then just make one quick post about it on your Facebook page. That's not too much to ask, is it? Seriously... just one post.

MAGIC PHRASES

Beyond liking, authority and reciprocity, there a few phrases that, when used at the right time, almost make you feel like a Jedi mind master when successful. These phrases are quite context-specific so you won't get a chance to use them every day, but when the opportunity arises, be bold.

Reactance. Psychological reactance is when someone pulls in the opposite direction from where they feel led. We do this with children, known as reverse psychology. "I'll bet you can't finish your broccoli before Daddy eats his chocolate cake!" Works great for kids but no adult will fall for this, right? Turns out it works just as well on adults, you just need more subtlety and context.

Last summer, I was stuck in southern Illinois and needed to rent a car for the three hour drive up to Chicago. This was late on a Sunday afternoon in a relatively small town and the only car rental place that was open didn't have any cars available. So, I did what any self-respecting Human Whisperer would do and bummed a ride over to the rental office anyway. The very first words I said to the rental agent were, "You probably don't have the authority to help me out here, but…" and then I proceeded to explain my situation in person. Let's just cut to the end of the story… yes, I got the car.

Perhaps it was the fact I showed up in person. Perhaps it was the genuine need seeping through my story. There's no way to know for certain, but I'm convinced that the opening phrase is the one that cemented the deal. As soon as I said it she straightened up, stood a little taller and slightly elevated her head. All signs of a person projecting importance and authority. Near the end of my explanation I hit the theme again, "I know that, by the book, you don't have any cars available today for someone without a reservation, I know your hands are tied, but educate me on our options." At least in part, to show me that she *did* have both the power and authority to take matters into her own hands, which were anything but tied, she finagled a way to get me a car.

The phrase, "you may not have the authority to help me out here, but…" is one of the strongest ways to use psychological reactance on a stranger to gain compliance for a request. Find the right moment to subtly use it and you'll be amazed at how well it works. If, however, it comes across as an obvious ploy to manipulate someone it will create an even stronger negative effect, from which you will not recover. Be subtle!

The phone call. Some people just won't return a phone call. Appeal to their curiosity to get that phone ringing! Create a mystery with your message:

- "Thanks so much! Give me a call so I can thank you personally." (This is a great option as it combines curiosity with gratitude.)
- "That's some exciting news you have! Can't wait to hear all about it."
- "You were right, I was wrong. And I'm big enough to admit it. Give me a call."
- "Hopefully you'll get this call before it's too late! Call me back soon and I'll give you the whole story."

Obviously, when they call back you need to have something to say that somehow relates to the message you left. There are many other ways to appeal to their curiosity as well. Think about your relationship to that person and what phrases might be applicable that achieve the same effect as the ones above.

This one works just as well when sending texts, and if you can pique their interest enough they will respond with a phone call (especially if you ignore their texts asking for clarification).

The free upgrade. This isn't something you can use use every day, but when the opportunity presents itself, get ready to pounce and expect the unexpected! It works well with just about everyone, regardless of mood–so even a cranky desk clerk who is over-worked and overtired will become intrigued. It's a line to use whenever you're asked your preference and you don't have one.

While staying in a lovely hotel off 7th Avenue in New York City at Christmastime (which is the best time to be in New York), a thirty-ish young man at the counter asked me if I had a floor preference. I thought about it for a second and said, "You know what? I'm more confident in your judgment than mine. Just put me in whatever room you would want."

"I'd pick a room overlooking the (Central) Park, but those cost a little more."

Dejected, I sighed, "Well, assuming I can't afford the upsell, where would you choose to stay?"

"I'd still take the room overlooking the park," and moving to a slightly quieter tone (but still above a whisper) said, "We can just set it up as a promotion…" A few clacking keyboard minutes later we had our room overlooking Central Park, and it was a bigger room than we had originally booked. Don't know what the original price was on the room, but I'm sure it was at least twice as much as we paid!

Since I stumbled across this little gem, I've used it over and over. In hotels, restaurants, airplanes, rental car agencies, and return departments. Whenever you hear a question and you don't have a preference, don't try to figure one out. Let them decide for you and your chances of maximizing the experience goes up.

It goes without mentioning, but I'll mention it anyway…It doesn't work every time. My success rate is hovering around 50%, which I find to be extraordinary. I continue to tweak the wording to see if I can get that number higher, but on balance am thrilled with its success.

Here's *why* this works:

"If someone was to say they trusted your judgment and then ask you to choose the best 'whatever' for them, it's human nature to give that person the best you have to offer. You don't want to put someone in a cheap room with a window that faces an alleyway after they asked you for the room you would want for yourself. It would reflect poorly on you. It also helps that it's not just some line. It *is* true. I do trust the judgment of the person who works there to know what's best.

"You might think this is no different than asking for someone's recommendation. 'What room do I want? Well, what do you recommend?' 'What seat do I want on the plane? Well, what do you recommend?' The difference is that they hear that said to them all day every day, so it carries significantly less weight. Also, a recommendation isn't binding. 'You recommend the Tiramisu? Hmmm… actually I'll go with the chocolate cake.' But when you give your power over to someone, when your attitude is, 'I couldn't possibly know better than you. Just choose for me.' People take that as a sign of some respect and want to do well by you. It's annoying when a friend foists the decision making onto you, but this is different. They're supposed to be the expert. Moreover, people in the service industry are often in a position where they're treated quite shabbily, so showing some deference is an attitude they appreciate." (Andy)

*   *   *

FORGET-ME-NOTS

- Asking for a simple favor is anything but simple! *When* you ask, the *way* you ask, how you *look*, who you *appear* to be, and how *likeable* you are, all contribute to your chances of success.
- Simple options like mood, timing, and framing the request as "us" instead of "me" are techniques that can be used in conjunction with the strategies of likeability, authority, and reciprocity.
- Pick a strategy that would be easiest for you to start with and try using it as much as possible to find the limits of that strategy in different situations.

*   *   *

Getting favors and preferential treatment is, by definition, self-interested. Eventually, you will want to go beyond this to exert influence on the way people make larger decisions, for their benefit. This is the focus of the next chapter.

11

Decisions, Decisions

Getting people to agree to a favor is one thing, but guiding a decision is quite another. A *favor* is a single instance action primarily for the benefit of the requestor. A *decision* may have long lasting effects, depending on the nature of the decision, and is often less self-interested. For example, obtaining a rental car without a reservation is a one-time request made for the sole benefit of the requestor. A decision to begin long-term investing may benefit the influencer in part, but the target is the main beneficiary; and unlike a favor, this decision is long-lasting.

Guiding decisions has long been an object of study in behavioral sciences and has yielded some important conclusions. For Whisperers, the principles behind guiding decisions are:

- *Social Proof:* Using the target's observation of authorities, organizations and peers to influence a decision is one of the most successful strategies to guide choice.
- *Framing Choices:* Decisions can be guided by shaping the nature and number of choices.
- *Priming:* Subtle exposure to words and concepts cause people to make choices in the direction of a desired outcome.
- *Embodied Cognition:* Positive and negative sensory experiences can influence a person's decisions.

SOCIAL PROOF

When my daughter was three years old she could sleep through the night without wetting the bed but insisted on sleeping with pull-up diapers overnight. Upon waking, she was dry but would call out, "Mommy, do I have pull-ups on?" If the reply was, "yes", then it wasn't dry for much longer. To our chagrin, she just enjoyed the convenience of not having to travel all the way to the bathroom in the morning. We tried reasoning with her. We tried bargaining. We explained that *we* didn't need diapers at night. We even tried good old fashioned bribery, but none of our efforts to wean her off this crutch proved fruitful.

The day before she turned four she announced she would no longer need overnight diapers. Thrilled, we said, "OK! But why not?" Her reply shouldn't have surprised me, "Because four year-olds don't wear diapers." Her willingness to change her entrenched behavior boiled down to her perception of how other four year-olds behave. The fact that Mommy and Daddy didn't wear diapers at night made no difference to her. *It was to other four-year olds that she looked to see what she could and should be able to do.* This way of thinking doesn't end in childhood but persists throughout our lifetime.

*   *   *

"Social proof" is the theory that we align our opinions to more closely match the opinions of authorities or social groups. Perhaps you agree with the theory in general but believe you would stand by your opinions no matter how great the pressure. Maybe, maybe not...probably not. The incredible power of social proof is most vividly demonstrated in its therapeutic use with children suffering from phobias and social detachment.

Children with extreme dog phobias were asked to watch another child play with dogs for 20 minutes a day. After just 4 days, two-thirds of the fearful children were willing to climb into an enclosure to play with a dog. It didn't matter whether they saw an actual child or a video clip.

The number of children seen also made a difference. A video montage of several children was more effective in elevating the power of social proof than a video of just one child. *The more people seen engaging in an activity the more it is viewed as correct* (Bandura). Importantly, this transformation persisted after a month without any further behavioral intervention.

Additional situations were modeled and found to provide genuine therapeutic benefit. Socially detached and withdrawn children watched a video clip where similarly isolated children joined in activity with other kids. After viewing this, the study group of children began interacting with others on the level of a typical child. After six weeks, those children were among the most socially active at their school (O'Connor). A single viewing of this video clip reversed a potential pattern of lifelong maladapted behavior.

(If you or someone you know has ever experienced a severe, debilitating phobia of flying, germs, spiders, heights, or being alone, you can recognize how incredible these results are.)

*   *   *

Social proof works on systematic thinking but is also effective in triggering heuristic thinking. Canned laughter from a "laugh track" is a staple in scripted situation comedies (sitcoms). Nobody claims to like it yet it is ubiquitous throughout the television industry. Why? Because people laugh longer, more frequently, and rate the show as funnier when it is accompanied by a laugh track. Not only do we use others' laughter to determine what is funny, but we respond to that laughter even when we *know* it is *fake*. In fact, we have become so acclimatized to taking others' reactions as evidence of what is funny that we respond to the sound of laughter and not the substance of actual comedy. This happens without thought!

Salting the tip jar

Salting tip jars and church collection plates operates on the same principle. An overflowing tip jar implants the idea that most people tip; therefore, it must be the appropriate thing to do. When advertisers say something is "fastest growing" or "largest selling" or "most preferred" they aren't convincing us the product is even good. Instead, they're only trying to prove that others think so. Our thoughts on political beliefs, what is funny, when to tip, and what to buy are just a small sampling of the myriad ways in which we subconsciously surrender our decision making autonomy to those around us. This works on the heuristic level by prompting action without critical thinking "Is the collected money being used for the welfare of others?," "How good was the service?", or "How good is the product?". Not only can analytical thought be short-circuited in simple decisions but it works with more consequential decisions as well.

Subjects charged with judging political policy perfectly illustrate the heuristic short-cut. Conservative test subjects were presented with a made-up welfare policy more generous than any real policy, but were told 95% of house republicans felt the policy "provided sufficient coverage without undermining a basic work ethic and sense of personal responsibility". The subjects bypassed their systematic processing and overwhelmingly fell into the party line. The same results were obtained when liberal subjects were likewise shown a welfare policy more restrictive than any modern policy but were told it was overwhelmingly supported by house democrats as it would "lighten the financial burden of the poor." Opinions rested entirely on who the policy was associated with. For both groups, content analysis only happened when not told about party preference (Cohen).

We are generally aware of the use of social proof with laugh tracks, salted tip jars and celebrity or authority endorsements, but the power of social proof and the extent to which it can affect our decisions to forgo critical examination (as in the welfare policy example) is extraordinary.

TIMEOUT: What are some of the decisions you try to guide on a regular basis? How can you effectively use modeled behavior or endorsements to guide decisions through heuristics?

Most of us would like to think *we* would be among the few giving deliberate thought to both small and consequential decisions no matter how others respond... especially in life and death decisions! Unfortunately, time and again, this has been shown to be untrue.

Whisper Alert: Social Proof engages heuristic decision making.

When the target observes authorities, organizations, peers, and modeled behavior which causes them to heuristically make decisions or initiate a response based on those observations, the power of social proof is undeniable. As a Whisperer, therefore, an additional look at social proof to see some of the dangers is warranted.

The dark side of social proof

On March 13, 1964, 28-year old Kitty Genovese was on her way to her Queens, New York, apartment around 3 A.M. When she reached her apartment complex courtyard, she was stabbed, sexually assaulted, and murdered. The attacker fled once but returned to continue the assault over a period of half an hour. A dozen people heard or saw "something", but no one saw "everything". They saw others looking from their windows on the other side of the courtyard. No one called police until the attacker fled the second time and Genovese had died (Manning). This brought about a scathing social critique of how city dwellers are a detached and unfeeling people. This thought was reinforced because no similar stories existed in rural areas.

One reason for the lack of intervention was the *diffusion of responsibility*. The prevailing thought process of each observer was that *someone* will call for help and probably already has, so in the end no one dials 9-1-1. While this provides a partial explanation, the bigger reason is less intuitive.

The forces of social proof insidiously camouflaged the situation. But how could people not have known that Kitty was in a fight for her very life? That seems like a reasonable question. Through closed windows in wintertime, screams and calls for help are muffled and unclear. They were unaware a murder was taking place. Some thought it was an argument, a drunken brawl, or friends goofing around. All of the witnesses took their cue about the situation *from the other witnesses.*

When we see something potentially alarming *but don't fully understand* the situation, we learn from the way the others react to determine if the event is an emergency. We forget that everyone else is looking to determine how *they* should react. Appearing calm, we maintain a stone-faced poise among strangers and are met by the same, so everyone sees everyone else looking unflustered and not stepping in to help. As a result, the event will be interpreted as a non-emergency, and no one will step in. This phenomenon has come to be known as "the bystander effect."

Conditions that increase chances of the bystander effect exist normally in cities, which are noisy, distracting, fast-moving places where it's hard to be certain of context for any given event. The dense population makes it likely that unusual and emergency situations will be seen by many people unknown to each other.

This is how it can happen that a man collapses in the center of a busy department store on "Black Friday" and dies of a heart attack with no shoppers or staff trying to help. We've all heard similar stories. It's not that people don't care about the welfare of others, nor is it because they assume an emergency call has already been made. Rather, the decision to act is shaped by those around us, once again highlighting the power of social proof.

*   *   *

Help is more likely if only *one* person sees an incident! Smoke appearing from under a door was reported 75% of the time by a lone observer but only 38% of the time in a three person group. When two of the three people were coached to not react to the smoke, it was only reported 10% of the time (Latané). The idea of "safety in numbers" is backwards.

However, the bystander effect can be overcome when it is clear an emergency exists. In a staged experiment with a utility worker, where it was clear he was in distress, assistance was rendered 100% of the time. In "unsafe" situations, assistance was rendered 90% of the time even when people thought they themselves might be in danger from downed power lines. This assistance was offered whether the people were alone or in a group (Clark).

So if you are in an emergency situation, how can you break the stalemate to get the help you need? The best strategy is to reduce the uncertainty of those around you. *Tell them*. If people understand there is an emergency, they will assist. Rather than making a general request to the group, request assistance of a specific individual. This will overcome the diffusion of responsibility. Finally, if you *witness* a questionable situation, be proactive in determining whether an emergency exists. Ask the person, "Are you alright?" Or in a case where they don't or can't answer, ask a fellow spectator. "Does this person need help?" If no one knows, assume the situation requires intervention and take action.

*   *   *

The bystander effect highlights the general principle of social proof: *the more uncertain we are about a situation, the more readily we look to others to determine how to think and act.*

Social norm exceptions

There is an inherent struggle in society between conformity and uniqueness, where the principle of social proof doesn't function as expected.

More so than other children, upper and upper middle class children are taught they are special. This type of rearing creates a need for uniqueness, which manifests as an aversion to conformity in choices of consumer behavior, i.e., the need to put a unique stamp on a car or home purchase. By contrast, the working class doesn't have an aversion to blending in. They pick the more popular item which is likely to be the most reliable and represent the best overall value per dollar spent.

Similarly, when purchasing a car, the drive to be unique causes the buyer to look for something that isn't *too* popular but *looks like* most of the other cars in its class and has similar, if not upgraded, features and amenities. There is an inherent struggle between nonconformity, which pushes us *away from* more popular items, and social proof, which pushes us *toward* those items. The net effect is to choose something *moderately similar* to more popular items. This principle is so strong that one can reliably predict how well a car will sell based solely on its looks and feature set, as opposed to cost, mileage, and reliability (Landwehr). The key is that *similarity* appeals to Social Proof but still scratches that itch to be different.

Why does it work so well?

> *"When you find yourself on the side of the majority, it is time to pause and reflect"*

> - MARK TWAIN

Is it possible to abandon the truth even when you know you are correct? Can the beliefs of others weaken your resolve to speak the truth to avoid standing alone?

Imagine seeing the following drawn on a whiteboard in a classroom:

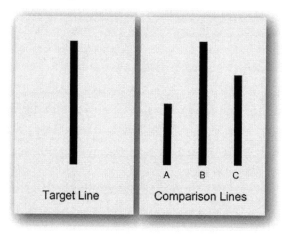

Target Line   Comparison Lines

A   B   C

You're seated with others in a semi-circle facing this whiteboard. The instructor asks the first person, "Which comparison line is the same length as the target line?" "Easy," you smile, but are quickly shocked to hear the first person answer "C". What?!, the second and third people answer "C" as well.

Your pulse speeds up a bit as you take a closer look. Maybe you missed something. Maybe the viewing angle creates a convincing optical illusion... No, "B" is definitely the same length as the target line. As the next few people answer "C" you begin to question your judgment. The person beside you answers "C", you feel a flash of heat as all eyes are now on you. There's only one thing to say, "Yes, 'C' is the same length."

While most people believe they would have been the lone dissenting voice, in this exact experiment, the results were quite different (Asch). When the line length was modified to be slightly harder to judge, the number of people conforming to the group went up. People tend to echo the group's decision. Why? The more we are unsure of a situation, the more likely we are to take the opinion of the group as correct.

There are two reinforcing ideas at work when appealing to social proof. The first is called "informational influence," where we question the accuracy of our beliefs when others' opinions differ from us. (Think "by-stander effect".) The second is "normative influence" which is the need to appear a member of the group (Schulman).

We also conform to avoid being stigmatized and potentially face social rejection. Peer pressure is a type of normative influence and everyone who has raised a teen or been a teen knows how strong its pull can be. Social proof is most effective when the target is more unsure of himself or when the situation is ambiguous. With these variables in play, the target is likely to look toward others for clarity and correctness.

Most test subjects gave the wrong answer because of both informational and normative influence. Informationally, the person double and triple-checked the board and then concluded they must not be seeing things correctly. Normatively, even when they knew the others were wrong, they went along with the group to avoid appearing deviant.

TIMEOUT: How might I use the impact of Informational (uncertain, complicated and/or confusing) and Normative (a part of the group) Social Proof to encourage heuristic decision making?

What follows is one example:

When working as a technical manager and seeking a consensus among the employees for a change many of them did not want, I tried my hand at guiding choice. A mandate is quick and easy, but unless you get genuine buy-in, true progress tends to stall. Convincing them their co-workers were on board with the new idea would make the transition easier.

Due to potential restructuring, it was important to educate each group on the workings of the other groups. This would require a fair amount of knowledge transfer and training. (Training that most didn't want, but was the best solution to achieve results.) I called small groups into a meeting room instead of speaking to the whole team at once. Pre-staged on the whiteboard for the first group I had written three options across the board in a row.

Option one "Business as usual" equated to no training at all. Option two "Knowledge transfer" equated to cross training (for which I was hoping to get some traction). Option 3 "Permanent switch" (a last minute idea) to permanently keep the groups in flux. (As most preferred their own working groups, I knew this would go over like a lead balloon.) Underneath each option I wrote a number *presumably* indicating the number of votes from a previous group (the first group to vote was unaware of their status as the first group.) Something like: "Business as usual" - 0 votes, "Knowledge transfer" - 6 votes, "Permanent switch" - 1 vote.

Once everyone was seated I spoke about the pros and cons of each option and when it was time to vote I turned around and erased the previous "tally" so everyone could vote. Even when I knew most people favored option one, I was able to get a nearly unanimous vote on the new strategy. After the first staged vote count, the tally was a true reflection of the employee votes, so no further staging was necessary.

Although I never explicitly stated the board reflected the tally of other people, some may feel this crosses an ethical boundary. If your conscience is uneasy with this specific example, then by all means don't feel pressured to use it. By applying a little creative problem solving, however, this principle can be used in a number of personal and professional situations to gain consensus.

(Unbeknownst to me at the time, adding a third choice is one of the "guiding" strategies that can be used in tandem with social proof.)

FRAMING CHOICES

Riddle: *When you have three, you have three. When you have two, you have two. When you have one, you have none. What am I?*
Answer: *Choices.*

The number of available choices affects the decision making process. If there is only one option, influence is moot as there is no alternative. As the number of choices grows, indecision grows. More mental effort is required to analyze each option and a wrong choice is more likely. A mistake might mean unpleasant consequences which further increases the mental stress of making the choice.

Take a trip to the local paint store. If you've ever tried to pick out a room color for your home you are more than a little familiar with the anxiety that can be brought on by too many choices. You want blue? Nope. You'll need to choose one of its 1,200 shades. Heaven forbid you should want a neutral color. You'll sift through 200 shades of white before you even get to *off-white*. And then there are the ecru and beige families after that. It's more than a little overwhelming. Even more so when there are two of you trying to reach a consensus on one of those little colored squares.

In his book "The Paradox of Choice", Barry Schwartz studied the effect of choices on our psyche and discovered some counterintuitive ideas. The biggest surprise is that we are *happier* when we know our decisions are *irreversible*. What? Let's say that again. We are *happier* when we know our decisions are *irreversible?* When a choice is changeable we focus on what we're *missing* and we remain in a constant state of dissatisfaction. An irreversible decision forces us to focus on how and why we made the right choice. We work to justify our decision and put all our psychological weight behind it. It's the difference between "what is" and "what if".

When we choose a college, a life partner, or employer, we end up thinking, "I'm so glad because...". The energy wasted on looking back at what might have been is replaced with looking ahead and discovering all the reasons why our decision was the right one.

Keeping our options open leads to less happiness, not more. Although people don't change their mind and reverse course very often, we just prefer having *options*. They are not normally as varied as what we find in a paint store, but are usually limited to a few.

* * *

How a target makes decisions from possible options is important to the Whisperer, as we all approach decision making differently.

Schwartz separates choosers into "maximizers" and "satisficers". Maximizers are not happy unless they have made "the best choice" in all circumstances. Satisficers have certain criteria, that if met, will make their decision acceptable without the need to obtain "the best," and so are willing to settle for "good enough."

Maximizers objectively make better decisions *but those choices do not make them happy*. Not only is anxiety increased during the decision making process, but afterwards, maximizers are still hyper-focused in re-examining if their choice was best. Being a maximizer exacts a toll on one's life because they crucify themselves for every choice that didn't turn out right.

Satisficers don't believe they can create an ideal world so are less bothered when the world turns out less than ideal. They don't focus on what might have been and are less likely to alter course even when making a reversible decision. A satisficer's TV may not be as good as his maximizer neighbor's, but he enjoys it a lot more.

Most people fall somewhere on a continuum, and become maximizers with some things they're particular about. Many of my friends are laid back about everything except their technology. They need "the best" phone, tablet and computer, dammit! Second best will not do. For others, it might be items such as home furnishings, club membership, exercise equipment, or the "stuff" we need for our hobbies.

* * *

If, upon careful self-examination, you conclude you are a habitual maximizer, work on altering your thought process to worry less about the choices you didn't make or the road you didn't take. Accept your decisions and the positives stemming from those decisions. Work to enjoy the quality of your life.

WHISPER ALERT: Identify your Maximizers for Maximum results!

Before shaping and directing choices, be aware of what kind of decision maker you're dealing with. If you're dealing with a maximizer, they aren't likely to rely on heuristics. For them, each decision is a thoughtful deliberation. If necessary, you can use the ideas in chapter 9 to move them into heuristic thinking, but your success will be lower than someone who is a satisficer in the same area. Know your target; are they maximizers or satisficers?

Fear of loss powers heuristics

At 7 years of age, I accompanied my father to Sears to buy a new washer and dryer. They were on sale and dad was always looking to save a penny. The sales clerk said those washer/dryer sets were all sold out but "maybe they misplaced one in the back, I'll go check it out." Wouldn't you know, a few minutes later he came back and told us there was "*one more* in the back".

It took an eternity to ring it up so I walked around the appliance department and heard another sales clerk say the *exact same thing*! As luck would have it, he was able to find just one more in the back too!

On the drive home I recounted how lucky the second customer was that there was still one more left. My dad laughed and said, "they've probably got 5,000 of those things in the back. That's just how they get you to buy it!"

This was my first exposure to the *scarcity principle*, which is the idea that opportunities seem more valuable when their availability is limited. We are awash with warnings of "limited availability" in advertising. And why not? It works.

Our heuristics are flipped on when something is limited. We unconsciously assume that it is scarce because everyone else has analyzed the product favorably and purchased so we better jump on the bandwagon.

Impacting a decision can be achieved by framing a choice in terms of losses or gains. The heuristic pull is that people are *more* motivated to avoid losing something than potentially gaining something of equal value. This is most clearly demonstrated in *comparisons between two choices.*

In staged transactions test groups more often finalized the deal to avoid a $5 surcharge than to gain a $5 discount. No difference in actual savings, but a surcharge is losing money, whereas the discount is thought of as a gain (Levin).

In a famous experiment from the 1980s, two groups of test subjects were faced with two options for a devastating scenario:

* * *

Imagine that the U.S. is preparing for the outbreak of an unusual Asian Disease, which is expected to kill 600 people. Two alternative programs to combat the disease have been proposed. Assume that the exact scientific estimate of the consequences of the two options are as follows:

Group 1 options:
If Program A is adopted, 200 people will be saved.
If Program B is adopted, there is 1/3 probability that 600 people will be saved, and 2/3 probability that no people will be saved.

Group 2 options:
If Program C is adopted, 400 people will die.
If Program D is adopted, there is 1/3 probability that nobody will die, and 2/3 probability that 600 people will die.

* * *

Which of the two programs would you favor? Stop and figure it out before reading further.

Reading these options carefully you realize all options predict the results will likely be the same. A and C are the same; B and D are also the same. Because of our innate aversion to loss, a majority of test subject from group 1 chose program A. Those in group 2 chose program D. Program C frames the result as a loss, i.e. people will die with the alternative choice stating a possible loss. Program A frames the results as a gain, i.e. people will be saved with the alternative choice stating the possible loss. Although the net result is the same, decisions can be altered simply by framing them as a gain or loss (Tversky).

The power of the decoy (The sneaky third choice)

In addition to framing, adding a third option can help guide a choice. When presented with two choices it is often easy to determine which is good and which is better. Consider the following choice for a magazine subscription:

- Option 1: online subscription $59
- Option 2: online and print $125

Only 32% of respondents chose option 2, because it was more expensive by a large margin. But as soon as a third option was added as shown below, option 2 was chosen 84% of the time!

- Option 1: online subscription $59
- Option 2: online and print $125
- Option 3: print subscription only $125

Why? No one chose option #3 because it was specifically tailored to be inferior to one of the other two options. This nudges a person in a specific direction between any two other choices (Huber).

Next scenario–two nearly identical cell phones:

Phone 1: $400, 50GB storage capacity
Phone 2: $300, 40GB

Given these choices, there is no clear winner. A third choice can be added to guide consumers to either phone. Look closely at each option.

Push toward phone 1:
Phone 1: $400, 50GB storage capacity
Phone 2: $300, 40GB
Phone 3: $425, 48GB (decoy)

Push toward phone #2:
Phone 1: $400, 50GB storage capacity
Phone 2: $300, 40GB
Phone 3: $325, 32GB (decoy)

We choose the phone that compares favorably to the third choice because any other choice means we are *losing* a tangible value–yes, it all comes back to loss. This has come to be known as *the decoy effect*. The decoy elevates the value of one of the other two choices drawing you to the preferred choice.

TIMEOUT: In my sphere of influence how might I frame choices (reorganization, suppliers, goals, regulations, rules) as a way to avoid a loss?

Most of us break away from any conversation to answer our cell phone or take a text. Why? Because if we don't take the call we *lose an opportunity* to engage another person. But by taking the call we are putting the live person next to us on hold. Since we already have their attention, we are more likely to deprioritize that which is closest to us. In short, the aversion to loss causes us to answer those phones and jeopardize the *quality* of the real conversation. We know it's bad form, we know we shouldn't do it, but....

Whisper Alert: The fear of loss is a powerful motivator to engage heuristic decision making.

PRIMING

In a general sense, priming is when you guide someone's thinking through stimulus. In a larger sense, one could argue that everything we've discussed in this chapter would fit that definition. What we're talking about here, though, is when you lead someone to a specific thought by initiating that thought at the outset of a conversation. Words, numbers, and actions are all perfect fodder for priming. Unless you make it obvious, the subject remains completely unaware of the implanted thought.

Words

More directly, *priming uses words and ideas to direct someone to a certain thought*. Words can create a mental state to change how people think and behave. We saw this in chapter 4 with the positive and negative impact on test scores.

In a similar way, if you want someone to be more open minded, then prime their mindset with **words** such as: change, flexible, malleable, pliable, and elastic. Working these into a conversation has been shown to create a more open minded attitude!

The same thing happens with "polite" words such as respect, honor, patiently, courteous, graciously, etc. You can generate more considerate feelings in your target which may manifest itself through less frequent interruption.

Words about sin, guilt and remorse caused more people to enjoy a guilty pleasure like a piece of chocolate. People primed with health related words felt more guilt when consuming a luscious dessert. So, if you're trying to steer someone away from making bad decisions at mealtime, prime them with the appropriate words (Hassin, Bargh, Goldsmith).

It may be difficult to use some of these words without sounding like you are reading from a Thesaurus. You don't need to use all of these words in a conversation, just a couple of words should be enough to prime your target. But let's take it beyond words.

*   *   *

Planting **ideas** through incident is even more influential than using specific words. Tell them about a time you were open minded. Better yet, tell them about a time *they* helped *you* and you listened to them: *"Remember when you told me not to use the old reporting tool with the new spreadsheets? I didn't want to hear it but …."*

Making this kind of a statement works on two levels because you're priming the idea of general open mindedness with a story about when *they* had a suggestion. Properly primed, they will be more likely to listen to your next idea.

If you don't know the person well enough to recall something that links the two of you together, a third party can be used. This time let's prime politeness: *"I just got off the phone with my friend, Sara. She is a great sounding board because she always lets me get my entire thought out before responding. Anyway, how are you doing?"* Next time you're about to start a conversation with someone who interrupts you a lot, make a similar statement or relevant anecdote.

*   *   *

Another great option is to use a first person perspective: *"My first reaction when someone asks me for money is to immediately say, 'No', but I have found when I overcame that knee jerk reaction, I always felt better about myself. It sounds corny, but giving does create a sense of satisfaction."* [3] For a statement like this, remember to wait a few minutes before moving from

---

3 This statement is much too heavy handed but is necessary to explain the principle behind priming. For this to work consistently, you'll need to come up with language that fits *your* voice.

the priming statement(s) to your request! Even better, make your donation request at the end of the conversation, the influence won't be recognized as such but the primed mindset is still very much in play.

Also keep in mind this type of priming is not designed for direct marketing where you meet someone and then immediately try to sell them something–it will *not* work in that context. There are already plenty of books for "making the sale". The focus here is where you are trying to affect thought processes in ways not for your sole benefit.

Numbers (Anchors)

- Is the temperature of the sun's surface greater or less than 2,385,900,502 degrees?
- Did Michael Jackson have more or less than 492 #1 singles?
- Is the average monthly cell phone bill more or less than $3,718?

These numbers are a little off. Come up with your estimates to these questions before reading further...

* * *

You most likely (rightly) assumed that my numbers were high in each case. What you may not realize is that those absurd numbers most likely caused you to estimate too high as well. (Although not important, the answers to the questions above are: ten thousand, thirteen, and seventy-three dollars, respectively). Unconsciously using the first set of numbers to guide you toward your final answer is called *the anchoring effect*. People tend to make judgments based on an initial anchor point (Tversky, 1974).

Anything that is quantifiable, typically through some numeric measure, is subject to the "anchor and adjust" heuristic. The numbers you saw were a type of priming where

Once anchored, our thoughts don't tend to float too far from that spot.

you start at that number and then adjust upward or downward until you hit a *plausible* number. The adjustment, however, will always end up at one extreme or the other of

---

Something *I* would say, and say *casually*, without making too big a deal out of it would be, "I just gave a little money to <fill in the blank>, and it always makes me feel good..."

what you consider credible, because as soon as you get into the range of possibility, you will stop there and not adjust any further.

A practical way to leverage this idea is when discussing your value, whether negotiating for a salary, or determining your hourly rate on a project or contract. Conventional wisdom dictates that you force the other party into naming a price first. This is wrong! To properly establish your worth, **you** need to name a number first, however difficult or socially awkward it might be. Now your value has been primed in their mind. If they make a counter-offer, it will be adjusted from your initial number.

You don't want your number to be ridiculously high as in the sample questions above, but it should be high enough so you don't sell yourself short.

Actions

We looked at the "foot-in-the-door" technique in the last chapter as a powerful means of getting someone to like you. Liking aside, this approach works for larger decisions that aren't directly related to personal favors. If you get someone to agree to a small request, then larger requests are *much* more likely to be honored. You're priming bigger decisions through requests for smaller ones. Once someone has overcome inertia and begun acting a certain way or thinking a certain way, we are more likely to continue along those same lines.

In the 60s, researchers Jonathan Freedman and Scott Fraser experimented with this hypothesis. When homeowners were asked to place a large "Drive Carefully!" sign in their front yard, only 17% of people agreed to request. Another group of homeowners were *first* asked if they would place a small sticker 3-inch sticker in their window to promote safe driving. Those who agreed were asked three weeks later to place a large "Drive Carefully!" sign in their front yard. 76% agreed! Just by granting a small innocuous request first, the larger request for support was more often granted (Freedman).

Whatever decision or thought process you're looking to initiate or alter, the first and smaller request must be easy. Gaining compliance for larger tasks will then become easier. If your end goal is a big one, increase the time between the first and second requests.

Timeout: How might I prime with words, numbers and actions to guide decisions?

EMBODIED COGNITION

An even more subtle way to influence decisions heuristically is by targeting the sensory system.

Although a relatively new concept in the field of behavioral psychology, the early evidence is both strong and encouraging that *selectively altering one's senses can effectively shape choices in subtle ways.* We know our conscious mind can control unconscious behavior which will in turn determine our mental state. The reception of sensory stimuli affects our unconscious thoughts and are explained and expressed through metaphorical language which in turn creates a bridge between our conscious and unconscious thoughts. Scientists using MRIs read sentences to subjects that contained tactile metaphors such as "She had a 'rough' day". When hearing these metaphors, the same regions of the brain were activated as when people physically sensed rough textures through touch. The sensory stimuli bridge between our conscious and unconscious thoughts is the study of embodied cognition.

* * *

It isn't magic. Sensory experiences make it more *likely* someone will make a certain choice. For example, sensory input that would increase one's willingness to take financial risks will not cause them to foolishly imperil their assets, nor will it even *guarantee* success for more moderate requests. Using specific sensory stimuli, however, does increase the likelihood that a *reasonable* invitation may be *positively* met. With that caution out of the way, let's get to the good stuff.

Temperature

Altering the temperature affects attitudes beyond the sensory experience alone. In one experiment, people were asked to hold a therapeutic pad for several minutes and then answer a survey to determine the pad's commercial viability. After the survey, they were offered a choice of a refreshment or a gift certificate in the name of a friend. In other words, they could choose something for themselves or something for another person.

The test group holding a *cold* therapeutic pad chose the gift certificate only 25% of the time. The test group holding a *hot* therapeutic pad chose the gift certificate 54% of the time. The only variable was the temperature of the pad (Williams). In other words, *people that are warmer are more* **generous** *than colder people.* A good thing to know when you want your target's choice to be either generous or more self-centered.

A similar experiment tested whether temperature had any effect on one's level of trust. While holding a therapeutic pad, subjects were asked to play an investment game where some were investors and others were trustees. Those holding a cold therapeutic pad invested less and expressed less faith in the trustees. Those holding a warm therapeutic pad invested more and expressed more faith in the trustees (Kang). The unambiguous results demonstrate that *warmer people are more **trusting***.

*   *   *

The generosity and trust effect of warmth vs. cold appears to be short-term. However, decisions made while "under the influence of heat" can be longer lasting. Additional research shows that if you are the one providing the physical warmth, you are perceived as metaphorically warmer and more sympathetic. By simply providing a warm room (not uncomfortably so) or offering a hot drink, you will be seen as warmer and more trustworthy and will have created a greater spirit of generosity and trust in your target. The implication beyond these experiments indicates comforting warmth tends to create a positive mindset.

Touch

Entire books have been written about the importance of human touch for our emotional, physical, and psychological development. We, however, are only interested in demonstrated choice that can be affected by the use of touch. For example, waitresses who touched customers on the hand or shoulder for one second received greater tips. They did NOT receive better ratings suggesting the customers were unaware of the effect of touch on their behavior (Crusco). Further studies show that when touching becomes excessive or blatant, it can have a negative impact on both tips and ratings. As with warmth, *a <u>subtle</u> touch can also influence generosity*. Remember, less is more.

An experiment from 2010 showed that a light tap on the shoulder *increased* financial risk taking. Overt touches, such as a handshake, actually *decreased* the level of financial risk subjects were willing to make (Levav). This supports the power that *subtle* touches have over the decisions of others. So if you're trying to convince someone to financially back a money-making idea, a light touch on the shoulder or upper arm can bring about both a feeling of generosity and a reduced aversion to risk.

Texture

As with the warm vs. cold therapeutic pads, having subjects touch objects of a certain *texture* can affect their thinking as well.

Playing soft ball or hard ball: When looking at pictures to determine the gender of sexually ambiguous faces, those squeezing a hard ball were more likely to identify the faces as male. In a follow-up experiment, people were asked to write the answer firmly or gently on the paper. Those who pressed the pen gently were more likely to categorize the faces as female (Slepian, 2011).

Politically, in the U.S., Republicans are viewed as carrying a hard-line view on issues like the economy, foreign affairs and social issues while Democrats are viewed as softer and more charitable (Hayes). Accordingly, squeezing a soft ball caused more people to identify random faces as Democrats instead of Republicans. Squeezing a hard ball caused more people to identify a picture as a physicist (a "hard" science) rather than a historian, which is considered a "soft science" (Slepian, 2012). These studies demonstrate how our sense of touch *unconsciously* affects the way we categorize things to align with cultural definitions.

Attributing "hard' or "soft" traits to others may similarly be affected. After reading an ambiguous passage about the interaction between a boss and an employee, those touching a soft blanket rated the boss less strict and rigid than those touching a hard block. Other traits, however, like social skills or intelligence were rated the same across both groups.

Those sitting on a soft chair are found to be more willing to budge on price than those sitting on a hard chair. The soft seat quite literally makes for a soft negotiator. This principle is in effect anytime you're dealing with someone where you need to find some common ground. Have you ever been in situations where you were too inflexible or caved too quickly? Your contact with hard or soft textures may heavily influence your willingness to compromise!

Texture is more than just hard or soft surfaces. When asked to participate in a "cognitive" test after completing a sandpaper rough puzzle or very smooth puzzle, those in the rough puzzle group found the interaction competitive, unfriendly and argumentative. Simply touching a rough or smooth object radically altered their perceptions of the subsequent interaction (Ackerman). So if you want to pave the way for a smooth dialogue, don't rub sandpaper on your target!

WHISPER ALERT: "Warm and fuzzy" is not just an empty cliche.

So it is not surprising when light subtle touch, squeezing a soft ball, touching a soft blanket, sitting on a soft cushion, handling a smooth puzzle....all positively correlate with viewing things on the "softer side of life". The importance here is to consciously make use of this information to tip the balance because sometimes the race is "won by a nose".

Recent research findings (beyond our scope) indicates that hyperactivity in kids with ADHD may not hurt their ability to learn, but rather is what helps keep them engaged. Allowing them to fidget and move freely increases their ability to concentrate and work through solutions to problems but can become a distraction for others. Finding non-disruptive ways to fidget such as squeezing and playing with soft objects allows for success of all students in the classroom by quietly keeping all children engaged

(Sarver). Many teachers now allow "fidget spinners" in their classrooms, which are small devices that serve the same purpose.

Weight

Popular metaphors and cliches signifying attitudes about weight are common. People *weigh their options* before *throwing their weight around.* Once you make a *heavy decision*, you feel *a weight has been lifted.* And, depending on the *gravity of the situation*, you may feel like *the weight of the world is on your shoulders.* Is there a common sensory link?

A study from 2010 sought to answer this question. When test subjects were asked to evaluate a job candidate based on a resumé attached to more heavily *weighted* clipboards, those with heavy clipboards rated candidates as *better qualified and more interested* in the position. There was no difference in rating for sociability and likeability, only traits related to performance and seriousness (Ackerman).

The association between importance and weight is bidirectional, not only does weight affect an individual's concept of importance, but the concept of importance also activates the physical perception of weight (Schneider). Earlier we learned that nonverbal behavior subconsciously changes our mental state to bring the two into harmony. This principle is reflected in embodied cognition theory. When holding a heavy book and told it was important, test subjects estimated the weight to be higher than if no mention were made of the importance of the book. This was *not* the case when the subjects only looked at the book.

This is heuristically important because if someone feels something is important, they will focus their attention on analysis. Increasing physical weight can be useful in situations where you want someone to thoughtfully consider what you're saying rather than using a mental shortcut to dismiss your thought out of hand.

Color and contrast

Color: Red is a conundrum, triggering a wide range of emotional states. Can we identify some overriding principle?

On one hand, it is associated with passion. From Valentine's Day cards to to roses, red is indelibly linked to love and lust. Using the color red as a background for women's portraits caused men to increase their perceptions of sexual attractiveness above that of the women placed before other colored backgrounds. By now, this shouldn't be surprising. Further, the red background had no effect on opinions of the women's likeability or intelligence (Elliot, 2008). As with other sensory stimuli, the subconscious influence of red alters our conscious evaluations in specific situations.

Additionally red has been shown to evoke fear of failure and cultivate avoidance behavior for students taking tests. Whether an entire cover page was red (or just the ID number at the top of the page), red had a consistent negative impact on test scores, regardless of the type of test or the test taker. Unlike the stereotype effect from chapter 4, red affects all test takers across gender, race, subject matter and academic level (Elliott, 2015).

Finally, a mind blower! Athletes in red win more often than athletes in other colors! In the 2004 Olympics, wrestlers were assigned random blue or red headgear and red won more fights. Too small a sample? A study of the success of English soccer teams from 1946-2003 was positively correlated to the color of their shirts (Hill, Attrill). Why? Possibly athletes were emotionally charged by the color and played *above* their ability level. (Consider the use of a red flag in the bullring.) Equally possible, it increases anxiety in their opponents who look at them just like a red cover sheet on an exam. That feeling generates enough fear of failure so they play slightly *below* their ability level. A third possibility is that it subconsciously affects the referees. When showing identical Tae Kwon Do competition videos to sport referees, the test subjects awarded more points to those wearing red (Hagemann).

How do we make sense of the apparent positive and negative implications for the color red? The confusion disappears if we view red as an *amplifier for existing feelings about people and situations*. Attractiveness and anxiety are both amplified in the examples of viewing photographs and taking tests, respectively. In the sports example, the color red has an amplifying effect on both the players and their opponents.

Contrast: The difference between light and dark isn't as open to context as the color red. Black is associated with negative connotations, experience, aggression and illicit activity: blacklist, black cloud, black sheep, black market, and blackmail; contrast this to the positive view of light: looking on the bright side, the light at the end of the tunnel, looking toward a bright future, and having a bright smile (Lobel). In fact, a "bright smile" is not just a figure of speech. Smiling faces are actually seen as physically brighter than frowning faces (Song).

Someone dressed in black will be viewed as more aggressive than someone wearing another color. A look at 15 years of NHL infractions shows that teams wearing black uniforms were penalized more often than teams in other colors. A closer look shows this was only true for aggressive penalties and not technical infractions (Frank).

The study went on to show that not only are people dressed in black perceived as more aggressive, the evidence suggests they actually *become* more aggressive. People were told to choose five of 12 games offered. Each game was ranked in increasing aggressiveness from block stacking all the way up to human chicken fights. Groups given black uniforms picked the most aggressive games to play. By contrast, those wearing white (and those without uniforms) chose equally non-aggressive games. This shows that wearing black can increase one's inclination toward aggression *and* increase others' perceptions of aggressive behavior.

Light Exposure: Seasonal Affective Disorder (SAD) was first diagnosed by the National Institute of Mental Health in the 1980's (Wikipedia). In winter, less daylight compounded by more time in darker interior space increases feelings and actions associated with depression. Complaints include hopelessness and worthlessness, suicidal thoughts, loss of interest in activities, social interaction, difficulty with concentration, decreased sex drive, a lack of energy, and agitation. Since that time subsequent studies have shown light deprivation is not just related to clinical disorders. All of us benefit from spending time in the light. Over 20 days, test subjects exposed to 30% more light reported better moods and more positive interactions during that time. Furthermore, the light source, whether sunlight *or brightly lit spaces*, didn't affect the results (Rot).

Dark and light may also affect our moral *behavior*. We know that criminals typically operate in darkness. Commission of a crime is easier, but perhaps there is a sensory link between darkness and immoral behavior. Students were given 5 minutes to solve 20 difficult problems. When finished, they dropped the results in an unattended box and in an adjacent box they dropped their record of how many problems they solved. Those in a dimly lit room cheated more than those in a well-lit one even though results were anonymous with no proctor for both groups. It seems the darker room fostered an inclination to cheat (Zhong). But light and darkness aren't the only things that affect our moral choices.

Cleanliness

Metaphors we use to describe our moral and ethical state of mind are often linked to cleanliness. Innocence is referred to as a *clean conscience* and immoral behavior is described as *feeling dirty*. Like other sensory experiences, our actions unconsciously link the metaphor to the literal meaning.

After a person acts unethically they feel not only emotionally, but physically dirty, possessing a desire to clean themselves. Researchers asked subjects to recall a time where they acted ethically or unethically and then were offered a free gift, either an antiseptic wipe or a pencil. The antiseptic wipe was chosen twice as often because dirtiness was physically and psychologically intertwined.

Devout believers pray for their sins to be washed away. This desire for cleansing can be surprisingly specific and even extends to part of the body. Test subjects were asked to deliver an unethical message via *email or voicemail*. Email senders more often chose hand sanitizer whereas voice mail senders chose mouthwash! The link between emotional state and choice is undeniable.

There is evidence physical cleaning actually succeeds in clearing one's conscience. After being asked to recall a situation where they acted unethically, some were asked to wash their hands with antiseptic wipes. Then everyone was asked to perform service volunteer activities. Those that didn't wash their hands volunteered at 74% vs. 41% for the hand washers. The hand washers volunteered far less since they had already purged their guilt via washing. Those who hadn't washed their hands volunteered to psychologically cleanse their previous guilt (Zhong, 2008).

The realization that people who feel inwardly unclean will engage in psychological *or* physical behaviors to alleviate their guilt is extraordinary. Thalma Lobel, PhD, at Tel Aviv University asked about the relationship between physical cleanliness and moral behavior. She went about asking the question in reverse. Instead of getting clean, she asked the question, "are psychologically dirty people more or less likely to engage in unethical behavior?"

In this study, people going to or from showers at the gym were asked to take a study on "general knowledge." There were four easy questions and nine very difficult ones, nearly guaranteeing a failing grade. However, it was a self-grading exam and only the score was recorded and handed in so there was no apparent way of "catching cheaters." Her studies revealed that physically clean students (having just taken a shower after a workout) were *more* likely to cheat on tests than those who were dirty (unshowered after a gym workout).

At first blush this may seem counterintuitive. In the previous study, those that felt dirty would physically or emotionally clean themselves to counteract their previous misdeeds and bring themselves into balance. In this study, those who felt clean on the outside felt clean enough on the inside to falsify their scores. It was as though they had a "morality surplus." So even after cheating, they too, were still in balance. The unshowered people already felt physically dirty and didn't want to add any more filth to their life, even if that dirt was metaphorical (Lobel, p.156-9).

We tend to view a company and its employees as more ethical, reliable and honest when in clean surroundings. Likewise, companies that operate in a less unkempt environment are viewed unfavorably if not with outright suspicion. To be seen in "the best possible light" (metaphor intended), make sure you and your surroundings are immaculately presentable.

*   *   *

Aside from the morality issues involved with cleanliness, our willingness to take risks is also affected. For most of us, our experience with previous risk plays a predominate role in our willingness to engage in future risk. If we invested a lot of money in high risk stocks and lost a bundle, we would be far less likely to invest very much again. Getting burned makes us gun shy. Conversely, if we rolled the dice, got lucky and received a windfall, we would be far *more* likely to make a risky investment in the future.

Cleanliness has been shown to alter the role of past influence on these decisions. In a 2012 study, participants were given actual money and played three rounds of simple 50:50 games of chance. Those that went on a winning streak were far more likely to continue the game for even higher amounts of money. Those on a losing streak were far more reticent to bet. Those from each group that washed their hands after the first round were equally willing to place additional bets! Although short lived, the simple act of handwashing negated the effects of the previous bets. The most surprising thing is that the handwashing negated the betting habits of those on a lucky streak as well, not just those experiencing bad luck (Xu). In effect, cleaning one's self washes away the impact of both good and bad luck on our subsequent decisions.

Taste and Smell

When our "sweetheart" makes a romantic gesture or someone performs an act of kindness or thoughtfulness, we say that was a "sweet thing to do." Unsurprisingly, given the MRI study and studies of temperature and texture, we link these actions to things that are physically sweet. This work in a bidirectional dynamic.

In the first part of a 2012 study, subjects were shown pictures of people alongside a picture of the subject's favorite food. When asked about the personality traits of the people in the photograph, those whose favorite foods were sweet, ranked the photographed person as more caring and giving–in a word, sweeter. Just the visual association of a sweet food with a person caused the target to view them as kinder.

Does the sensation of sweet taste transfer to behavior? Two groups of volunteers were given either salty or sweet snacks, participated in an unrelated activity, and were then asked to help out in a "separate" study. The sweet milk chocolate snack group were more willing to help out (Meier).

Behavioral change doesn't actually require the ingestion of sweet food, they just need to be able to *smell* it. For years, realtors fill an open house with the smell of fresh baked bread or cookies because those smells leave a favorable impression on potential buyers. In retail sales, pleasant aromas influence the amount of money spent and increase the likelihood of revisiting the store. For parents with messy kids, smelling a cleaning-related scent influences our cleaning behavior and makes it more likely we will clean a room (Douce, Holland).

Odors influence our personal interactions with other people. If someone smells like they just climbed out of a garbage truck, we want our interaction with that person to be as brief as possible. Sweet odors influence us as well. Good samaritans changed a dollar bill more often in front of Cinnabon or Mrs. Fields than in front of relatively odorless clothing stores. More women gave their phone numbers to men in areas with pleasant smells. Waiting rooms scented with geranium essence oil fostered more interaction between strangers—more conversation, eye contact, and even physical contact, with overall shorter social distance (Baron, Guéguen, Zemke).

Odors also influence mental and athletic performance. Peppermint and cinnamon scents have been shown to increase cognitive performance with video games, typing and alphabetizing records. Attention and memory improved. Subjects more easily endured a treadmill stress test in peppermint scented rooms than subjects in rooms with no aromas (Moss, Barker, McCombs).

Office personnel smelling citrus-scented cleaning products kept their desks cleaner than the control group (Holland). The participants in the study were completely unaware of this influence on their behavior, they just "behaved cleaner."

We would like to believe that our behaviors and moral judgments are determined by our unchanging values, not by the smell of the room or whether we've just taken a shower. The evidence is compelling, however, that these sensory experiences have a strong impact on how we think and behave. Embodied cognition works so well, in part, because it such a well camouflaged phenomenon.

If someone has been burned on money making ideas in the past, having them wash their hands before presenting them with a new opportunity is by no means a guarantee of success, but based on the results in these studies, using sensory experiences to promote a change in behavior provides a significant advantage over those blissfully unaware of this phenomenon.

Timeout: How do temperature, touch, texture, weight, color, cleanliness and taste affect our unconscious thoughts? Which ones would I use in subtly guiding decisions, and how?

* * *

FORGET-ME-NOTS

- People will heuristically follow the lead of others particularly when they are uncertain of how to proceed (social proof).
- Framing choices as a way to avoid a loss is a simple way to activate heuristic thinking in order to achieve the desired outcome.
- Priming words, numbers, and actions at the outset of a conversation gets a person to make decisions in line with the primed concepts.

- Affecting the target's senses can create heuristics all their own. Altering temperature, weight, and color are a few ways by which people can be subconsciously nudged into a desired decision.

*　*　*

While affecting the decision-making process is significantly more complex than getting someone to do you a favor, the greatest level of influence a Human Whisperer can wield is to change a person's *mindset*. If you stop someone from littering in the park you've changed one decision, but haven't affected their underlying mindset of being an environmentally conscious person. That type of change requires a few additional tools that don't seek to change individual decisions directly but, rather, to *actually alter how people think.*

12

Altering mindsets

A fanatic is one who can't change his mind and won't change the subject.

--WINSTON CHURCHILL

A s previously discussed, the laugh track is one example of how decisions can be affected. It is a tangible demonstration that social proof can generate a *behavior-altering* decision–to laugh. But does it really alter our *mindset* about the show? A recent study found that while canned laughter creates heuristic cues as to when to laugh, it makes the story harder to relate to and prevents the viewer from thoughtfully engaging with the characters and the narrative (Gillespie). In short, changing a decision does not change the deeper thought processes. In order to change a mindset, additional tools are needed to alter the way a person thinks about themselves and the world around them. This is the most difficult form of persuasion, and if you can gain insight into this process, you will become a Human Whisperer in the truest sense.

WHY IS IT SO HARD TO CHANGE SOMEONE'S MIND?
People don't tend to change course when they've made up their mind about something. We first must understand *why* before learning how to affect those deeper thought processes. The three primary reasons people refuse to reconsider their decisions are: commitment, message radius, and cognitive dissonance. The first obstacle, *commitment*, is a heuristic barrier. *Message radius and cognitive dissonance* combine elements of both heuristic and systematic thinking.

Commitment
When someone has accepted a belief, internal and external pressure is exerted to think and behave in ways consistent with that belief.

Once committed to a position, we are free to think about connected ideas without questioning our accepted belief. This shortcut provides a way to more easily navigate an increasingly complex world, as it would be impractical to systematically re-analyze all our fundamental decisions due to new information and/or ever changing circumstances. In short, this becomes a touchstone.

Continuously changing one's mind projects a lack of commitment to our ideals. Even occasional mindset change can sometimes be viewed negatively. In politics, dogmatically sticking to one's guns in spite of all evidence to the contrary is still considered a virtue! While new information and changing circumstances should get people to reevaluate their position, fear of being seen as inconsistent or confused prevents them from doing so.

This fundamental commitment is a heuristic stronghold and must be overcome before tackling the subsequent issues of message radius and cognitive dissonance.

Message radius

When someone is listening to a new idea or persuasive argument, they categorize it by comparing it to their current beliefs, and then determining whether to accept it, reject it, or remain undecided (also called noncommitment). Social judgment theory refers to this as the "latitudes of acceptance." The very center of their belief on a given topic is the anchor point. After travelling some distance from that point, one will reach the latitude of noncommitment, and outside of that lies the latitude of rejection.

The size of these latitudes vary from topic to topic, but reflect an overarching rule: _the more closely the topic is linked to our self-identity, the smaller the latitudes of acceptance and noncommitment, and the greater the latitude of rejection._

If you're speaking to a staunch gun rights activist, any argument that proposes to heavily regulate gun ownership will immediately, and heuristically, land in the latitude of rejection with no hope of winning that person over, no matter how well formed or structured the argument. The same holds true for anyone with a fervent belief on either side of any volatile issue like abortion rights, the environment, health care, immigration, or the death penalty. When someone holds one of these issues near and dear to their heart, it forms part of their core identity, and so has a very small latitude of acceptance for ideas that fall outside the center of belief.

Conversely, latitudes of acceptance and noncommitment are larger for issues with which the individual is not emotionally invested. Someone who has taken up a fierce stand in support of environmental issues may more easily be swayed by arguments for or against school vouchers, as that is not related to their core issue. In that case, their latitude of acceptance for new ideas, such as an educational voucher system, will be larger. Further, when discussing whether to raise the retirement age, your target may be swayed in either direction by a compelling argument unless they find themselves directly affected, i.e. they are nearing retirement age. In general, issues that people are not as passionate about, or are not directly affected by, will find larger latitudes of acceptance and noncommitment.

The issues can be *anything!* The political examples are only given to clarify the principle. Let's say you want to convince people that Superman is the greatest comic book hero of all time. While you may find easy success with a retired suburban housewife from the midwest, the Comic-Con attending, cosplay-wearing, role-playing millennial will prove more difficult.

WHISPER ALERT: The closer the issue is to the individual's core identity the smaller the latitude of acceptance.

Too often, we attempt to persuade others with information that falls well outside their latitude of acceptance and is summarily dismissed. Information must be structured so that our message falls near the acceptance boundary. Only then will it be systematically analyzed.

If you follow the advice in chapters 4 and 5, you know where your target's acceptance boundaries are positioned. Repeatedly making arguments on the fringe of the acceptance boundary causes the anchor point to gradually adjust, increasing the range of acceptance. Ideas offered within the latitude of rejection are heuristically dismissed out-of-hand, no movement toward changing the mindset has been made and further efforts are more difficult.

So start small. Choose issues that are unrelated or only tangentially related to the issues most important to them. Pick ideas your target will agree with, even begrudgingly. Keep the message radius as close to the boundary of acceptance as possible. Once you get their anchor point moving, you can alter your message accordingly to stay at or near the boundary. At first, you should not pick issues with which your target most closely identifies; rather, choose topics with which they have no deep association.

Time out: What is my core identity? What is the core identity of family members, friends and peers? What would be targeting strategies to initiate any move from center?

Cognitive Dissonance

Cognitive dissonance is when you hold two incompatible ideas in your head at the same time <u>or</u> when you believe something but act in a manner contradictory to that belief. We saw in chapter 2 how our *conscious* body language affects our mindset, and in chapter 3 how our mindset affects our *unconscious* body language. Both directions of this mind/body relationship preserve harmony between our thoughts and actions. This process is also in play when our mind holds two competing ideas.

The struggle to preserve consistency between incongruent thoughts is a powerful, yet often overlooked concept as people try to reduce dissonance and increase *cognitive harmony*. Creating this harmony is achieved through a *systematic* analysis, resulting in a reduction of dissonance by:

- Changing one's mind about one of the elements
- Reducing the importance of an element
- Increasing the overlap between elements
- Re-evaluating the cost/reward benefit

Someone who overeats and leads a sedentary, heart-unhealthy lifestyle lives with a dissonance that must be overcome. They know the importance of healthy living, they know their lifestyle is unhealthy, yet they act in opposition to that belief. To reduce the clash of these competing ideas, the person will use one of the above strategies and:

- Change their lifestyle and begin eating healthy and exercising
- Conclude that a healthy lifestyle isn't really important after all
- Determine there is no true dissonance as the lifestyle isn't really unhealthy
- Decide that this lifestyle is worth the health cost

* * *

The mind will go to extraordinary lengths to eliminate cognitive dissonance.

Capgras' Delusion, in which the sufferer believes their family, friends and loved ones have been replaced by imposters, is such an example. This normally presents in people that have suffered some form of neurological damage, preventing them from generating an emotional response to others. Its victims can identify their family and friends but they have no emotional connection to them due to the nature of their impairment. Recognition without emotion creates a cognitive dissonance in the mind of the sufferer that must be resolved. Capgras' delusion patients have opted to resolve that dissonance by changing their mind about one of the elements–that the people in question are not, in fact, their friends and loved ones. It becomes easier to reconcile that lack of emotion and connection if those people are seen as imposters.

Cotard's Syndrome is a rarer and more bizarre condition where the patient believes they are either dead or that they don't exist at all! Here, the lack of emotion caused by neurological damage isn't just limited to people, but to all aspects of the patient's life. Since they feel no emotion at all they disengage from life. The brain makes sense of this emotional deadening by presuming they are no longer alive. Once again, the brain accepts a preposterous conclusion in order to avoid cognitive dissonance (Ramachandran).

Unusual mental conditions aside, the larger point is not to dismiss the limits of what the mind will construct to reduce dissonance. When you attempt to alter someone's thoughts about an issue, and if this new idea is in conflict with an existing idea, a dissonance is created that must be resolved before the new mindset is accepted.

People will think, behave, decide, and pursue whatever course of action allows them to maintain cognitive harmony and reduce the conflict between competing thoughts.

> **Timeout**: Can I identify any cognitively dissonant beliefs in my own life? How did I resolve these to maintain cognitive harmony? What examples can I identify in family, friends and peers?

ALTERING BELIEFS

Before trying to alter someone's beliefs, the first thing to ask yourself is why. Is it to show that you're right and they're wrong? Is it just to win them over "to your side?" If so, these motivations are more about your ego than anything else, and so are bound to fail. However, if your goals are in the best interest of others and you approach the situation with the right frame of mind, you will become powerfully persuasive. The plan outlined below only works if you adopt the right frame of mind.

The objective

Before focusing on the compelling points and counterpoints, the primary objective is getting the subject into the right frame of mind. They need to be psychologically open to listening to, and considering, your viewpoint. This is primarily done by appealing to systematic thinking. You want them to critically assess the information and ultimately decide to change course. To alter someone's beliefs, you must overcome both the heuristic and systematic obstacles outlined above and get them into a receptive state of mind. Rather than attacking each obstacle one-by-one, all of them can be overcome by getting your target to:

- Drop their defensiveness and desire to talk over you to "get their point out."
- Understand that it is not a contest but a conversation. There are no winners or losers, just people having a sincere dialogue.
- Reject attitudes of intellectual superiority and recognize they may not have all the answers and may not grasp the full extent of the situation.

Sounds impossible. We've all had conversations with people that seemed so bullheaded, self-righteous and sure of themselves that they would never allow a foreign idea to pass through their noggin. But even they can be convinced.

"Fine, fine. But how do we get people into this state of mind?"

The key rests upon four simple words: ***You do it first.***

You have been practicing this principle in small ways while learning to read and connect with others–from the smile and handshake, to listening skills, developing curiosity, helping others reach their goals, and elevating the status of your target.

You can't ask someone *else* to drop their defensiveness and accept their fallibility unless you are willing to do the same. If you are unwilling to accept the possibility that *they* might be right about a few things, why should they extend that same courtesy to you? You can't get someone to understand that the discussion is an open dialogue unless it really is. Stop working to prove "you're right and they're wrong."

If your mindset is one of openness and willingness to explore the subject matter together, with no preconceptions about where you'll wind up, you're in the right headspace to alter beliefs--either yours or theirs! If you are unable or unwilling to do this, then your ego and need to be proven right outweigh your desire to persuade.

Is this how you see your subject, or is this how they see you?

Ultimate influence is only for those secure enough in themselves to do this without artifice or subterfuge. The following four-step process demonstrates this open mindset to your subject, and if successful, will be reciprocated.

As with charismatic default settings, if you learn to naturally default to these process behaviors, *you will become a master persuader.*

The process

Stay calm. This is always the first step. An emotional mind always believes it is right, regardless of all evidence to the contrary. No matter how powerful the argument, it falls on deaf ears. If you can master your emotions and help others do the same, your ability to influence skyrockets.

You must reign in your emotions (which, for some, will be a very difficult thing to do) and listen to the other person with every ounce of presence you can muster, even if... no, *especially if* you are being verbally attacked. Interrupting someone that is agitated only increases their defensiveness. No matter the situation, or how they are responding, remaining calm must become your go-to response.

Remain calm and be SUBTLE!

How you respond to pressure directly corresponds to your ability to influence and persuade.

Maintaining your composure will have a calming effect on others and get them into a position to have a meaningful conversation. This works not only by calming others through example, but staying calm when others aren't makes you appear more powerful and you will be more highly regarded.

If their heated emotional state persists despite your good example, say, "If I said something to upset you, it wasn't my intention." As a pattern interrupt, this phrase is a good way to make them conscious of how they're reacting without getting them more defensive. With this sudden realization, their response will usually be something like, "No, it's not you, it's just that this topic gets me all riled up," or, "No, I've just been under a lot of stress lately." In either case, they will see that their level of emotional investment in the conversation is disproportionate to your expectation and they will adjust accordingly. If they say, "Yes, you did upset me when you said...(*which gives you important information*)" even then they know you're not trying to rile them up and are willing to listen. In either case, watching them move from excited to calm after asking this question will start to make you feel like a true Whisperer!

Account for differing perspectives. Most attempts at persuasion amount to one blind man urging the other blind man to see the elephant as he does. As noted in chapter 4, we tend to overestimate how much others opinions are similar to ours, and when we become aware of differences, we immediately assume they are wrong. Remember that our entire belief system may not align with someone else's; in fact, it may be diametrically opposed!

Get to the root of the disparity. Often, you'll find the *true* difference represents a larger philosophical divide in the way we view the world and therefore runs deeper than the issue under discussion. Ask more probing questions to get at the root of the disparity. It's *where these differences begin* that the most meaningful conversations take place because the farther from the point of origin the greater the divide.

A good way to uncover those differences is starting with points on which you both *agree.* Focus on those areas and move outward until you uncover where those differences lie. Doing this before communicating your persuasive message will save you time, instead of possibly pursuing lines of thought that won't move your subject. Once aware of that boundary between agreement and dissimilarity, only then can you target your argument to correspond within their worldview (think message radius).

Protect their Ego. We are all controlled to some extent by our emotions. If we are made to feel important, we will treat those who made us feel that way more favorably. Conversely, we remember those that hurt our pride, however insignificantly, and aren't likely to grant favors to those in this group.

The effect of kind and harsh words are magnified in public, which is why you often hear the adage, "criticize privately, praise publicly." If you need to criticize someone, do it one-on-one as it reduces the sting of the message. Conversely, if you praise someone while others are around, it magnifies the power of those words too, and will have a much greater effect than if the praise was delivered alone.

This same principle is important when trying to persuade. Therefore, don't do it publicly, because you're asking them to change their mind or consent to a course of action that wasn't their idea *and* represents a departure from their current line of thinking. Ego is involved, so it is far more difficult for them to publicly change their mind. Don't put them on the spot.

Moving someone to your position comes down to how you make them feel about themselves. Publicly or privately, you can be a source of encouragement and positivity without pandering to your target. If they leave the conversation feeling better about themselves than when they came into it, your chances of exerting influence are good.

Speak __confidently__ with __empathy__ and __tact__. Make your request (or state your case) with the __confidence__ that it will be well-received. Expecting a positive result changes your emotional state and your body language will support this. They, in turn, are more likely to accede to your thinking if you maintain the "assumption of success." If you waffle, or ask in a way that you assume they're going to say no, that's what they'll do. Author Bob Burg elegantly sums it up,

> *"Expecting someone to be helpful doesn't change them. It changes you. And that is what changes them."*

When attempting to persuade, the best way to convey *empathy* is go beyond the places you agree and state their position as honestly and openly as you can. This shows you have a real understanding of their point of view and effectively disarms the other person and puts them in a conciliatory state of mind. Also, if you've made a false assumption, they can clear up any misconception. It shows you are fair-minded and open (even if you aren't). Give a genuine accounting of both arguments. Talk about what ways, if any, their point of view captures elements of truth. Then talk about how, on balance, why you feel your position is either more ethically or practically defensible.

Rule of thumb: *If you can't intelligently argue both sides of the issue, then you don't understand the issue well enough to take a stand for either.* In which case, neither exhibiting empathy nor championing your position will bear fruit.

Tact means paying attention to the *how* and *when* of your message. As for the how, you must convey your ideas in ways that people can hear without becoming threatened or defensive. Word choice and tone are two key considerations in how a message is communicated. Also remember to listen more than you speak. The greatest persuaders all have one thing in common–they are great listeners. When someone feels heard they will allow you to be heard in kind.

The "when" is as important as the "how." Before saying anything, think about how what you're about to say will make the other person feel. If the message would be better received later, then be patient for the opportune time. When it comes to tact, the greatest thought comes from the Buddhist mantra,

> *"If you propose to speak, always ask yourself, is it true, is it necessary, is it kind, and is it timely?"*

Another way to think about tact is to remember the words of Abraham Lincoln, "Tact is the ability to describe others as they see themselves."

An example will demonstrate this process:

A number of years ago, the company I worked for did not allow telecommuting for any of its employees. This was a directive from the CEO himself and he was adamantly against it. Others had tried to explain to him the benefits, but his stated concerns were that without the proper amount of face time, projects would suffer due to lack of adequate communication. Given that we could call, text, email and connect to the corporate network through a Virtual Private Network (VPN), this argument seemed assailable.

As time went by, we had casual chit-chat in the hallway and break room. When possible, I steered the conversation toward telecommuting (I only brought it up when he was in a good mood.) Because I <u>stayed calm</u>, listened and tried to <u>account for his perspective</u>, he realized I didn't have an ulterior motive (and I didn't, because I was more than willing to accept that his perspective could be a better representation of reality than mine). Turns out his *real* objection was the perception that teleworkers weren't really engaged in doing their job and weren't as committed to the company goals as those who show up each day. Therefore, their work product wouldn't be as good. A-Ha! Now, I had something to work with.

Meanwhile, most other people asked him in group settings, "Why can't we telework? You've gotta change that policy!" They unwittingly made my job harder because the public assault on his ego was causing him to dig into that position. I made sure to only speak about this when no one else was around, and I never indicated his position was unreasonable–all important factors in <u>protecting the ego.</u>

I *agreed* with him that any teleworking solution would have to provide as good a work product as what you would expect from the on-site employees (<u>empathy</u>). Then I found other managers who had worked for previous employers where telecommuting was allowed. One at a time (never as whole group) they would extol the virtues of this way of working from their first-hand experience. I was also able to bring up studies which showed telecommuters are *more productive* than their on-site counterparts, take fewer days off, and report a greater level of job satisfaction.

Once I sensed he had shifted far enough from his center of belief that telecommuting was inherently flawed and would never be tolerated at his company, finally, mustering my <u>confidence</u> and <u>tact</u>, I tried to close the deal, "You know, if these managers and the trade studies are accurate, we need to give telecommuting a shot on at least a trial basis to know if it's worth pursuing in the long term. If we did a limited roll-out for 6 months, we'd have a good idea how well it will work for us." Asked with the expectation of agreement, I got it. One year later, the policy went company-wide for all employees that were in a position to work remotely. If I had made the request without those intervening steps and moving his anchor point over time, it would have never worked.

Did I mention the word "patience"?

Timeout: What beliefs of others, if altered, would be of benefit to them? How might I pursue the right frame of mind and implement the process?

Overcoming objections

Even with the right mindset and the perfect talking points, people usually express some objections before altering their mindset. Real persuasion requires intellectual humility and an awareness that you may not always be right. If you aren't willing to change your position, you won't be able to effectively persuade others to change theirs. "Faking" being open to new ideas is a failing strategy and only serves to create feelings of frustration for you, and feelings of being manipulated and coerced for your subject, which is actually quite the reasonable response considering that by faking, you _were_ trying to manipulate and coerce them. These practical considerations for overcoming objections aren't designed to be used in lieu of being genuine, but rather in conjunction with the process outlined above.

Pre-empt the objection. One of the most common sales techniques is pre-empting an objection. If you know the primary objection to an idea, you can overcome it by <u>bringing it up first</u> and getting them to agree to an idea that runs _counter_ to their primary objection. Once you bring up the solution, they can't reasonably hold onto an inconsistent position so they're only left with secondary (weaker) objections that are more readily overcome.

Let's say you are trying to convince a friend or family member, let's call her Sue, to go back to school to earn a degree or begin post-secondary education. If you know Sue's main issue is the time it would take, you can pre-empt that objection before it comes up by saying, "A lot of people in your position would be faced with a time crunch if they went back to school, but you have such a well-developed support network that, for you, time isn't as much a factor when deciding whether to go back to school or not."

You need to spend time crafting your responses to the primary objections. They need to be true and they need to resonate with the subject. Frame the response _before_ it becomes an objection.

Responding to objections. You won't be able to pre-empt every objection. There will always be lines of argument you didn't account for and you'll need to handle them the right way. If you hear an objection, immediately _agree_! Too many people immediately _disagree_ and try to convince the person that the thought or concern is incorrect. This is a great way to put people on the defensive and get them to shut down. To keep them in the conversation, agree with them. Don't contradict.

Once they know you have truly heard their concern, only then can you attempt to overcome the objection.

Providing additional information before asking again frames their answer as a _new decision_, and <u>not</u> just a case of _changing their mind_. People are more likely to adopt a new mindset in the presence of new information, instead of "caving in."

You've overcome the time issue, but now Sue says, "Yeah, but it's still a lot of effort, and in the end, I'm not sure it would be worth it." Now, we've uncovered a new objection which speaks to Sue's mindset that college isn't worth the commitment necessary to achieve it. Saying, "Are you kidding me!?! Do you have any idea the difference in average salaries between those with degrees and those without?" will only create resentment and defensiveness, whether you are right or not. Think Buddha, *is it true, is it necessary, is it wise, is it timely.*

Instead, agree and only then counter the objection, "Sue, I think a lot of people think this way. Sometimes, it can be hard to know if the grass truly is greener on the other side. In this case, though, I think it is. Let me show you the numbers I ran across the other day. Not only do grads make more, they have lower unemployment, and studies show they are not only happier, but healthier as well. So, while at first blush, it may not seem like a big difference, when you really look at all the facets involved, the difference is quite substantial." Be sure to give details and point to additional resources she may want to examine.

Agree. Reframe their point of view so they feel heard, respected, and understood. Then counter the objection with new information and seek agreement again.

Whisper Alert: Demanding your target say "Uncle" is never a good strategy.

Timeout: For a mindset change I've identified, how would I agree, reframe then counter?

ONE BIG EXCEPTION (DIRECT SUGGESTION)

The previous section focused on altering minds by _overriding heuristic thinking_ to engage a *systematic* process that causes the target to reassess their position and determine if cognitive harmony can be maintained in spite of a shift in that position. This is accomplished by staying calm, accounting for differing perspectives, protecting the ego, and speaking with empathy and tact.

The one exception, and it's a big one, where we can _leverage heuristic thinking_, is for issues related to self-image. (So far, we've only talked about topics, opinions, and worldviews that don't relate to how we view ourselves). Being generous, kind-hearted, environmentally conscious, punctual, and open-minded are all examples that fall into these self-image categories. Remember that commitment, or remaining *consistent* in our beliefs, has both an external and internal component. Both are equally susceptible to a little "heuristic tinkering" through a technique I call "direct suggestion."

Expectations (external consistency)

The consistency heuristic is that we adjust our self-image in ways that reinforce the perception others have of us. The "stereotype threat" discussed in chapter 4 is a good example of this. (A black student becomes aware of the perception others have of him and his mindset and subsequent testing performance follows suit.)

When a telemarketer asks you, "How are you doing today?" they aren't just trying to curry favor by pretending to be warm and friendly. They are attacking the consistency heuristic. Once you say, "I'm fine," it's easier to get you to comply with a request to help others that aren't doing so well. Even when said as a perfunctory response, you will have increased psychological pressure to comply. Simply by saying the words out loud, you've created the perception that you are, in fact, doing well. And the best way to live up to that perception is to agree to help out.

A cold-calling study differentiated this heuristic from routine courtesy which led to an eye-opening finding. During a fundraising call, an experimental group was asked, "How are you feeling tonight?" The control group was told, "I hope you're feeling well tonight." With no other difference in the calls, the group that needed to verbalize their answer to a question agreed to give a donation 33% of the time vs. 15% of the time for the control group. That single question more than doubled the success rate! (Howard)

This heuristic is typically applied to sales, but Human Whisperers can make use of reflected perceptual dynamics as well. We simply verbalize the trait or ideal that we want our target to live up to, and they will! A few years ago I had dinner with a number of friends, one of whom monopolized every conversation. He would one-up every story and had the compulsion to get both the first *and* last word on every topic. We all liked him well enough, but this particular behavior could get tiresome. Even good-natured ribbing, designed to make him aware of this quirk, had no effect.

He and I were the first to arrive and after some routine chit-chat I (very casually) said to him, "There's something I've noticed about you lately. You've been increasingly reserved...letting others get their ideas out and once everybody has had a say, you drop some knowledge on us. I guess you've figured out that it's what the last person says that's remembered." It wasn't remotely true, *but it changed his idea of what my perception of him was.* The entire evening went swimmingly, and much to everyone's surprise, he didn't take over the conversation even once. Of course, to reinforce this, when he would say something at the end any given topic, I would make sure to ponder it, nod and point at him across the table as if to say, "yeah, excellent point." With nothing more than a couple of sentences, I altered the way he thought about himself by altering the way I thought about him. This is as close to real magic as it gets.

A couple of things to keep in mind when using this technique.

First, this is not something to use to *change* someone's mind, rather you're *altering* their mindset by implanting an idea they hadn't previously considered. Telling a pro-life devotee, "Wow! You really seem to have embraced the pro-choice agenda," would be met with derision. But tell a dyed-in-the-wool political partisan (either a Republican or Democrat), "You don't lack for an opinion on things, but you are better than most at understanding the nuances of these issues and knowing there is a lot more gray area than people realize." If a political discussion does break out, they will work to reinforce this perception that you have of them. Their normally fiery rhetoric will be toned down and they will tend to moderate from extreme viewpoints. You can also use this as a springboard to alter a particular belief once you have implanted the idea that they are more open-minded than most people. Try it. It will make you feel like a true Jedi... I mean, Whisperer.

Second, external consistency is a short-term effect that is localized to you. Since you're the one whose perception needs to be maintained, this change in mindset, whatever it might be, won't last when you're no longer around (unless they think what is said might get back to you, in which case there may be some residual effect.) If you don't reinforce this new perception from time to time as well, then it won't last even if you are present. Understand its limitations.

The range of possibilities with this technique is enormous. Get people to behave in any way you tell them to! Not only can you get someone to stop monopolizing the conversation or temper someone's political fervor, but this will work with just about anything else you can come up with. It works with people you know well or have never met before. Just a couple more things I've achieved in the last two weeks with this technique (all temporarily, of course): got a husband to pay closer attention to his wife, changed a litterbug's habit, and stopped a bouncer from being so aggressive with customers. None of it was achieved with threats or even requests, but by relying on the heuristic that people will live up to our perceptions of them.

Self-concept (internal consistency)

The consistency heuristic works internally as well by causing people to behave in a way that is consistent with their assessment of themselves.

Just as with external perception, this too can be leveraged by telemarketers by getting a person to implant a thought into their own mind! In an Indiana study, one question on a survey asked, "What would you say if the American Cancer Society asked you to help them by going door-to-door for three hours?" Most people said "yes," because they weren't asked to *do* anything, as it was just a survey. Three weeks later a representative of the ACS called them and asked them to do just that. There was a 700% increase in the number of people that agreed over the control group that wasn't preconditioned! (Sherman)

This didn't change their view of others' perceptions, but rather their feeling about themselves. When the ACS representative made the second call, there was no need to stay true to the perception of the pollster from three weeks earlier. Rather, by saying "yes" to the earlier question, the seed was planted that they *are* the kind of person that would help out if needed. That seed produced fruit which carried forward.

Whisperers can also leverage this idea by appending a question to our previous statements that asks them to confirm whether our assessment is correct. Let's modify the political persuasion statement, "You don't lack for an opinion on things, but you are better than most at understanding the nuances of these issues and knowing there is a lot more gray area than people realize. *Why do you feel that's a part of your thinking?*"

The difference now is that we're asking for an explanation of how our perception matches their internal feelings. For lack of a better term, their answer almost works like a "mind-virus" that rewrites their assessment of themselves. The heuristic part of their brain is thinking they said it, so it must be true. Case closed. Nothing else to think about. Therefore, the change is more likely to be longer lasting, and the behaviors associated with this idea are more likely to persist even when you are not present, because they have internalized it and now see themselves in this new light.

"Why do you *feel* that's a part of your thinking?" is more effective at creating that internal linkage than a phrase like, "Don't you *think* so?" The first question cannot be answered with a simple "yes" or "no", and requires cognitive analysis which is internalized rather than dismissed. Also, for some reason, the word <u>feel</u> seems to work better at accessing the heuristic trigger than the word <u>think</u>, and upon reflection seems like a somewhat intuitive conclusion. Another excellent question would be, "How did you develop this way of thinking?"

Bi-directional impact

Public statements make an impact on both the speaker and the listener.

As demonstrated above, such a public affirmation creates a commitment in the speaker to which they will remain consistent. Even if they don't believe it at first, they'll *come to believe it.* American POWs captured during the Korean War were asked to make non-inflammatory statements like, "America is not perfect." The statements became slightly more critical and over time, very critical of America. The POWs came to believe these things simply by publicly communicating these ideas to others. Ultimately, the captives provided full confessions and valuable intelligence used by the Chinese Communists during the conflict. This effectively demonstrated that public acknowledgements affect the mind of the speaker (Schein).

On the receiving end, anyone listening to that public acknowledgement will infer the speaker believes what they are saying, even when given information to the contrary. A pro-Fidel Castro essay (so you know this isn't a new study) was shown to two groups of people and then asked if the writer was really pro-Castro or not. *Before* they were asked this question, the control group was told the writer *chose* to write it, while the test group was told the writer *was forced* to write it. For both groups, people assumed the writer was pro-Castro. The public statement created the automatic belief that the writer believed what he had written, even when told otherwise (Jones & Harris).

"Maybe not lead off with, 'I don't give a damn what you think'."

Moving from the theoretical to the practical, one way to leverage the bi-directional heuristic belief of public statements is to pit two opposing views against one another. In any situation where two people disagree on an issue, let's say the issue du jour is whether or not Walmart should be allowed to build a giant store in some small town. Find two people, one pro and one con, and ensure they are in the right frame of mind by staying calm, acknowledging their egos, etc. If they are defensive, combative, or adversarial, wait until they are in a better frame of mind.

Tell them they need to make the *other side's argument*. Victory goes to the one that can best capture the spirit of the opposing viewpoint, which indicates they best understand that viewpoint. Make sure to sell the idea that whoever can best make the others' argument will have demonstrated a better understanding of all sides of the issue.

This creates a complex event cascade. First, by tying the success of their argument to their understanding of the issue and your subsequent trust in them, they are incentivized to do well, so they won't try to "tank it." Second, by making the counter argument (like the POWs) the speakers may not come to completely believe what they're saying, but they will at least have a better appreciation of the other side. Third, by listening to the other person make *their* argument (like the pro-Castro listeners) they will come to believe that the other person at least respects and appreciates their position, and due to the second point, they actually *will*. Finally, the net effect (and objective) is that both individuals' anchor points will move toward the center. The amount of movement is dictated by how invested they are in the issue (think latitudes of acceptance), so even a minor change is a major victory.

When you are only dealing with one other person, *you* can play devil's advocate in place of one of the other parties. After using this technique for a multitude of issues where people disagree, it is striking how much people will talk about what they agree on afterwards. If you sell the premise properly, and they are in the right frame of mind, it is transformational.

THE PRICE OF PERSUASION

"The first rule of persuasion club is, 'don't talk about persuasion club.'"

-STEVEN KEYL

So what's the downside? In a word... anonymity.

After working to get the telecommuting policy instituted, I received neither credit nor recognition. In fact, the CEO would probably not even remember our conversations about it. Why? Because it was never a big deal (in his mind). The conversations were low-key and he never got the feeling I was trying to "hit him up for something." Afterwards, I told no one.

What would have happened if I had loudly and triumphantly proclaimed that I was able to convince the CEO to change the policy through my masterful use of persuasion? That would have been the last thing I accomplished at that job. The CEO would have felt like he was played, and others would have assumed I was always trying to put one over on them in every conversation. Staying quiet and forcing your pride to take a backseat allows you to continue invisibly getting results. And I did.

Until writing this book, I've never mentioned any successes related to wielding persuasion and influence. Whether getting a friend to stop monopolizing the conversation or getting a bouncer to stop misbehaving, these stories weren't even told to people with no connection to the people involved! Doing so would have planted the seed that I was a person to be careful around–which is the opposite of what you want.

During my career in the Intelligence Community, appearing to be just a "normal guy" has allowed me to wield tremendous influence with no one the wiser. These professional successes are conspicuously absent here as I wish to maintain that level of success!

Discussing your accomplishments is about ego, which you need to put aside if you're going to be a

The greatest Whisperers melt into the crowd. You'll never know who they are.

successful influencer. You *must* subvert your desire for others to see how smart, gifted, or skilled you are. As soon as people become aware of your talents, your ability to persuade disappears. This is best summed up by Salvador Dali who said, "The secret of my influence has always been that it remained secret." Amen, Sal!

What starts externally as a means of demonstrating consistency matures into an internal commitment which leads to lasting inner change. <u>This can only happen if they believe they are the agent of their own metamorphosis.</u> By taking credit, you would destroy your anonymity, your ability to wield influence in the future, *and* the ability to create a lasting change in the life of your subject. This is the price of all persuasion (favors, behavior, and mindset) - that no one will ever know the true extent of your talents.

* * *

FORGET-ME-NOTS

- Don't try to alter a mindset too far too quickly, as it will result in a heuristic rejection. Focus on ideas that land in the target's *range of non-commitment*, so they will systematically analyze the information.
- Moving people into a frame of mind that is open and receptive to new ideas requires that <u>you</u> be the first to adopt that frame of mind, and they will follow suit.
- Change others' self-image (and related behavior) by telling them how you see them (or how you would *prefer* to see them). They will alter their mindset to align with your stated perception. (Direct suggestion)
- Stay anonymous!

* * *

Epilogue

From charisma to psychopaths, from cold reading to embodied cognition, from detecting deception to altering beliefs, this has been quite a trip! What appears to be an array of diverging branches all come down to the same roots: understanding, connecting, influencing.

You can't exert real influence until you make a genuine connection, which you can't do until you truly understand a person. It's a process that is simple to conceptualize, but a good degree more difficult to achieve. Work at it. Use the ideas here to become more effective in dealing with people. Even if you meet an occasional failure, don't let it dissuade you from dusting yourself off and trying again.

Your ultimate success with this material hinges on how well you can adapt it to your environment. See how the various concepts come into play in your personal and professional lives.

Disappointed it's over so soon? Not to worry, there's a LOT more left to this book… and you're the one who is going to write it! Remember that <u>whispers are far more effective than shouts</u>. Don't pass up a single opportunity to change the world, in however small a measure. Let it begin with you.

Appendix A

Charismatic body language reference

Behavior	Detail
Smiling	Boosts warmth. Too much smiling reduces power. Smile less to boost authority and power.
Listening	Boosts presence. Don't think about your response until they have finished.
Speaking	Mirror their vocabulary and tempo to boost warmth and presence. Increase vocabulary slightly above their level to boost power.
Handshake	A firm, palm down handshake increases power, but can be seen as arrogant. When someone offers you a palm down handshake you can counter it to maintain social equality.
Eye contact	Maintain eye contact ⅔ of the time to increase presence. An inviting social gaze boosts warmth. A power gaze boosts...not surprisingly... power.
Gestures	Reduce gestures to increase power. To further boost power, selectively use arms akimbo, hand steepling, and hooding.
Mirroring	Boosts presence and warmth. Delay the mirrored behavior and reduce the magnitude to keep the movements "socially invisible".
Spacing	Let others choose the appropriate spacing between you to keep them comfortable. If someone is uncomfortable you cannot generate the rapport necessary to generate charisma.

Appendix B

Nonverbal communication reference

Type	Detail
Feet	They point in the direction the body wants to go.
Legs	Splayed outward shows dominance. Crossed legs can mean many things, not just a withdrawn or defensive attitude.
Torso	Note its angle in relation to the other party. Also look for torso barriers, such as crossed arms or held objects, as indicators of low confidence.
Arms	The meaning of crossed arms can be uncovered by looking at both the context and type of display–it doesn't mean just one thing, but most often indicates low confidence. When the elbows are prominently shown, it is normally interpreted as a high confidence display, i.e. arms akimbo (Wonder Woman) and hooding with the hands clasped behind the head.
Hands	Palm up displays are more open and submissive; palm down are more authoritative and dominant. Rubbing the hands together, or otherwise keeping them "busy" with tasks like picking lint and straightening a tie generally indicate stress and low confidence.
Eyes	Eye blocking is a flight response displayed by refusing to look at the stressor, closing the eyes, or physically blocking the line of sight with the hands and fingers. Looking away from someone during a conversation should _not_ be considered suspicious. This is a normal behavior.
Mouth	A real smile involves the entire face accompanied by pronounced wrinkles around the eyes. Other types of smiles are affectations meant to convey or hide specific thoughts like sarcasm, flirtation, anger, or contempt.

Appendix C

Deception cue reference

Nonverbal

Hands	Scratching the head and face in direct response to questions *may* indicate deception, but look for confirming cues. Rubbing hands together, adjusting clothing, or inspecting hands and fingernails indicate anxiety, <u>not</u> deception.
Legs	Look for *changes* in leg movement in response to stimulus.
Face	Hard swallows and throat clearing in response to stimulus indicates stress. Liars smile less and show less expression, but when they do smile it lasts unnaturally long. Amount of eye contact and other facial expressions should not be a consideration in determining deceptive responses.

Verbal

Evasion	Every type of evasion seeks to avoid answering the question. Listen for responses that *imply* an answer but don't actually answer the question.
Denial	Denials made by a liar tend to be too general or too specific. Truth tellers make clear, unambiguous statements about the matter at hand. Liars also bury denials inside of a larger, off-the-topic narrative.
Qualifiers	Words or phrases that preface a denial. Meant to alter your perception and/or make the denial more psychologically palatable.
Word Choice	Most importantly, look for <u>text bridging</u> statements where an answer seeks to "skip over" parts of the the story with phrases like, "...later on..." and "...after that..." Also look for <u>convincing statements</u> where the person acts as a character witness for themselves. Liars overuse these.

Misdirection	Statements that lead you away from your line of inquiry and seek to alter perception, such as being overly polite, feigned nonchalance, and commenting on things unrelated to the matter at hand.

Paralinguistic

Response length	Truthful people offer full explanations and stay on topic. Liars tend to offer minimal information and tend to drift off topic.
Response latency	Liars must figure out answers, so there is a longer delay before they begin answering a question. Asking you to repeat a question or clarify an obvious word or phrase is a delaying tactic used to subtly buy more time.

References

Abel, E. L., and M. L. Kruger. "Smile Intensity in Photographs Predicts Longevity." *Psychological Science* 21.4 (2010): 542-44. Print.

Ackerman, J. M., C. C. Nocera, and J. A. Bargh. "Incidental Haptic Sensations Influence Social Judgments and Decisions." *Science* 328.5986 (2010): 1712-715. Print.

Amodio, D.M., and C.D. Frith (2006). "Meeting of minds: The medial frontal cortex and social cognition." *Nature Reviews Neuroscience* 7: 268-77.

Anand, K. J. S., and Patrick J. McGrath. *Pain in Neonates.* Amsterdam: Elsevier, 1993. Print.

Andreas, Steve, and Charles Faulkner. *NLP: The New Technology of Achievement.* New York: Morrow, 1995. Print.

Andy, "Magic Words", The Jerx Blog, (http://www.thejerx.com/blog/2016/8/14/magic-words), 14 August 2016. (Edited) Web.

Argyle, Michael, Veronica Salter, Hilary Nicholson, Marylin Williams, and Philip Burgess. "The Communication of Inferior and Superior Attitudes by Verbal and Non-verbal Signals*." *British Journal of Social and Clinical Psychology* 9.3 (1970): 222-31. Print.

Ariely, Dan. *Predictably Irrational: The Hidden Forces That Shape Our Decisions.* New York, NY: Harper, 2008. Print.

Aron, A., E. Melinat, E. N. Aron, R. D. Vallone, and R. J. Bator. "The Experimental Generation of Interpersonal Closeness: A Procedure and Some Preliminary Findings." *Personality and Social Psychology Bulletin* 23.4 (1997): 363-77. Print.

Asch, Solomon E. "Studies of Independence and Conformity: I. A Minority of One against a Unanimous Majority." *Psychological Monographs: General and Applied* 70.9 (1956): 1-70. Print.

Attrill, Martin J., Karen A. Gresty, Russell A. Hill, and Robert A. Barton. "Red Shirt Colour Is Associated with Long-term Team Success in English Football." *Journal of Sports Sciences* 26.6 (2008): 577-82. Print.

Bandura, Albert, and Frances L. Menlove. "Factors Determining Vicarious Extinction of Avoidance Behavior through Symbolic Modeling." *Journal of Personality and Social Psychology* 8.2, Pt.1 (1968): 99-108. Print.

Bargh, John A., Mark Chen, and Lara Burrows. "Automaticity of Social Behavior: Direct Effects of Trait Construct and Stereotype Activation on Action." *Journal of Personality and Social Psychology* 71.2 (1996): 230-44. Print.

Barker, Shannon. "Improved Performance On Clerical Tasks Associated With Administration Of Peppermint Odor." *Perceptual and Motor Skills* 97.7 (2003): 1007. Print.

Baron, R. A. "The Sweet Smell Of... Helping: Effects of Pleasant Ambient Fragrance on Prosocial Behavior in Shopping Malls." *Personality and Social Psychology Bulletin* 23.5 (1997): 498-503. Print.

Berman, Mark. "The seven racist e-mails the Justice Department highlighted in its report on Ferguson police", The Washington Post, (https://www.washingtonpost.com/news/post-nation/wp/2015/03/04/the-seven-racist-e-mails-the-justice-department-highlighted-in-its-report-on-ferguson-police/?utm_term=.d4ac11dd1f9a), 4 March 2015. Web.

Berrios, G.e. "Classic Text No. 37: J. C. Prichard and the Concept of 'moral Insanity'" History of Psychiatry 10.37 (1999): 111-16. Print.

Bickman, Leonard. "Social Roles and Uniforms: Clothes Make the Person." PsycEXTRA Dataset. Print.

Blair, R.j.r. "Responding to the Emotions of Others: Dissociating Forms of Empathy through the Study of Typical and Psychiatric Populations." Consciousness and Cognition 14.4 (2005): 698-718. Print.

Bless, H., G. Bohner, N. Schwarz, and F. Strack. "Mood and Persuasion: A Cognitive Response Analysis." Personality and Social Psychology Bulletin 16.2 (1990): 331-45. Print.

Board, Belinda Jane, and Katarina Fritzon. "Disordered Personalities at Work." Psychology, Crime & Law 11.1 (2005): 17-32. Print.

Bolton, Robert. People Skills: How to Assert Yourself, Listen to Others, and Resolve Conflicts. New York: Simon & Schuster, 1986. Print.

Bond, Jr. Charles F., and Bella M. Depaulo. "Accuracy of Deception Judgments: Appendix A." Personality and Social Psychology Review 10.3 (2006). Print.

Bono, Edward De. Lateral Thinking: A Textbook of Creativity. London: Penguin, 1990. Print.

Bornstein, Robert F. "Exposure and Affect: Overview and Meta-analysis of Research, 1968-1987." Psychological Bulletin 106.2 (1989): 265-89. Print.

Bouie, Jamelle. "There's No Such Thing as a Good Trump Voter." Slate Magazine. 15 Nov. 2016. Web. 31 Mar. 2017.

Brake, Terence; "Cultural Stereotypes Lead to Misunderstandings." Country Navigator. 24 Feb. 2017. Web. 11 Apr. 2017.

Broeder, D. "The University of Chicago Jury Project." Nebraska Law Review 38 (1959): 760-74.

Burg, Bob. Adversaries into Allies: Win People over without Manipulation or Coercion. Print.

Burnkrant, Robert E., and H. Rao Unnava. "Effects of Self-Referencing on Persuasion." J CONSUM RES Journal of Consumer Research 22.1 (1995): 17. Print.

Buss, David M. "Sex Differences in Human Mate Preferences: Evolutionary Hypotheses Tested in 37 Cultures." Behavioral and Brain Sciences 12.01 (1989): 1. Print.

Cabane, Olivia Fox. The Charisma Myth: How Anyone Can Master the Art and Science of Personal Magnetism. New York: Portfolio/Penguin, 2012. Print.

Carney, D. R., A. J. C. Cuddy, and A. J. Yap. "Power Posing: Brief Nonverbal Displays Affect Neuroendocrine Levels and Risk Tolerance." Psychological Science 21.10 (2010): 1363-368. Print.

Chaplin WF, Phillips JB, Brown JD, Clanton NR, Stein JL. "Handshaking, gender, personality, and first impressions." Journal of Personality and Social Psychology. 79.1 (2000): 110-7. Print.

Cialdini, Robert B., and Et Al. "Basking in Reflected Glory: Three (football) Field Studies." Journal of Personality and Social Psychology 34.3 (1976): 366-75. Print.

Cialdini, Robert B. Influence: The Psychology of Persuasion. New York: Collins, 2007. Print.

Cialdini, Robert B., and Et Al. "Reciprocal Concessions Procedure for Inducing Compliance: The Door-in-the-face Technique." Journal of Personality and Social Psychology 31.2 (1975): 206-15. Print.

Clark, Russell D., and Larry E. Word. "Where Is the Apathetic Bystander? Situational Characteristics of the Emergency." Journal of Personality and Social Psychology 29.3 (1974): 279-87. Print.

Cohen, Geoffrey L. "Party Over Policy: The Dominating Impact of Group Influence on Political Beliefs." Journal of Personality and Social Psychology 85.5 (2003): 808-22. Print.

Crusco, A. H., and C. G. Wetzel. "The Midas Touch: The Effects of Interpersonal Touch on Restaurant Tipping." Personality and Social Psychology Bulletin 10.4 (1984): 512-17. Print.

Curley, Allison, "The Truth About Lies: The Science of Deception", Brainfacts.org, (http://www.brainfacts.org/in-society/in-society/articles/2013/the-truth-about-lies-the-science-of-deception/), 20 March 2013. Web.

Darwin, Charles and Phillip Prodger. "The Expression of the Emotions in Man and Animals" Oxford University Press, 1998. Print.

Dean, Jeremy. "Why We All Stink as Intuitive Psychologists: The False Consensus Effect", PsyBlog, (http://www.spring.org.uk/2007/11/why-we-all-stink-as-intuitive.php), 21 September 2015. Web.

Dijksterhuis, Ap, and Ad Van Knippenberg. "The Relation between Perception and Behavior, or How to Win a Game of Trivial Pursuit." Journal of Personality and Social Psychology 74.4 (1998): 865-77. Print.

Douce, L., and W. Janssens. "The Presence of a Pleasant Ambient Scent in a Fashion Store: The Moderating Role of Shopping Motivation and Affect Intensity." Environment and Behavior 45.2 (2011): 215-38. Print.

Drahota, Amy, Alan Costall, and Vasudevi Reddy. "The Vocal Communication of Different Kinds of Smile." Speech Communication 50.4 (2008): 278-87. Print.

Dulaney, Earl F. "Changes In Language Behavior As A Function Of Veracity." Human Communication Research Human Comm Res 9.1 (1982): 75-82. Print.

Dunbar, Robin I.m. "The Social Brain Hypothesis." Evol. Anthropol. Evolutionary Anthropology: Issues, News, and Reviews 6.5 (1998): 178-90. Print.

Eibach, Richard P., Lisa K. Libby, and Thomas D. Gilovich. "When Change in the Self Is Mistaken for Change in the World." Journal of Personality and Social Psychology 84.5 (2003): 917-31. Print.

Eibach, Richard P., and Steven E. Mock. "The Vigilant Parent: Parental Role Salience Affects Parents' Risk Perceptions, Risk-aversion, and Trust in Strangers." Journal of Experimental Social Psychology 47.3 (2011): 694-97. Print.

Ekman, Paul. Emotions Revealed: Recognizing Faces and Feelings to Improve Communication and Emotional Life. New York: Times, 2003. Print.

Ekman, Paul, and Maureen O'sullivan. "Who Can Catch a Liar?" American Psychologist 46.9 (1991): 913-20. Print.

Elliot, Andrew J. "Color and Psychological Functioning: A Review of Theoretical and Empirical Work." Frontiers in Psychology 6 (2015). Print.

Elliot, Andrew J., and Daniela Niesta. "Romantic Red: Red Enhances Men's Attraction to Women." Journal of Personality and Social Psychology 95.5 (2008): 1150-164. Print.

Epley, N., and E. Whitchurch. "Mirror, Mirror on the Wall: Enhancement in Self-Recognition." Personality and Social Psychology Bulletin 34.9 (2008): 1159-170. Print.

Epley, Nicholas. Mindwise: How We Understand What Others Think, Believe, Feel, and Want. Print.

Erez, Amir, Vilmos F. Misangyi, Diane E. Johnson, Marcie A. Lepine, and Kent C. Halverson. "Stirring the Hearts of Followers: Charismatic Leadership as the Transferal of Affect." Journal of Applied Psychology 93.3 (2008): 602-16. Print.

Eyal, T., and N. Epley. "How to Seem Telepathic: Enabling Mind Reading by Matching Construal." Psychological Science 21.5 (2010): 700-05. Print.

Falk, E. B., R. P. Spunt, and M. D. Lieberman. "Ascribing Beliefs to Ingroup and Outgroup Political Candidates: Neural Correlates of Perspective-taking, Issue Importance and Days until the Election." Philosophical Transactions of the Royal Society B: Biological Sciences 367.1589 (2012): 731-43. Print.

Farroni, Teresa, Enrica Menon, Silvia Rigato, and Mark H. Johnson. "The Perception of Facial Expressions in Newborns." The European Journal of Developmental Psychology. Taylor & Francis. Web. 03 Dec. 2015.

Fitzsimons, Grainne M., and John A. Bargh. "Thinking of You: Nonconscious Pursuit of Interpersonal Goals Associated with Relationship Partners." Journal of Personality & Social Psychology 84.1 (2003): 148-63. Print.

Forouzan, Elham, and David J. Cooke. "Figuring Outla Femme Fatale: Conceptual and Assessment Issues concerning Psychopathy in Females." Behavioral Sciences & the Law Behav. Sci. Law 23.6 (2005): 765-78. Print.

Fox, Michael W. Concepts in Ethology: Animal and Human Behavior. Minneapolis: U of Minnesota, 1974. Print.

Frank, Mark G., and Thomas Gilovich. "The Dark Side of Self- and Social Perception: Black Uniforms and Aggression in Professional Sports." Journal of Personality and Social Psychology 54.1 (1988): 74-85. Print.

Freedman, Jonathan L., and Scott C. Fraser. "Compliance without Pressure: The Foot-in-the-door Technique." Journal of Personality and Social Psychology 4.2 (1966): 195-202. Print.

Gillespie, Brian, Mark Mulder, and Manja Leib. "Who's Laughing Now? The Effect of Simulated Laughter on Consumer Enjoyment of Television Comedies and the Laugh-Track Paradox." Journal of the Association for Consumer Research 1.4 (2016): 592-606. Print.

Gilovich, Thomas, Dale W. Griffin, and Daniel Kahneman. Heuristics and Biases: The Psychology of Intuitive Judgement. Cambridge, U.K. ; New York: Cambridge UP, 2002. Print.

Givens, David B. Love Signals: A Practical Field Guide to the Body Language of Courtship. New York: St. Martin's, 2005. Print.

Goldsmith, Kelly, Eunice Kim Cho, and Ravi Dhar. "When Guilt Begets Pleasure: The Positive Effect of a Negative Emotion." Journal of Marketing Research 49.6 (2012): 872-81. Print.

Goleman, Daniel. Working with Emotional Intelligence. New York: Bantam, 1998. Print.

Greengross, Gil. "Does Racist Humor Promote Racism?" Psychology Today, (https://www.psychologytoday.com/blog/humor-sapiens/201107/does-racist-humor-promote-racism), 18 July 2011. Web.

Gustafson, Sigrid B., and Darren R. Ritzer. "The Dark Side of Normal: A Psychopathy-linked Pattern Called Aberrant Self-promotion." Eur. J. Pers. European Journal of Personality 9.3 (1995): 147-83. Print.

Guéguen, N., Jacob, C., Martin, A., "Mimicry in Social Interaction: Its Effect on Human Judgment and Behavior", European Journal of Social Sciences 8, no. 2 (2009)

Guéguen, Nicolas. "The Sweet Smell Of... Courtship: Effects of Pleasant Ambient Fragrance on Women's Receptivity to a Man's Courtship Request." Journal of Environmental Psychology 32.2 (2012): 123-25. Print.

Hadnagy, Christopher. Social Engineering: The Art of Human Hacking. Indianapolis: Wiley, 2011. Print.

Hadnagy, Christopher, Paul Ekman, and Paul F. Kelly. Unmasking the Social Engineer: The Human Element of Security. Print.

Hagemann, Norbert, Bernd Strauss, and Jan Leißing. "When the Referee Sees Red ...." Psychological Science 19.8 (2008): 769-71. Print.

Harris, Lasana T., and Susan T. Fiske. "Dehumanized Perception." Zeitschrift Für Psychologie 219.3 (2011): 175-81. Print.

Haslam, Nick, Paul Bain, Lauren Douge, Max Lee, and Brock Bastian. "More Human than You: Attributing Humanness to Self and Others." Journal of Personality and Social Psychology 89.6 (2005): 937-50. Print.

Hassin, Ran R. "Being Open Minded Without Knowing Why: Evidence from Nonconscious Goal Pursuit." Social Cognition 26.5 (2008): 578-92. Print.

Hatfield, Elaine; Cacioppo, John T.; Rapson, Richard L. Clark, Margaret S. (Ed), "Primitive emotional contagion" Review of personality and social psychology, Vol. 14., (1992) : 151-177.

Hayes, Danny. "Candidate Qualities through a Partisan Lens: A Theory of Trait Ownership." American Journal of Political Science 49.4 (2005): 908. Print.

Heath, Chip. "On the Social Psychology of Agency Relationships: Lay Theories of Motivation Overemphasize Extrinsic Incentives." Organizational Behavior and Human Decision Processes 78.1 (1999): 25-62. Print.

Hemphill, James F., Robert D. Hare, and Stephen Wong. "Psychopathy and Recidivism: A Review." Legal and Criminological Psychology 3.1 (1998): 139-70. Print.

Herrmann, E., J. Call, M. V. Hernandez-Lloreda, B. Hare, and M. Tomasello. "Humans Have Evolved Specialized Skills of Social Cognition: The Cultural Intelligence Hypothesis." Science 317.5843 (2007): 1360-366. Print.

Hill, Russell A., and Robert A. Barton. "Psychology: Red Enhances Human Performance in Contests." Nature 435.7040 (2005): 293. Print.

Hirsch, A. R., & World, C.J. (2001). "Practical methods for detecting mendacity: A case study." The Journal of the American Academy of Psychiatry and the Law, 29, 438-444.

Hofling, Charles K., Eveline Brotzman, Sarah Dalrymple, Nancy Graves, and Chester M. Pierce. "An Experimental Study In Nurse-Physician Relationships." The Journal of Nervous and Mental Disease 143.2 (1966): 171-80. Print.

Holland, R. W., M. Hendriks, and H. Aarts. "Smells Like Clean Spirit: Nonconscious Effects of Scent on Cognition and Behavior." Psychological Science 16.9 (2005): 689-93. Print.

Holland, Rob, Merel Hendriks, and Henk Aarts. "Smells like Clean Spirit: The Unconscious Influence of Scent on Cognition and Behavior." PsycEXTRA Dataset. Print.

Holt-Lunstad, Julianne, Timothy B. Smith, Mark Baker, Tyler Harris, and David Stephenson. "Loneliness and Social Isolation as Risk Factors for Mortality." Perspectives on Psychological Science 10.2 (2015): 227-37. Print.

Houston, Philip. Spy the Lie: Former CIA Officers Teach You How to Detect Deception. New York: St. Martin's, 2012. Print.

Howard, Daniel J. "The Influence of Verbal Responses to Common Greetings on Compliance Behavior: The Foot-In-The-Mouth Effect." Journal of Applied Social Psychology 20.14 (1990): 1185-196. Print.

Hsee, Christopher K., Elaine Hatfield, and Claude Chemtob. "Assessments of the Emotional States of Others: Conscious Judgments Versus Emotional Contagion." Journal of Social and Clinical Psychology 11.2 (1992): 119-28. Print.

Huber, Joel, et al. "Adding Asymmetrically Dominated Alternatives: Violations of Regularity and the Similarity Hypothesis." Journal of Consumer Research, vol. 9, no. 1, 1982, p. 90., doi:10.1086/208899.

Human, Lauren J., and Jeremy C. Biesanz. "Target Adjustment and Self-other Agreement: Utilizing Trait Observability to Disentangle Judgeability and Self-knowledge." Journal of Personality and Social Psychology 101.1 (2011): 202-16. Print.

Inbau, Fred Edward. Criminal Interrogation and Confessions. Burlington, MA: Jones & Bartlett Learning, 2013. Print.

Jencks, Christoper; Phillips, Meredith (Edited) "The Black-White Test Score Gap", The New York Times on the Web, (https://www.nytimes.com/books/first/j/jencks-gap.html), 15 December 2016

Jones, Edward E., and Victor A. Harris. "The Attribution of Attitudes." Journal of Experimental Social Psychology 3.1 (1967): 1-24. Print.

Kachalia, Allen. "Liability Claims and Costs Before and After Implementation of a Medical Error Disclosure Program." Annals of Internal Medicine Ann Intern Med 153.4 (2010): 213. Print.

Kang, Yoona, Lawrence E. Williams, Margaret S. Clark, Jeremy R. Gray, and John A. Bargh. "Physical Temperature Effects on Trust Behavior: The Role of Insula." Social Cognitive and Affective Neuroscience 6.4 (2010): 507-15. Print.

Karren, Keith J., N. Lee. Smith, Brent Q. Hafen, and Kathryn J. Gordon. Mind/body Health: The Effect of Attitudes, Emotions and Relationships. Print.

Kenny, David A. Interpersonal Perception: A Social Relations Analysis. New York: Guilford, 1994. Print.

Knapp, M. L., & Hall, J.A. (2002). Nonverbal communication in human interaction, (5th Ed.). New York: Harcourt Brace Jovanovich.

Kohut, Heinz, and Charles B. Strozier. Self-Psychology and the Humanities: Reflections on a New Psychoanalytic Approach. New York: W.W. Norton, 1985. Print.

Kolenda, Nick. Methods of Persuasion: How to Use Psychology to Control Human Behavior. Print.

Kruger, Justin, and Thomas Gilovich. ""Naive Cynicism" in Everyday Theories of Responsibility Assessment: On Biased Assumptions of Bias." Journal of Personality and Social Psychology 76.5 (1999): 743-53. Print.

Kunda, Ziva, Paul G. Davies, Barbara D. Adams, and Steven J. Spencer. "The Dynamic Time Course of Stereotype Activation: Activation, Dissipation, and Resurrection." Journal of Personality and Social Psychology 82.3 (2002): 283-99. Print.

Kuykendall, David, and John P. Keating. "Mood and Persuasion: Evidence for the Differential Influence of Positive and Negative States." Psychology and Marketing Psychol. Mark. 7.1 (1990): 1-9. Print.

Landwehr, Jan R., Aparna A. Labroo, and Andreas Herrmann. "Gut Liking for the Ordinary: Incorporating Design Fluency Improves Automobile Sales Forecasts." Marketing Science 30.3 (2011): 416-29. Print.

Lane, Richard D., Lynn Nadel, and Geoffrey Ahern. Cognitive Neuroscience of Emotion. New York: Oxford UP, 2000. Print.

Langer, E.J. "Minding Matters," Advances in Experimental Social Psychology, vol. 22, ed. L. Berkowitz. New York: Academic Press, 1989.

Latane, Bibb, and John M. Darley. "Group Inhibition of Bystander Intervention in Emergencies." Journal of Personality and Social Psychology 10.3 (1968): 215-21. Print.

Lefkowitz, Monroe, Robert R. Blake, and Jane Srygley Mouton. "Status Factors in Pedestrian Violation of Traffic Signals." The Journal of Abnormal and Social Psychology 51.3 (1955): 704-06. Print.

Levav, J., and J. J. Argo. "Physical Contact and Financial Risk Taking." Psychological Science 21.6 (2010): 804-10. Print.

Levin, Irwin P., Sandra L. Schneider, and Gary J. Gaeth. "All frames are not created equal: A typology and critical analysis of framing effects." Organizational behavior and human decision processes 76.2 (1998): 149-188.

Levy, Becca R., Alan B. Zonderman, Martin D. Slade, and Luigi Ferrucci. "Age Stereotypes Held Earlier in Life Predict Cardiovascular Events in Later Life." Psychological Science 20.3 (2009): 296-98. Print.

Levy, Becca, and Ellen Langer. "Aging Free from Negative Stereotypes: Successful Memory in China among the American Deaf." Journal of Personality and Social Psychology 66.6 (1994): 989-97. Print.

Leyens, Jacques-Philippe, Paola M. Paladino, Ramon Rodriguez-Torres, Jeroen Vaes, Stephanie Demoulin, Armando Rodriguez-Perez, and Ruth Gaunt. "The Emotional Side of Prejudice: The Attribution of Secondary Emotions to Ingroups and Outgroups." Personality and Social Psychology Review 4.2 (2000): 186-97. Print.

Lieberman, David J. Get Anyone to Do Anything and Never Feel Powerless Again: Psychological Secrets to Predict, Control, and Influence Every Situation. New York: St. Martin's, 2000. Print.

Lieberman, David J. Never Be Lied to Again: How to Get the Truth in 5 Minutes or Less in Any Conversation or Situation. New York: St. Martin's, 1998. Print.

Lonegunman. "Derren Brown's Forer Experiment Text." Micro.Lone Gunman. 31 Jan. 2010. Web. 24 May 2017.

Maddux, W. W., E. Mullen, and A. D. Galinsky. "Chameleons Bake Bigger Pies And Take Bigger Pieces: Strategic Behavioral Mimicry Facilitates Negotiation Outcomes." Academy of Management Proceedings 2007.1 (2007): 1-6. Print.

Manning, Rachel, Mark Levine, and Alan Collins. "The Kitty Genovese Murder and the Social Psychology of Helping: The Parable of the 38 Witnesses." American Psychologist 62.6 (2007): 555-62. Print.

Marist Poll "2/8: Holy Super Powers, Batman! Mind Reading and Time Travel Top List." Top Super Powers Wanted by Americans. (http://maristpoll.marist.edu/28-holy-super-powers-batman-mind-reading-and-time-travel-top-list/) Web. 21 Dec. 2015.

Martin, Pearl Y., Victoria E. Hamilton, Blake M. Mckimmie, Deborah J. Terry, and Robin Martin. "Effects of Caffeine on Persuasion and Attitude Change: The Role of Secondary Tasks in Manipulating Systematic Message Processing." European Journal of Social Psychology 37.2 (2006): 320-38. Print.

McCombs, K., Raudenbush, B., Bova, A., Sappington, M., "Effects of peppermint scent administration on cognitive video game performance." North American Journal of Psychology 13.3 (2011): 383-90.

Meier, B. P., Moeller, S. K., Rimer-Peltz, M., Robinson, M. D., "Sweet taste preferences and experiences predict prosocial inferences, personalities, and behaviors." Journal of Personality and Social Psychology, 102.1: (2012), 163-74.

Miller, Richard L.; Seligman, Clive; Clark, Nathan T.; Bush, Malcolm "Perceptual contrast versus reciprocal concession as mediators of induced compliance." Canadian Journal of Behavioural Science / Revue canadienne des sciences du comportement, Vol 8(4), Oct 1976, 401-409.

Mitnick, Kevin D., and William L. Simon. The Art of Deception: Controlling the Human Element of Security. Indianapolis, IN: Wiley Pub., 2002. Print.

Moore, Richard. The High Blood Pressure Solution: A Scientifically Proven Program for Preventing Strokes and Heart Disease. Rochester, VT: Healing Arts, 2001. Print.

Moss, Mark, Steven Hewitt, Lucy Moss, and Keith Wesnes. "Modulation Of Cognitive Performance And Mood By Aromas Of Peppermint And Ylang-Ylang." International Journal of Neuroscience 118.1 (2008): 59-77. Print.

Myers, David G. Exploring Psychology. New York, NY: Worth, 2005. Print.

Navarro, Joe, and Marvin Karlins. What Every BODY Is Saying: An Ex-FBI Agent's Guide to Speed-reading People. New York, NY: Collins Living, 2008. Print.

Nicholls, Tonia L., James R. P. Ogloff, Johann Brink, and Alicia Spidel. "Psychopathy in Women: A Review of Its Clinical Usefulness for Assessing Risk for Aggression and Criminality." Behavioral Sciences & the Law Behav. Sci. Law 23.6 (2005): 779-802. Print.

Nisbett, Richard E., and Timothy D. Wilson. "Telling More than We Can Know: Verbal Reports on Mental Processes." Psychological Review 84.3 (1977): 231-59. Print.

O'Connor, Robert D. "Relative Efficacy of Modeling, Shaping, and the Combined Procedures for Modification of Social Withdrawal." Journal of Abnormal Psychology 79.3 (1972): 327-34. Print.

O'Doherty, J., Winston, J., Critchley, H. Perrett, D., Burt, D.M., and Dolan R.J., (2003) "Beauty in a smile: the role of medial orbitofrontal cortex in facial attractiveness." Neuropsychologia, 41, 147–155.

Palermo, Elizabeth, "Truth Be Told, White Lies Can Keep Relationships Strong." LiveScience. TechMedia Network. Web. 17 May 2016.

Pease, Allan, and Barbara Pease. The Definitive Book of Body Language. New York: Bantam, 2006. Print.

Perrett, David I., D.michael Burt, Ian S. Penton-Voak, Kieran J. Lee, Duncan A. Rowland, and Rachel Edwards. "Symmetry and Human Facial Attractiveness." Evolution and Human Behavior 20.5 (1999): 295-307. Print.

Perry, Raymond P., Philip C. Abrami, and Les Leventhal. "Educational Seduction: The Effect of Instructor Expressiveness and Lecture Content on Student Ratings and Achievement." Journal of Educational Psychology 71.1 (1979): 107-16. Print.

Petty, Richard E., John T. Cacioppo, and Martin Heesacker. "Effects of Rhetorical Questions on Persuasion: A Cognitive Response Analysis." Journal of Personality and Social Psychology 40.3 (1981): 432-40. Print.

Pinker, Steven. The Better Angels of Our Nature: Why Violence Has Declined. New York: Viking, 2011. Print.

Pocheptsova, Anastasiya, Aparna A. Labroo, and Ravi Dhar. "Making Products Feel Special: When Metacognitive Difficulty Enhances Evaluation." Journal of Marketing Research 47.6 (2010): 1059-069. Print.

Pohlmann, Tom; Neethi, Mary Thomas, "Relearning the Art of Asking Questions", Harvard Business Review, 27 March, 2015, (https://hbr.org/2015/03/relearning-the-art-of-asking-questions)

Porter, Stephen, Angela R. Birt, and Douglas P. Boer. "Investigation of the Criminal and Conditional Release Profiles of Canadian Federal Offenders as a Function of Psychopathy and Age." Law and Human Behavior 25.6 (2001): 647-61. Print.

Pronin, E., and M. B. Kugler. "People Believe They Have More Free Will than Others." Proceedings of the National Academy of Sciences 107.52 (2010): 22469-2474. Print.

Ramachandran, V. S., and Sandra Blakeslee. Phantoms in the Brain: Probing the Mysteries of the Human Mind. New York: William Morrow, 1998. Print.

Ratey, John J., and Albert M. Galaburda. A User's Guide to the Brain: Perception, Attention, and the Four Theaters of the Brain. New York: Pantheon, 2001. Print.

Regan, Dennis T. "Effects of a Favor and Liking on Compliance." Journal of Experimental Social Psychology 7 (1971): 627-39.

Ross, L. D., Y. Lelkes, and A. G. Russell. "How Christians Reconcile Their Personal Political Views and the Teachings of Their Faith: Projection as a Means of Dissonance Reduction." Proceedings of the National Academy of Sciences 109.10 (2012): 3616-622. Print.

Ross, Michael, and Fiore Sicoly. "Egocentric Biases in Availability and Attribution." Judgment under Uncertainty Heuristics and Biases: 179-89. Print.

Rot, M. Aan Het, D.s. Moskowitz, and S.n. Young. "Exposure to Bright Light Is Associated with Positive Social Interaction and Good Mood over Short Time Periods: A Naturalistic Study in Mildly Seasonal People." Journal of Psychiatric Research 42.4 (2008): 311-19. Print.

Rowland, Ian. The Full Facts Book of Cold Reading. London: Ian Rowland, 2012. Print.

Rudacille, Wendell C. Identifying Lies in Disguise. Dubuque, IA: Kendall/Hunt, 1994. Print.

Ryan, C. S. "Accuracy of Black and White College Students' In-Group and Out-Group Stereotypes." Personality and Social Psychology Bulletin 22.11 (1996): 1114-127. Print.

Sanbonmatsu, David M., and Frank R. Kardes. "The Effects of Physiological Arousal on Information Processing and Persuasion." J CONSUM RES Journal of Consumer Research 15.3 (1988): 379. Print.

Santos, Michael D., Craig Leve, and Anthony R. Pratkanis. "Hey Buddy, Can You Spare Seventeen Cents? Mindful Persuasion and the Pique Technique1." Journal of Applied Social Psychology 24.9 (1994): 755-64. Print.

Sapir, A. (1996). Scientific Content Analysis (SCAN). Phoenix, AZ: Laboratory of Scientific Interrogation.

Sarver, Dustin E., Mark D. Rapport, Michael J. Kofler, Joseph S. Raiker, and Lauren M. Friedman. "Hyperactivity in Attention-Deficit/Hyperactivity Disorder (ADHD): Impairing Deficit or Compensatory Behavior?" Journal of Abnormal Child Psychology 43.7 (2015): 1219-232. Print.

Savitsky, Kenneth, Boaz Keysar, Nicholas Epley, Travis Carter, and Ashley Swanson. "The Closeness-communication Bias: Increased Egocentrism among Friends versus Strangers." Journal of Experimental Social Psychology 47.1 (2011): 269-73. Print.

Schafer, Jack. "Text Bridges: The seven commonly used Text Bridges that signal deception." Psychology Today. (https://www.psychologytoday.com/blog/let-their-words-do-the-talking/201103/text-bridges) 6 March, 2011. Web.

Schafer, John R., and Joe Navarro. Advanced Interviewing Techniques: Proven Strategies for Law Enforcement, Military, and Security Personnel. Springfield, IL: Charles C. Thomas, 2010. Print.

Schafer, John R. Psychological Narrative Analysis: A Professional Method to Detect Deception in Written and Oral Communications. Springfield, IL: Charles C. Thomas, 2010. Print.

Schein, Edgar H. "The Chinese Indoctrination Program for Prisoners of War." Psychiatry 19.2 (1956): 149-72. Print.

Schneider, I. K., B. T. Rutjens, N. B. Jostmann, and D. Lakens. "Weighty Matters: Importance Literally Feels Heavy." Social Psychological and Personality Science 2.5 (2011): 474-78. Print.

Schouten, Ronald, and Jim Silver. Almost a Psychopath: Do I (or Does Someone I Know) Have a Problem with Manipulation and Lack of Empathy? Center City, MN: Hazelden, 2012. Print.

Schulman, Gary I. "Asch Conformity Studies: Conformity to the Experimenter And/or to the Group?" Sociometry 30.1 (1967): 26. Print.

Schwartz, Barry. The Paradox of Choice: Why More Is Less. New York: Ecco, 2004. Print.

Seaward, Brian Luke. Managing Stress: Principles and Strategies for Health and Well-being. Sudbury, MA: Jones and Bartlett, 2004. Print.

Sensation: The New Science of Physical Intelligence. S.l.: Atria, 2014. Print.

Serin, R. C. "Psychopathy and Violence in Criminals." Journal of Interpersonal Violence 6.4 (1991): 423-31. Print.

Serin, Ralph C., Ray D. Peters, and Howard E. Barbaree. "Predictors of Psychopathy and Release Outcome in a Criminal Population." Psychological Assessment 2.4 (1990): 419-22. Print.

Sherman, Steven J. "On the Self-erasing Nature of Errors of Prediction." Journal of Personality and Social Psychology 39.2 (1980): 211-21. Print.

Silvia, Paul J. "Deflecting Reactance: The Role of Similarity in Increasing Compliance and Reducing Resistance." Basic and Applied Social Psychology 27.3 (2005): 277-84. Print.

Slater, Seth M.F.A. "Why Do We Lie?" Psychology Today. Web. https://www.psychologytoday.com/blog/the-dolphin-divide/201309/why-do-we-lie, 17 May 2016.

Slepian, M. L., N. O. Rule, and N. Ambady. "Proprioception and Person Perception: Politicians and Professors." Personality and Social Psychology Bulletin 38.12 (2012): 1621-628. Print.

Slepian, M. L., M. Weisbuch, N. O. Rule, and N. Ambady. "Tough and Tender: Embodied Categorization of Gender." Psychological Science 22.1 (2010): 26-28. Print.

Slepian, Michael L., E. J. Masicampo, Negin R. Toosi, and Nalini Ambady. "The Physical Burdens of Secrecy." Journal of Experimental Psychology: General 141.4 (2012): 619-24. Print.

Smith, Tom; Rasinski, Kenneth; Toce, Marianna, "America Rebounds: A National Study of Public Response to the September 11th Terrorist Attacks", National Organization for Research at the University of Chicago, (http://citeseerx.ist.psu.edu/viewdoc/download?doi=10.1.1.458.6605&rep=rep1&type=pdf), 25 October 2001. Web.

Sobel, Andrew, and Jerold Panas. Power Questions: Build Relationships, Win New Business, and Influence Others. Hoboken, NJ: Wiley, 2012. Print.

Sobel, Andrew, and Jerold Panas. Power Relationships: 26 Irrefutable Laws for Building Extraordinary Relationships. Print.

Song, Hyunjin, Andrew Vonasch, Brian Meier, and John A. Bargh. "Brighten Up: Smiling Faces Appear Brighter than Frowning Ones." PsycEXTRA Dataset. Print.

Steele, Claude M., and Joshua Aronson. "Stereotype Threat and the Intellectual Test Performance of African Americans." Journal of Personality and Social Psychology 69.5 (1995): 797-811. Print.

Stephey, M.J. "A Brief History of the Fist Bump." Time. Time Inc., 05 June 2008. Web. 02 Dec. 2015.

Strack, F., and R. Neumann. "Furrowing the Brow May Undermine Perceived Fame: The Role of Facial Feedback in Judgments of Celebrity." Personality and Social Psychology Bulletin 26.7 (2000): 762-68. Print.

Tversky, Amos, and Daniel Kahneman. "Rational Choice And The Framing Of Decisions." Decision Making: 167-92. Print.

Tversky, Amos, and Daniel Kahneman. "Judgment under Uncertainty: Heuristics and Biases." Judgment under Uncertainty: 3-20. Print.

Valins, Stuart. "Emotionality And Information Concerning Internal Reactions." Journal of Personality and Social Psychology 6.4, Pt.1 (1967): 458-63. Print.

Vorauer, Jacquie D., Verena Martens, and Stacey J. Sasaki. "When Trying to Understand Detracts from Trying to Behave: Effects of Perspective Taking in Intergroup Interaction." Journal of Personality and Social Psychology 96.4 (2009): 811-27. Print.

Webster, G. D., G. R. Urland, and J. Correll. "Can Uniform Color Color Aggression? Quasi-Experimental Evidence From Professional Ice Hockey." Social Psychological and Personality Science 3.3 (2011): 274-81. Print.

Wenner, Melinda. "Smile! It Could Make You Happier." Scientific American Mind Sci Am Mind 20.5 (2009): 14-15. Print.

Williams, L. E., and J. A. Bargh. "Experiencing Physical Warmth Promotes Interpersonal Warmth." Science 322.5901 (2008): 606-07. Print.

Willis, J., and A. Todorov. "First Impressions: Making Up Your Mind After a 100-Ms Exposure to a Face." Psychological Science 17.7 (2006): 592-98. Print.

Wilson, Paul R. "Perceptual Distortion of Height as a Function of Ascribed Academic Status." The Journal of Social Psychology 74.1 (1968): 97-102. Print.

Witherington, Laurence. "Which Country Drinks the Most Alcohol?" The Wall Street Journal. Dow Jones & Company, 22 Aug. 2014. Web. 11 Apr. 2017.

Wojcieszak, M. "False Consensus Goes Online: Impact of Ideologically Homogeneous Groups on False Consensus." Public Opinion Quarterly 72.4 (2008): 781-91. Print.

Xu, Alison Jing, Rami Zwick, and Norbert Schwarz. "Washing Away Your (good or Bad) Luck: Physical Cleansing Affects Risk-taking Behavior." Journal of Experimental Psychology: General 141.1 (2012): 26-30. Print.

Zemke, D. M., and S. Shoemaker. "A Sociable Atmosphere: Ambient Scent's Effect on Social Interaction." Cornell Hospitality Quarterly 49.3 (2008): 317-29. Print.

Zhong, C.-B., V. K. Bohns, and F. Gino. "Good Lamps Are the Best Police: Darkness Increases Dishonesty and Self-Interested Behavior." Psychological Science 21.3 (2010): 311-14. Print.

Zhong, C.-B., and K. Liljenquist. "Washing Away Your Sins: Threatened Morality and Physical Cleansing." Science 313.5792 (2006): 1451-452. Print.

About the author

Steven has spent the last 20 years working in the United States Intelligence Community (IC) where his services are still employed by various "three-lettered agencies." His insights come directly from his time working for the U.S. Government, where his diverse work situations allowed him the opportunity to hone the skills of understanding, connecting with, and influencing others.

He maintains a sense of wonder at how our minds work. The material in *The Human Whisperer*, available through seminars and training, are the outgrowth of real-world experience and exhaustive research.

While the foundation of his experience rests on time-tested strategies, he's also studied the techniques of psychics, magicians, and social engineers, who work through various forms of misdirection. He's left no stone unturned in his quest to understand why we think and behave the way we do.

Assuming his lifelong dream to become a rock star fails to materialize, he will continue helping people become the most powerful version of themselves on:

- Facebook (www.facebook.com/stevenkeyl)
- Twitter (www.twitter.com/stevenkeyl)
- His website directly (www.stevenkeyl.com)

He also knows a few fun card tricks and more than a few face-melting guitar riffs.

Made in the USA
Columbia, SC
13 February 2018